Research in Psychology

D0405251

To Sue
With love and thanks

Research in Psychology

A Practical Guide to Methods and Statistics

Colin Dyer

Blackwell
Publishing

© 2006 by Colin Dyer

BLACKWELL PUBLISHING
350 Main Street, Malden, MA 02148-5020, USA
9600 Garsington Road, Oxford OX4 2DQ, UK
550 Swanston Street, Carlton, Victoria 3053, Australia

The right of Colin Dyer to be identified as the Author of this Work has been asserted in accordance with the UK Copyright, Designs, and Patents Act 1988.

All rights reserved. No part of this publication may be reproduced, stored in a retrieval system, or transmitted, in any form or by any means, electronic, mechanical, photocopying, recording or otherwise, except as permitted by the UK Copyright, Designs, and Patents Act 1988, without the prior permission of the publisher.

First published 2006 by Blackwell Publishing Ltd

1   2006

Library of Congress Cataloging-in-Publication Data

Dyer, Colin.
    Research in psychology : a practical guide to methods and statistics / Colin Dyer.
        p. cm.
    Rev. ed. of: Beginning research in psychology.
    Includes bibliographical references (p.) and index.
    ISBN-13: 978-1-4051-2526-0 (pbk. : alk. paper)
    ISBN-10: 1-4051-2526-8 (pbk. : alk. paper)
    1. Psychology—Research—Methodology—Textbooks.   2. Psychometrics—Textbooks.   I. Dyer, Colin.
Beginning research in psychology.   II. Title.

    BF76.5.D94 2007
    150.72—dc22

                                                                              2006001996

A catalogue record for this title is available from the British Library.

Set in 10 on 12.5 pt Dante
by SNP Best-set Typesetter Ltd, Hong Kong
Printed and bound in Singapore
by COS Printers Pte Ltd

The publisher's policy is to use permanent paper from mills that operate a sustainable forestry policy, and which has been manufactured from pulp processed using acid-free and elementary chlorine-free practices. Furthermore, the publisher ensures that the text paper and cover board used have met acceptable environmental accreditation standards.

For further information on
Blackwell Publishing, visit our website:
www.blackwellpublishing.com

CONTENTS

FIGURES

BOXES

ACKNOWLEDGEMENTS

I am very grateful to all those friends and colleagues who have in some way contributed to the writing of this book. I am particularly happy to acknowledge the contributions of the anonymous reviewers who saw sections of the book at various stages. Without their helpful and constructive comments I doubt whether it would ever have been finished. Any errors and omissions that remain, however, are my responsibility alone.

I would like to thank all the people at Blackwell Publishing who have been involved in the gestation and production of this book. I am particularly grateful to Sarah Bird for doing so much in the early stages, to Will Maddox for providing such excellent support as it started to take shape and to all who saw the project through to completion.

I would also like to record my gratitude to Dr Donald Jenni for allowing me to reproduce Figure 1 from Jenni, D. A. and Jenni, M. A. (1976). Carrying behaviour in humans: Analysis of sex differences. *Science*, *194*, 859–60.

The following material is reproduced from the public domain:

Box 5.3: reproduced from Experiment 1 in Stroop, J. R. (1935). Studies of interference in serial verbal reactions. *Journal of Experimental Psychology*, 18, 643–662.
Table 4.3: reproduced from Chart 1 in Bales, R. F. (1950). A set of categories for the analysis of small group interaction. *American Sociological Review*, *15*, 257–68.

1

PSYCHOLOGY AND SCIENCE

CHAPTER MAP

The prediction
The test of prediction
The conclusion

Popper, Kuhn and the Debate about the Nature of Scientific Progress

Psychology Paradigms Old and New

'Old paradigm' psychology and its problems
The wider context of the 'paradigm crisis'
'New paradigm' research in psychology

Chapter Summary

Further Reading

THIS CHAPTER

* *Identifies three key characteristics of science.*
* *Considers why the philosophical doctrine of empiricism is central to all scientific research.*
* *Outlines four goals of scientific activity.*
* *Describes the stages of 'the scientific method' as a route to developing better scientific theories and introduces the idea of falsification as means of testing hypotheses.*
* *Considers some of the features of 'good' scientific theories.*
* *Introduces Kuhn's notion of 'paradigm' as a way of understanding recent developments in psychology as well as scientific progress in general.*
* *Reviews the factors leading to the emergence of 'new paradigm psychology' and outlines some of its characteristics.*

KEY CONCEPTS

Empiricism	falsification
epistemology	positivism
hypothesis	anti-positivism
prediction	paradigm
theory	quantitative
induction	qualitative
deduction	

● SCIENCE AND PSYCHOLOGY ●

The words, 'science' and/or 'scientific' are found in almost every attempt to encapsulate the essence of modern psychology in the form of a concise definition (for example Eysenck, 2000, p. 3). Their presence reminds us that, alongside the substantive material, the study of psychology also necessarily involves an encounter with an array of more general questions that link the psychological subject matter to its methodological roots. The processes of learning how to 'do science', to think scientifically, and to appreciate some of the reasons why science proceeds in the way it does, are all at least as important as (say) understanding the various theories of human memory. In fact, one could argue that they are more important because, although theories in psychology may rapidly be discarded when they no longer serve a useful purpose, the features that define the scientific approach to generating new knowledge appear to be virtually immutable.

The purpose of this book is to provide an introduction to some of the methods of data collection and analysis that are used in psychology and in this first chapter we begin by considering what science is and what it means to study psychology scientifically. The following passage, taken from a recent psychology text, provides a good starting point.

'Under close scrutiny by outside observers, reported ESP phenomena often fail to occur (Swets and Druckman, 1990). However, several laboratory experiments have apparently demonstrated clairvoyance, telepathy, or psychokinesis (e.g., Rao and Palmer, 1987). Some blindfolded subjects do far better than chance would predict at clairvoyance tasks such as naming the colors of cards by touching them (Youtz, 1968). Others do slightly better than chance at telepathy or psychokinesis tasks such as describing or altering the output of a machine that is generating random numbers in another room (e.g., Honorton and Harper, 1974; Jahn, 1982; Schmidt, 1969).' (Bernstein, et al., 1997, p. 132)

This extract makes some important points about the nature of science.

Science requires transparent reasoning

Each statement in the extract is supported by one or more citations consisting of name(s) and a date of publication. Citations refer to sources of evidence that are relevant to the argument being presented. Reasoning in psychology, as in other sciences, therefore possesses transparency in the sense that an author's arguments are based on evidence that may be independently examined and judged. Science is committed to the idea of public knowledge: to the idea that information, both 'facts' and the reasoning about them, should be available to anyone who has acquired the necessary skills and expertise.

Science is rational

Scientific statements are rational in the sense that they are the result of an explicit process of reasoning that follows the rules of logic and can thus, in principle, be followed by anyone. This means that scientific knowledge is trans-cultural – a scientific statement carries the same information in any part of the world.

Science acknowledges only a single source of authority

All sciences, including psychology, are evidence-based disciplines. The presence of citations in the extract means that we are not being asked to accept any of the statements about ESP solely on the authority of Bernstein and his co-authors. We can, if we wish, see the evidence by following up the references and thus examine the factual basis for any of Bernstein's assertions. Put another way, we can say that the source of authority of a scientific statement lies in the facts themselves, and the rationality of the argument provided rather than in the identity of the person who makes it.

There is one further point. The extract tells us nothing about how or why psycho-kinesis, or any other ESP phenomenon, might occur (if in fact it does). Any explanation of ESP can only be provided by a theory, of which there is no sign in the extract. As we shall see shortly, scientific knowledge builds on twin foundations composed of theories on the one hand and evidence on the other, and both are needed if we are to hope to understand any natural phenomenon. We will look more closely at this important relationship between data and theory later on.

● EMPIRICISM: THE FOUNDATION OF SCIENCE ●

The reason why the collection and evaluation of evidence is given such a prominent role in science is to be found in the philosophical doctrine known as 'empiricism'.

Empiricism is the closest thing there is to one central idea in science because it has provided the underpinning rationale for all the immensely successful scientific work of the past three hundred years. It consists, in essence, of a single powerful insight: that reliable knowledge about the world can only be acquired if it is based on information that is available in some form to the senses. By implication, therefore, it also asserts that information obtained from other sources, such as the human imagination, can never provide a sound basis for constructing explanations of the world as it is.

However, as Viney (1993) points out, the doctrine of empiricism by itself provides only the necessary, but not the sufficient, conditions for the generation of new knowledge. That is, direct experience of the world is an essential ingredient of knowledge, but it is not enough by itself. Something further is required before it can provide a basis for knowledge. This something, as the philosopher Karl Popper (1974) argues, is human reason. The information acquired by the senses always requires some degree of interpretation by the person whose senses they are. Sensory information cannot, therefore, 'speak for itself' but always requires a reasoned act of interpretation by the observer.

The historical and practical importance of empiricism as an epistemological position (see box 1.1 below) has been its emphasis that what counts as knowledge must be acquired through the active exploration of material reality. In this view, explanations of why the world is as it is are only valid if they are based on evidence that has been obtained through some kind of practical information-gathering activity – that is, by empirical research. In psychology, such data-gathering may involve the application of any of the methods discussed in this book, as well as some others that are not mentioned.

Why has empiricism been so successful?

There seem to be three main reasons why empiricism has been so effective as a guiding principle in science.

BOX 1.1 Epistemology

Epistemology is the branch of philosophy that is concerned with questions about what knowledge is and how it may be achieved. It asks two fundamental questions. First, how can true information or ideas be distinguished from false? (This question arises because claims of truth, in science as in other areas of life, cannot be taken at face value.) Second, it asks what general approach or procedure is most likely to provide access to the truth about things. How may knowledge be reliably achieved?

The term 'epistemology' also refers to the specific arguments of philosophers, and others, about these fundamental questions. In this sense, empiricism should be seen as one among a number of different epistemologies. However, as implied above, empiricism seems to occupy a unique position because the collective experience of those researchers who have put its principles into practice over the past three hundred years suggests that it offers a highly reliable and effective approach to generating new knowledge.

- By focusing on the active collection of evidence empiricism ensures that there will be a correspondence between what is discovered and the reality that is external to the observer. Although an investigation may be handicapped by poor research technique, a researcher can nevertheless be confident that there is an essential link between the phenomenon that is being investigated and the empirical data.
- If evidence is collected it means that, in principle at least, it can be made public and hence available to others. This in turn offers a way of correcting errors, because any one set of research findings can be verified by others working in the same field.
- Empiricism asserts that there are no esoteric (hidden) sources of knowledge that may be acquired only by initiates. On the contrary, the only source of knowledge about the world is the world itself and this can be acquired by anyone who is able to acquire the necessary skills and techniques.

● SCIENCE: THE PROCESSES ●

We noted earlier that psychology identifies itself as one of the sciences and we should now start to explore in more detail what may be meant by the complex concept 'science'. As a starting point, science may be defined as the process of inquiry that aims to generate an understanding about why the natural world is as it is. One way of understanding more clearly what this involves is to look for the underpinning principles and concepts that guide the activities of the people engaged in 'doing science'. Arguably, it is these that make science most distinctive as a human activity, and differentiate it most clearly from other, non-scientific, activities. We shall first look briefly at what seem to be goals of science, and then go on to consider the process of knowledge generation itself.

As Scriven (1968) points out, the classical view of science is that it is concerned with a distinctive set of activities such as description (including observation and measurement), explanation, prediction and control. These have been seen to constitute the 'goals' of scientific activity. However, they can probably be more usefully seen as activities that scientists pursue as part of the more general goal of generating new knowledge rather than as ends in themselves.

Description

Description represents the first step towards the generation of new knowledge since it is only by means of accurate description of a phenomenon that the real shape of a problem may become clear. The construction of a description is thus the first step towards probing more deeply into a scientific question. Thus, to refer again to the extract from Bernstein et al. (1997) the first step towards determining whether ESP phenomena really occur is to obtain accurate descriptions of those situations in which it appears to take place. Accurate description always requires careful observation of the phenomenon being studied though, as we noted earlier, observation also requires the exercise of reason and thus always involves more than 'just looking'.

Explanation

In science, simple descriptions of phenomena are rarely enough to satisfy. The goal is explanation. Researchers always want to know why (how) some phenomenon (such as, for example, ESP) takes place. That is, they are interested in the conditions under which it occurs (or fails to occur), and in the kinds of natural processes on which it is based. It is through the construction and evaluation of answers to questions on these matters that our knowledge of the world develops incrementally.

As we mentioned earlier scientific explanations frequently take the form of theories. The question of how exactly theories are developed and evaluated is central to understanding how science operates, and we will return to it later.

Prediction

As Anthony O'Hear (1989) suggests, there is a close and two-way connection between explanation and prediction in modern science. The existence of a theory that explains some phenomenon is also quite likely to permit predictions to be made, and conversely, the ability to make an accurate prediction implies that some degree of understanding of the phenomenon has already been achieved.

Clearly, a prediction can only be as good as the accuracy of the underpinning theory. Thus a process of generating new predictions and then checking them out provides a very practical test of the explanatory power of a theory and represents the principal way in which theories are refined and developed.

In the physical sciences, the predictive power of theory has led to spectacular feats such as the ability to place and sustain human life in space. In the human sciences, such as psychology, on the other hand, the variable nature of the human subject matter means that theory is relatively undeveloped and it is extremely difficult to make precise predictions of human behaviour.

Control

Sometimes, a theory that possesses good predictive power may also allow control to be exercised over the phenomena it deals with. Clearly, if a phenomenon can be explained in detail so that accurate predictions can be made, then it may be possible also to manipulate it at will. It is equally clear that this is not possible in all areas of knowledge, no matter how good the theory. For example, the ability to control a phenomenon is present in many areas of physics and chemistry, but not, for obvious reasons, in cosmology.

In psychology, the possibility of controlling human behaviour and experience exists in some applied areas of the discipline. For example, clinical psychologists may use techniques based on the principles of conditioning to help people whose lives have been disrupted by maladaptive forms of behaviour. Although this particular example of the application of psychological knowledge to change behaviour is largely uncontentious, the wider ethical issues raised by the question of behavioural control are severe and it is not therefore generally regarded as one of the goals of psychology.

We now move on to consider the process of scientific inquiry itself and how it is that new knowledge may come into existence through the procedures known as 'the scientific method'.

● SCIENCE AS KNOWLEDGE DEVELOPMENT: 'THE SCIENTIFIC METHOD' ●

The process of scientific inquiry follows a characteristic pattern involving what is sometimes known as 'the scientific method' or, more formally, 'the hypothetico-deductive method'. This is the picture of science that is now strongly associated with the name of the philosopher Karl Popper. As it is presented here, Popper's account of what is involved in 'doing science' appears unproblematic and straightforward and indeed, for many scientists, it represents an accurate picture of how they go about their work. On the other hand, there are many who would argue that it represents a narrow and idealized view of science that simply does not square with the reality. It should certainly be recognized from the outset that, at least as far as psychology is concerned, it may not be the whole story. Nevertheless, within its limitations – which we mention later – it provides a useful starting point for the exploration of what it means to 'do science'.

In this view, the scientific method is to be understood as forming a sequence of discrete stages that moves the researcher from a position of relative ignorance to one of (somewhat) greater knowledge. Figure 1.1 below represents these stages.

Identify a problem

The process of knowledge generation can only begin once something has been defined as a problem that is worthy of investigation. Popper (1972) has suggested that a researcher usually

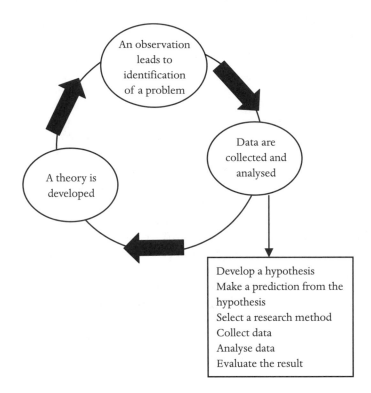

Figure 1.1   The research cycle

experiences some sense of puzzlement as he finds himself, in Popper's words, in a 'problem-situation'. It is this sense of puzzlement that motivates the subsequent search for an answer. But how does this come about? Where do problems come from? For psychologists there are two important sources of research ideas.

- Casual observation (in the sense of observation not carried out systematically) is one important source of ideas. It may be that some new phenomenon is spotted for the first time or, equally, that something quite well known or obvious is seen as a problem that is worthy of further investigation. Since human behaviour is everywhere, and is easily observed, it is no surprise that the list of examples of psychological research that have been started in this way is an extremely long one.
- Published accounts of research carried out by other investigators are vitally important forms of scientific communication, as was implied at the beginning of the chapter. In these, scientists report on their investigations, and attempt to account for their findings in terms of new or existing theories. The information presented in such reports frequently acts as a starting point for new investigative work. This can happen for one of any number of reasons as the analysis in box 1.2 shows.

As was noted earlier, the publication of new data is an expression of two important values in science – first, that knowledge should be public and held communally, and, second, that nothing should be immune to criticism and evaluation. Publication not only makes new

---

BOX 1.2 Some ways that published research may stimulate new work

- The earlier work is methodologically flawed – a method of research has been used that is inappropriate to the way the problem has been defined.
- An appropriate method has been applied inadequately.
- It appears the results have been interpreted incorrectly.
- The theory on which the investigation was based has been interpreted or applied incorrectly.
- There is a need for a replication of the original research in order to increase confidence in the original result.
- There is an inconsistency in the results of earlier research, as when one set of results contradicts or is inconsistent with an existing theory.
- Some of the ideas in the earlier research cause an entirely new problem to be recognized.

---

results accessible to other scientists, but also exposes them to the scrutiny of the rest of the scientific community so that any errors can be identified and corrected.

Develop a hypothesis

Once a problem has been identified a research hypothesis may be developed. This is an initial (and tentative) explanation proposed for the phenomenon in question. Previous research or theories about similar situations or problems may often assist a researcher in the task of formulating the research hypothesis since they may contribute insights, ideas (or even the hypothesis itself). It is this research hypothesis that is tested in the subsequent investigation.

Form a prediction from the hypothesis

From the initial research hypothesis the next step is to form a specific prediction. This is a precise and testable statement about what data can be expected to be found if the hypothesis is correct. It is, of course, always possible that several predictions may be derived from the same hypothesis, so that each tests different aspects of the hypothesis or looks at different conditions or situations under which the hypothesis might hold true.

Test the prediction: collect and analyse data

Next, the prediction is subjected to empirical test. This is the most visible part of research since it requires the researcher to select a method of research that is appropriate to the problem and then to use it to collect information. The raw data thus collected need to be processed further in order to find out whether the prediction was correct. Quantitative data (data in the form of numbers) will require some form of statistical analysis while qualitative data (data in verbal form, such as an interview transcript) will generally require to be reduced to a more succinct form, for example, by means of thematic analysis. The end result in either case will be a decision about whether the prediction that has just been tested is, or is not, correct.

Evaluate the result

The decision about whether a prediction has been confirmed involves comparing the prediction against the data obtained. If the data are as predicted, the prediction, and hence the hypothesis from which it was derived may be accepted. Alternatively, if the data are not as predicted, both the prediction and the hypothesis must be rejected as incorrect, and the position must be reconsidered. We return to this point, from a slightly different angle, a little later in the chapter.

Develop a theory

The ultimate goal of science is the development of theory. A theory is essentially an explanation that encapsulates current knowledge and represents what we believe we know about a given topic. Because all human knowledge is incomplete it follows that our theories are also incomplete, and can, therefore, in principle be shown to be so at any time, as new information is uncovered.

Theories vary widely from those that are highly general and large scale – such as the theory of relativity in physics – to those that are much more specific and small scale. Very general theories may support many specific hypotheses and many more predictions from those hypotheses, while small scale, specific theories are likely to generate comparatively few hypotheses. In psychology much of the theorizing is small scale and specific.

● HOW THEORIES DEVELOP:
POPPER'S EXPLANATION ●

How does this process of theory development operate? You will recall that the prediction that was tested was derived from a more general statement, called a hypothesis. This, in turn, is very likely to be based on a theory. Now clearly, if the prediction is shown by empirical test to be correct in a specific instance, then it implies that the more general hypothesis is also correct. Similarly, if a hypothesis continues to receive this kind of confirmation (that is, if the same result can be replicated time and time again) it suggests that the theory, on which the hypothesis itself was based, may also be accurate as a description of the underlying reality. It is only through continued successful replications that beliefs about the correctness of the hypothesis, and thus of its underlying theory, can be strengthened. Figure 1.2 illustrates this process.

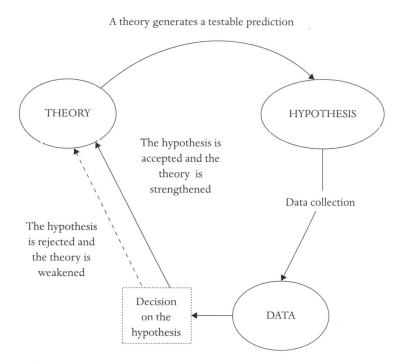

Figure 1.2   The relationship between theory, hypothesis and data

This seems straightforward enough. However, what is not obvious from the above is the logic of the hypothesis-testing process. What exactly does it mean to 'test' a hypothesis in this context, and how may a researcher be certain that an adequate test has been carried out?

The standard explanation of how hypotheses may be tested centres on the concept of falsification. Popper (1972) argued that any scientific statement (whether hypothesis, prediction, or theory) can only be said to have been tested satisfactorily if an attempt has been made to show that it is false. At first sight, this view appears to run against the grain of logic, since one would expect researchers to engage in collecting evidence that supports their hypotheses rather than the reverse. It is therefore worth looking at Popper's argument in a little more detail.

First, Popper points out that one can never be certain that a hypothesis or theory is correct. No matter how much convincing evidence is collected, there is always the possibility that somewhere there are data that show it to be false. Therefore, Popper argued, certain knowledge may only be achieved by attempting to falsify the theory or hypothesis, that is, *by actively searching for negative evidence*. Although it is impossible to prove a theory or hypothesis to be correct, it *is* always possible to show that it is incorrect because this takes only one piece of negative evidence. (Box 1.3 gives Popper's own illustration of the logic of this argument.)

The crucial importance of falsification to science is that it offers a way of obtaining conclusive knowledge. Although it is impossible ever finally to confirm a theory or show that a

BOX 1.3   Popper's argument for falsification

Popper illustrates the logic of his position on falsification by inviting us to imagine a scientist, who lives on a desert island and who spends his time watching birds fly overhead. If, in his observations, he sees only black swans and never a white one, could the scientist have confidence in the hypothesis that all swans everywhere are black? Popper says not because in that situation the theory would not have been subjected to an attempt at falsification. He points out that no matter how many black swans are seen there is always the possibility that somewhere there is a white swan that has never flown anywhere near the island, and thus has never been observed. The hypothesis that all swans are black may indeed be correct, although it is impossible to say so with certainty. On the other hand, the scientist has only to see a single white swan to know immediately *and with certainty* that his conjecture that all swans are black is false.

hypothesis is correct (because negative evidence may exist somewhere) it is nevertheless possible to disconfirm (i.e. prove them false) with certainty with just one piece of negative information.

Popper's principle of falsification provides a powerful way of distinguishing between science and other fields of knowledge, such as astrology and psychoanalysis, whose claim to be scientific is regarded as controversial by mainstream sciences. In Popper's view, the criterion of what makes a subject scientific is whether its theories are falsifiable, or not. Psychoanalysis, it is argued, provides a classical example of a 'pseudoscience' because the 'self-sealing' character of its ideas makes it impossible for psychoanalytic statements ever to be conclusively falsified (see box 1.3).

For the researcher, the practical consequence of the falsification principle is that it is entirely possible that after data are collected and considered, the hypothesis cannot be confirmed. What happens in this case and how does this influence theory development? There are a number of possibilities.

- The original link between the prediction and hypothesis may be unsound (remember that predictions are constructed on the basis of the hypothesis). In this case the prediction itself may need revision.
- On the other hand, if the reasoning that links a prediction to the hypothesis appears valid, then the repeated failure to confirm a prediction suggests that the hypothesis itself is erroneous. This weakens the hypothesis and in such cases, often the hypothesis may need to be revised to take account of the data. (Note that failure to confirm a prediction must normally be repeated, perhaps many times, before a hypothesis is sufficiently weakened to require revision. A single failure to confirm would be unlikely to be sufficient.)
- Sometimes, the failure to support a hypothesis also damages the underlying theory. This is particularly likely if the attempt to test the prediction throws up results that cannot be explained by the existing theory, in which case a single failure to confirm a hypothesis may be sufficiently convincing to completely sink a theory (see box 1.4 for an example).

BOX 1.4 An example of theory development

Donald Broadbent's (1958) 'filter' theory of attention provides a particularly clear example of how theories are modified in response to new data. Initially, the experimental results obtained by Broadbent, and others, appeared to show that when different messages are channelled to different ears nothing other than the physical characteristics of a message, such as pitch and volume, could be processed by the unattended ear. Broadbent's theory provided an explanation of how this might occur. However, subsequent research by Gray and Wedderburn (1960) showed that under certain conditions, people were able to process the meaning of two different messages arriving simultaneously at both ears, even though instructed to attend to only one of them. Broadbent's theory could not accommodate these new findings and it was therefore almost immediately superseded by the more comprehensive explanation, known as the Attenuator Model, proposed by Anne Treisman (Treisman 1960).

If the novel results can be confirmed by sufficient instances of replication, then a new theory must be developed in order not only to explain the results that were dealt with by the old theory, but also the new results too. This emphasizes the temporary nature of all theories. In a sense every theory awaits the critical data that will result in its being overthrown or improved. In practice however, it is fairly unusual for a theory to be overturned as decisively as Broadbent's. More often, negative data are balanced by other sets of positive results so that the overall picture is unclear.

This also suggests that there is a two-way relationship between theories and their supporting data. Note that figure 1.1 contains a feed-back loop between theory and the stages of observation and hypothesis formation. This shows that some kind of theory (however loosely it may be expressed) is always needed to guide and direct what happens in the earlier stages. It is only by using a theory as a starting point that a researcher is able to decide what is to be investigated, so while it is true that a theory is only as good as the data on which it is based, it is also the case that data collection cannot avoid being guided by theory. (See box 1.5 on inductive and deductive reasoning.)

It is important to recognize that these two elements, a theory and its data, are interdependent. Given data without an accompanying theory to explain them we will find we have only a mass of uncoordinated facts that by themselves explain nothing. On the other hand, without supporting data, a theory is merely a set of suppositions of unknown validity. Theories need data to ground them in reality, and equally, data need theories to elucidate their meaning.

As well as providing an explanation of how knowledge develops, Popper's work also helps to identify the criteria for separating the good theories from the less good ones. Clearly, not all theories are equally good. Some appear obviously to be better than others, in the sense that they seem to explain more about the world and are more resistant to refutation. However, the most important characteristics of a good theory are not necessarily those that are most apparent.

BOX 1.5   Inductive and deductive reasoning

Scientific reasoning employs both inductive and deductive reasoning to move between theories and data.

Induction is the reasoning that constructs a generalization (theory) on the basis of specific observations (data). For example, the cognitive psychologist Donald Broadbent determined, by means of 'dichotic listening' experiments, that when different information was transmitted to each ear, and the participants were directed to attend only to the information arriving at one ear, then most of the information arriving at the other ear was lost. By inductive reasoning from these data Broadbent subsequently devised his 'filter' theory, of selective attention.

Deduction is the reverse of induction, involving reasoning from a generalization to draw a conclusion about a specific case. Thus, deductive reasoning from Broadbent's filter theory (Broadbent, 1958) allows one to make specific predictions about performance in dichotic listening tasks.

● WHAT MAKES A GOOD THEORY? ●

Refutability

A good theory is not only one that is clearly expressed: it is also one that can be effectively tested and, if necessary, shown with certainty to be incorrect. In practice this means that it must be possible to say in advance of any test exactly what data would provide decisive refutation. This point may seem the opposite of the commonsense view that it is the business of scientists to show that theories are right, rather than wrong. However, to see why refutability is a desirable quality in a theory, consider the opposite possibility. An irrefutable theory is one for which it isn't possible to say what data would certainly show it to be incorrect. And if one can't specify the grounds on which it would be judged to be incorrect then it is equally impossible to say whether it is correct. An irrefutable theory thus simply presents a logical cul de sac: it doesn't lead anywhere.

This is an important issue because a theory or hypothesis that cannot, at least in principle, be shown to be incorrect cannot be regarded as scientific. Refutability is thus the critical test that, as Popper shows, allows us to demarcate sciences, such as psychology and chemistry from non-sciences such as astrology, psychoanalysis or bio-rhythm theory. These latter are characterized by the 'self-sealing' nature of their ideas which renders conclusive refutation impossible.

Economy

It has long been recognized that a good theory is one that is economical. This means it should aim to provide an explanation of the known facts that is as simple, and involves as few special assumptions, as possible. There are two reasons for this. The first is that a theory which is simple is likely to be more easily testable, and, as we have just seen, testability (refutability) is another criterion against which a theory can be measured. The second reason is that the simpler the theory, the easier it is to scrutinize the quality of the thinking. A simple, clearly expressed theory is clearly better than one which is complicated, and which could contain, all manner of ill-defined concepts, inadequate arguments or incorrect assumptions.

Predictive power

One result of research is the ability to make predictions about what will happen when certain conditions are met. Such predictions represent the application of a theory to a specific situation and can therefore only be as good as the theory. If a theory provides an accurate explanation of a phenomenon then it should also allow for accurate prediction of what will happen under certain conditions.

Productivity

A good theory is able to stimulate new thinking, leading eventually to the production of new knowledge. A common misperception of theories in general is that they try to provide a final and complete answer to a problem. On the contrary, a good theory will provide an open rather than a closed system of explanation in the sense that it suggests new ideas for further investigation, new interpretations of existing data, or new ways of tackling difficult problems. Far from closing off a line of inquiry with a final explanation, a theory should open up new avenues to be explored.

Testability

As we have seen above, a theory must be tested to confirm that the explanation it offers actually accounts for the problem being explored. This requires predictions from the theory to be compared to data. If the two agree then the theory can be considered upheld and can begin to count as a contribution to knowledge. If they do not agree, then it is necessary to reconsider – either the theory itself, or the predictions from the theory or the process of collecting data to compare with the predictions. (Strictly speaking, testing shows only that the theory is either incorrect or not incorrect. The latter is logically distinct from showing that it is correct.) Testability also implies clarity. A theory should be clear and explicit, so that it is obvious how the predictions follow from it. Unclear theories, obviously, are difficult to test with any confidence.

To summarize, this is how, according to Popper's account, science operates in its quest for certain knowledge. Predictions are derived from initial hypotheses, that are themselves based on formal or informal theories. These predictions are subjected to test by attempts to show them to be incorrect. Each confirmed prediction strengthens both the hypothesis and the underlying theory. After many such unsuccessful attempts at disconfirmation a theory may come to be regarded as virtually unassailable – that is, as essentially correct as an explanation. Conversely, each failure to confirm a validly derived prediction weakens the hypothesis and possibly also the underlying theory as well. When repeated tests of different predictions throw up a series of discrepant results over a period of time a theory becomes progressively weakened and eventually is replaced.

When we examine examples from psychology we see that this account offers an accurate picture of how knowledge generation proceeds. Reference has already been made to the part played by negative data in theory development in relation to Broadbent's case. The section below provides a further example, this time from social psychology, of how a theory was developed to explain the puzzling phenomenon of 'bystander apathy' (Latane and Darley, 1970).

● THE 'SCIENTIFIC METHOD' IN ACTION: THE 'BYSTANDER APATHY' RESEARCH ●

The observation

At around 3 a.m. on the night of 13 March 1964 in the New York borough of Queens, a 28-year-old woman called Kitty Genovese parked her car and set off for her nearby apartment. Before she could get there, however, she was attacked by a man who stabbed her several times. She screamed, attracting the attention of neighbours, several of whom put their apartment lights on and opened their windows. The attacker then walked away but came back after an interval and stabbed her again. Again she screamed, and again windows were opened in the apartment block. The man then drove away, but came back after a short while and stabbed her a third time, killing her. Despite the fact that the whole episode had lasted about 15 minutes, and had taken place before many witnesses, the police apparently received only one telephone call, 30 minutes after the first assault and 15 minutes after Ms Genovese's death, at 3.50 a.m. (based on the account in Brigham, 1986).

This was hardly the first time a young woman had been stabbed in New York at night in front of witnesses. However, what made it an exceptional case was the fact that she was stabbed several times over a period of some minutes, while many of the tenants in a nearby apartment block looked on, but made no effectual attempts to intervene. It was the latter features of the case that caused Bibb Latane and his co-workers to define the Kitty Genovese murder as a worthy research problem. They began a series of investigations that eventually led to the development of a new theory of bystander influence to explain the apparently incomprehensible behaviour of those who watched the series of assaults on Kitty Genovese.

The hypothesis

Latane and Darley called on earlier theories of social influence in proposing a theory of 'bystander influence' to account for the failure of the witnesses to intervene in the Genovese case. They began by proposing a model of the 'intervention process' – a series of decision points that a potential helper must pass through before offering aid (Latane and Darley, 1969). They believed that in the Genovese case the witnesses' behaviour was partly caused by a breakdown in the sequence of decisions that normally leads to the offer of assistance. They suggested that this is most likely to occur either at the point at which an event is defined as an emergency or at the point at which an onlooker decides that he has a responsibility to take some action. This led to the hypothesis that the failure to act at the latter point was caused by a 'diffusion of responsibility' among the witnesses in which they perceived the obligation to act to be shared among them.

The prediction

From this hypothesis, the specific prediction was made that the greater the number of bystanders to an emergency situation the greater would be the perceived sharing of responsibility and the lower would be the likelihood of any one of them intervening.

The test of prediction

This prediction was tested by Latane and his co-workers in a series of investigations that explored bystander responses to a number of different emergency situations, such as 'the fake seizure' (Darley and Latane, 1968), 'the fake fire' (Latane and Darley, 1968) and 'the collapsing bookcase' (Latane and Rodin, 1969). In the latter experiment, participants were conducted to a waiting room by a female confederate, who then went into an adjacent office. After a few minutes, a loud crash followed by moans was heard from the office. As predicted, it was found that the probability that help would be offered was closely related to the number of participants in the waiting room: the more participants there were, the lower the probability that help would be offered.

The conclusion

Since the prediction was confirmed, Latane's hypothesis, that responsibility diffusion occurs among witnesses to an emergency, could be provisionally accepted. Further successful tests of this and related predictions subsequently took place under a range of different circumstances, thereby providing support both to the hypothesis of responsibility diffusion and the underlying theory of bystander influence.

● POPPER, KUHN AND THE DEBATE ABOUT THE NATURE OF SCIENTIFIC PROGRESS ●

Popper's views on the development of theories also constitute an account of how science progresses: that is, how it is that reliable knowledge gradually replaces ignorance. In his view, progress occurs when an inadequate theory is replaced by one more adequate (or rather by one less inadequate) such replacement being triggered by the acquisition of some reliable new facts (data) about the world. The development of knowledge is thus, for Popper, a gradual and cumulative process in which the explanation of a natural phenomenon expressed in a theory is gradually refined and extended in scope.

At first sight, Popper's account may seem difficult to challenge, if only because with hindsight this is often how the sciences seem to have developed. The first hundred years of the history of psychology, for example, is strewn with discarded theories that have been superseded, as well as with some that are recognized as offering better explanations than those they replaced. However, in the 1960s an alternative account emerged that, among other differences, recognized that science is a highly social activity – a perception that is largely absent from Popper's somewhat idealized and abstract description.

The challenge to Popper came in the 1960s in *The Structure of Scientific Revolutions* (Kuhn, 1970) which proposed a quite different account of the growth of scientific knowledge. Kuhn's central idea was that each scientific discipline organizes itself around a core system of ideas that is shared by workers in that field and provides them with a distinctive way of viewing the world. Kuhn refers to this kind of shared world-view as 'a paradigm', arguing that progress in science occurs by means of revolutionary change from one paradigm to another.

In his book, Kuhn subjects the transition from one paradigm to another to detailed analysis. He begins by defining the pre-revolutionary state, which he calls 'normal science'. During periods of normal science there is a single dominant paradigm that constitutes the accepted world-view for most practitioners of a discipline. In effect, this defines and organizes the field of knowledge by identifying the questions that researchers should try to answer (i.e. questions that the paradigm defines as being likely to have answers) and by pointing to acceptable ways of getting answers. Disagreements among scientists are also structured by the paradigm in that they mainly occur about phenomena or interpretations of data that can be located within accepted limits. The paradigm in the stage of 'normal science' thus constitutes a powerful formative influence on the thinking of researchers that is extremely resistant to change.

However, change can, and does, occur. Periodically, scientists may encounter an anomaly – a fact or observation that cannot be accommodated within the framework provided by 'normal science'. According to Kuhn, the failure of an existing theory to account for discrepant data, or to allow recognized problems to be solved may trigger a 'paradigm crisis'. In this, a rival paradigm emerges and begins to gather support from members of the scientific community and a period, characterized by Kuhn as 'paradigm wars', ensues. If the new paradigm gathers sufficient support it may eventually supplant the old paradigm as the dominant world-view of the scientific community. If support for the new paradigm is not forthcoming after a period of turbulence normal science continues. Note that it is not necessary for the old paradigm to be shown to be false for it to be replaced, but merely that the new one provides a better fit to the observed facts than the old.

If a fundamental re-envisioning of the world does take place, it constitutes what Kuhn calls a 'paradigm shift' that affects all the workers in that discipline and defines a new set of problems at a fundamental level. Examples of such paradigm shifts might be the transition between Creationism and Evolution in nineteenth-century biology or in psychology, the anti-behaviourist 'cognitive revolution' of the 1960s (Leahy, 1992).

This account of the genesis of scientific revolutions may seem to take us quite a long way from our earlier concerns with hypothesis testing and theory development. However, it does have significant implications for an understanding of how science operates.

First, Kuhn's account rejects the idea that the growth of knowledge involves the simple accumulation of ideas in which old theories are replaced by newer, better ones. Rather, his account asserts that knowledge grows through violent revolutionary change as old paradigms are overthrown and replaced by new.

Second, Kuhn argued that theories are not just evaluated on their objective merits as explanations for data. In periods of normal science they are also assessed in terms of how well they fit the dominant paradigm. Theories that don't fit the paradigm are likely to be rejected no matter how persuasive an explanation they provide. Similarly, existing theories within the normal paradigm are not easily rejected just because they have been falsified. They may in fact be retained, despite their manifest inadequacies. For this reason, Kuhn rejected the idea (which he characterized as 'naive falsificationism') that in general science proceeds by simply replacing any theory shown to be incorrect with one more satisfactory. Clearly, simple replacement may sometimes occur (as we saw in the case of Broadbent) but Kuhn was sceptical of falsification as a description of the usual method of testing ideas at the level of theories, preferring to think in terms of rivalry between alternatives. For Kuhn, different theories that attempt to explain the same data can co-exist in a state of competition until one eventually emerges as the accepted view.

Third, Kuhn sees science as essentially a social activity. Scientists do not work alone, but are part of a community, formed by the common experience of socialization into a specific field of knowledge that is organized by an overarching paradigm. This, in part, explains why, for Kuhn, a paradigm shift necessarily involves a revolutionary change. The transition from old paradigm to new cannot be smooth simply because it involves an attack on the ideas of the established scientists by members of a new generation. It is almost inevitable under such circumstances, that change will be resisted for as long as possible and that only when the pressure in favour of the new paradigm becomes irresistible will the transition occur. The growth of knowledge is thus seen as fundamentally a social as well as a scientific process.

Popper and Kuhn each provide convincing, but competing, accounts of an important, complex and largely hidden area of human activity. But each applies a different perspective to the problems of scientific development. Popper's analysis invokes the power of logic but largely ignores the social context while Kuhn places social factors at the centre of his analysis. It is thus no surprise to find that they differ so markedly. However, neither Popper nor Kuhn can claim to have had the final word in the argument. Kuhn's ideas have been extremely influential over the last third of the twentieth century, but equally, Popper's account still has many adherents and the debate over their respective positions continues with apparently undiminished vigour (see e.g. Fuller, 2003). Nevertheless, Kuhn's ideas have a particular point for psychologists, since it may be argued that, in the methodology of research at least, psychology has only lately passed through a paradigm shift of its own. Kuhn thus not only gives us an interpretation of how science operates in general, but also provides a frame of reference for making sense of the very recent history of psychology.

● PSYCHOLOGY PARADIGMS OLD AND NEW ●

'Old paradigm' psychology and its problems

Old paradigm psychology is identified with the approach established during the nineteenth century by figures such as Fechner, von Helmholtz and Wundt. These 'founding fathers' had initially been trained in natural science, and naturally carried on their psychological work in

BOX 1.6   Positivism and anti-positivism

'Positivism' refers to the ideas developed in the mid-nineteenth century by the French philosopher, Auguste Comte. His aim was to establish strong connections between the established 'natural' sciences, such as physics and chemistry, and the newly emergent social sciences. One essential principle of his programme was that, since experimental research in the natural sciences was proving so successful as a way of generating new knowledge, research in the social sciences should adopt the same approach by making quantitative measures of variables under standardized conditions.

'Anti-positivism' is a twentieth-century challenge to the positivist view that denies that questions about human behaviour and experience can successfully be addressed by such means. There are a number of different, though closely related strands to anti-positivism that include realism in philosophy, postmodernism in cultural studies, feminism in politics and the humanistic or 'new paradigm' approach in psychology (see below).

the same vein. Their approach to research which was strongly positivistic in temper (see box 1.6) was aimed at the generation of objective knowledge that could be understood without reference to its social context, and from the beginning they adopted the experiment as the primary (though not exclusive) method of data collection.

This approach to 'doing psychology' remained the norm into the twentieth century. The methodological legacy of the 'founding fathers' became one of the central tenets of the behaviourism of Watson and Skinner, and was largely accepted even by non-behaviourists. Although there were important exceptions (most notably Freud and Piaget), in the main research participants were viewed as experimental 'subjects', sources of 'variables' whose contribution to research was largely limited to making responses to specific stimuli in tightly controlled laboratory situations. For the first hundred-odd years of its history psychology was largely defined by its commitment to this single method of research.

By the 1960s, public questioning of the traditional approach had begun to appear, and from the perspective offered by Kuhn's work, it could be said that a 'paradigm crisis' had begun. There was evidence of growing awareness within the psychological community that experiments, with their narrow focus on the quantitative testing of hypotheses about variables, were inadequate for the purposes of developing a proper understanding of human persons.

Thus, George Miller in his 1969 Presidential Address to the American Psychological Association (Miller, 1969) was prompted to ask why it was that psychology, despite its vast potential as an applied social science, had failed to live up to its early promise and had delivered so little of importance. He concluded that part of the answer lay in the 'misplaced scientism' involved in the application of the experimental method to questions about the behaviour and experience of human beings. This, he argued, was no more than a hangover from behaviourism which should be jettisoned. He proposed instead that better progress towards understanding could be achieved if, instead of using people as experimental 'subjects', researchers instead tried to enlist them as active co-participants in the research. Others followed Miller's

BOX 1.7   The experiment as a social situation

Martin Orne showed that research participants typically attempt to 'read' the 'demand characteristics' of a situation (the various cues provided by the immediate environment, the research procedure, and the behaviour of the researcher) in order to decide how they should react (Orne, 1962). Orne's work shows that research participants cannot be treated as merely passive emitters of responses because they are always actively engaged in trying to construct their own interpretation of what is happening. To the extent that they act on such interpretations, they introduce an entirely unpredictable set of influences into the research.

Robert Rosenthal (1963) identified a further source of bias in the form of an experimenter's own expectations on research results. The 'experimenter effect' as it is known, occurs when the experimenter fails adequately to control his/her behaviour towards the participants (e.g. by behaving differently to different groups) thereby again introducing a source of uncontrolled and unquantifiable error into the situation.

lead and among the dissatisfactions subsequently voiced about 'old paradigm' research were such issues as:

- The lack of ecological validity of most experimental studies meant that it was questionable whether experimental results obtained in one laboratory could be generalized to other situations and especially to the 'natural' environment outside it.
- The unrepresentative nature of volunteer samples. Largely for reasons of convenience, much experimental research was conducted using student volunteers who, as a group, were clearly younger, healthier and better educated than the general population. Nevertheless, it was routinely assumed that the results of such research held good for people in general.
- The social psychology of the psychology laboratory was itself suspect. Orne (1962) and Rosenthal (1963) among others, showed how the laboratory was far from being the neutral environment that earlier researchers had assumed. On the contrary, they showed that the social relations between experimenter and research participants could act as major sources of bias (see box 1.7).
- The problematic ethics of some research. Sensitized, perhaps, by such controversial investigations as Stanley Milgram's famous (or notorious) investigations of obedience (Milgram, 1963) and by Diana Baumrind's subsequent critique of his work on ethical grounds (Baumrind, 1964) there was increasing concern among psychologists about research ethics.

These debates on these issues provided an accumulation of evidence that led eventually to a rejection of the positivist argument that only by taking the same techniques and approaches that had been used in Chemistry and Physics could reliable psychological insights be achieved. Human persons enjoy a wholly different order of existence from inanimate nature (and much of animate nature as well) and it was beginning to be acknowledged that this difference should not only be recognized in research practice, but should be its founding principle. Three human characteristics in particular came to be seen as being of particular importance,

- *Humans are conscious.* That is, they are aware of their environment, and of their interactions with others. More importantly, they are also self-conscious and capable of experiencing, and reflecting on, the varieties of mental phenomena such as thoughts and emotions.
- *They are active and autonomous agents in the world,* experiencing the mental self as the cause and controlling force in their behaviour.
- *They are social entities.* Both behaviour and experience are largely driven by the presence of others and people are able to use their capacity for self-conscious awareness to manage their responses to others' behaviour.

The wider context of the 'paradigm crisis'

However, the 'paradigm crisis' was not simply triggered by dissatisfaction with the experiment as a method of research. It was also influenced by a number of other currents of thought that were present in western society at about the same time, including realism in philosophy, postmodernism in cultural studies, and feminism in politics. Each of these contributed ideas that pointed in essentially the same direction.

The realist philosophers (e.g. Harre and Seccord, 1972) argued that a truly scientific approach to the study of human beings must take into account the fact that it is the nature of human beings to reflect on their experiences and to act according to those reflections. The subjective understanding of one's own behaviour represents a uniquely privileged source of information that should not be ignored by the researcher. Therefore, to be truly understood, any account of behaviour and experience should always be interpreted in the light of what can be discovered about the individual actor's understanding of why the phenomena in question occurred.

Similarly, postmodernism, a cultural movement of the second half of the twentieth century, proposes that reality (knowledge) is a social construct, subjectively determined, rather than an objective phenomenon which is somehow located 'out there' beyond the individual observer. Examples of such constructs in psychology might be 'mental disorder' or 'psychological research' or 'attention'. Language is seen as crucial to this constructive process in that it helps to create reality rather than merely providing a reflection of it. Second, postmodernism sees knowledge as always located in a particular cultural environment: there are no context-free general laws to be discovered. Finally, it argues that the human person is not stable – but rather is a fluid, continuously changing entity. Polkinghorne (1992) argues that these ideas contributed significantly to the undermining of the 'old paradigm' way of doing psychology.

Feminist psychologists, offered a trenchant critique of 'masculinist' psychology that focused on the way research work is produced – including particularly the nature of the relationships between researchers and participants created within the traditional approaches to research. From this perspective, the 'old paradigm' research methods such as the experiment (but including other methods also), are seen as binding researcher and researched into an asymmetrical power relationship that is both exploitative and ultimately self-defeating. They therefore advocate the adoption of the more collaborative and reflexive stance offered by qualitative research methods. Criticisms of the experiment from this direction, such as those by Bell and Roberts (1984) both reflected and energized the discussions of the paradigm crisis.

'New paradigm' research in psychology

By the 1990s the evidence for a 'new paradigm' was beginning to be more clearly visible and there was growing interest within the British psychological research community. A significant watershed was a 1992 symposium on research methodology sponsored by the British Psychological Society (Henwood and Nicolson, 1995) that debated many of the issues, and clearly acknowledged the value of the qualitative approach. Since then, researchers in psychology have been encouraged to look for ways of addressing the experiential and cultural aspects of their research problems and have begun to borrow and develop a collection of methods that serve this goal. These include techniques as varied as discourse analysis, grounded theory, protocol analysis and ethnography. (See Richardson, 1997, for a more complete list.)

In what ways is new paradigm research different from what went before? The main differences between the old and new approaches can be summarized as follows:

- New paradigm research represents a shifting of research goals. Under the new paradigm the goal is to try to reach an understanding of the subjective world of the participant rather than (as under the old paradigm) simply accumulating quantitative data by measuring variables. Consequently research becomes more complex, requiring new methods and approaches. It also involves accepting that any explanations (theories) that emerge from research are largely specific to that situation (the principle known as indexicality). Thus, research can best be evaluated by the extent to which it can cast light on similar situations rather than by the 'old paradigm' notion of generalizability.
- New paradigm research also offers a different conception of the participant's role. Research participants are seen less as passive sources of data than as privileged routes of access to the subjective realm. The active co-operation of the participant thus becomes essential to successful research. A participant's awareness of being studied that under the old paradigm was seen as a source of error is, in the new paradigm, turned into a guiding principle.
- Different research methods are used to collect a wider range of data. Qualitative (descriptive) methods such as interviewing have come to the fore as the key to collecting data about the participant's experiential world. Consequently, research becomes a matter of interpreting qualitative data in order to extract meaning, and the analysis of language (e.g. using discourse analysis) becomes a key activity (see chapter 6 below).
- New paradigm research offers two important extensions to the role of the researcher. First, a researcher seeks the active co-operation of participants rather than treating them as passive sources of 'data'; second, the researcher's role becomes informed by the notion of reflexivity, in which her own experience is allowed to contribute to the process of research. For example, someone making a qualitative study of family relationships might draw on her own experiences as a child and sibling as a source of ideas when planning the research and in her discussions with participants.

Modern psychology now presents a methodologically varied picture. It is a multi-method discipline, employing a range of techniques in its quest for information that not only reflect the increasing interest in applied knowledge and the varied nature of the subject matter, but also the increasing sophistication of researchers. A range of qualitative methods is now available, from which researchers can select whichever seems to best suit a particular purpose. Employing a qualitative approach does not, of course, exclude the possibility of using the experiment when it offers the best means of attacking a particular problem, possibly as part of a combined quantitative/qualitative strategy. Even in such fields as cognitive psychology, where the experiment is likely to remain the method of choice of most researchers, a qualitative approach has proved fruitful (e.g. Reason 1990). What has clearly changed since the 1970s, is that the narrowly quantitative approach is no longer dominant: modern psychology is now much more open to the very interesting possibilities offered by qualitative research.

Chapter Summary

1   Science is characterized by transparency, rationality and the production of objective evidence as the source of authority for its statements. Transparency refers to the fact that the evidence for any statement is provided; rationality means that the logic of any scientific arguments should be clear; and authority rests on the presentation of verifiable facts.

2   Empiricism – the idea that reliable knowledge can only be obtained by interacting with the world and collecting information about the matter in question – represents the foundation of all scientific activity. Adherence to this principle guarantees that any knowledge thus acquired will be connected to reality, and will be available to others.

3   Science exists to provide a way of developing knowledge of the natural world. Among its characteristic activities are description, based on careful and accurate observation; the construction of explanation in the form of theories; the prediction of events using theory, and, in some disciplines, the exercise of control, in which natural events can be made to occur, or prevented from occurring.

4   The development of knowledge by empirical investigation can be represented in terms of a 'scientific method' consisting of a sequence of stages, though it is also widely recognized that the sequence may be truncated or otherwise varied from the ideal pattern. In the model, the stages of observation; problem identification; and the development and testing of predictions from hypotheses lead ultimately to the construction of a new theory or the revision of an existing one.

5   Theory development is the ultimate goal of science since theories represent statements of existing knowledge. In this, following Karl Popper, the central idea is that true knowledge represented by accurate theories can only be attained by attempting to falsify hypotheses – that is, by attempts to show that a hypothesis is *not* true rather than that it *is* true.

6   Popper's view of science and the growth of scientific knowledge has been challenged by Thomas Kuhn, whose central concept is the 'paradigm' – the framework of ideas that structures a field of knowledge. In his view, the development of a field of science requires the community of practitioners to transfer its allegiance from an old to a new paradigm

in the phenomenon of 'paradigm shift'. Some recent developments in psychology can be interpreted as involving just such a paradigm shift

7   'Old paradigm' psychological research can be characterized by its essentially positivist stance, as evidenced by its reliance on the experimental method and tendency to treat the human participants of research as 'subjects' – passive data sources.

8   From the 1960s there was increasing evidence of an impending 'paradigm shift' in psychology. Among the specific causes of dissatisfaction with the old paradigm approach were concerns about validity, sampling, the experimental procedure and research ethics. With hindsight, this development can be seen to be part of a much wider current of anti-positivist ideas that ran through other academic disciplines such as philosophy, politics and cultural studies.

9   The 'new paradigm' psychology that had emerged by the 1990s was characterized by a multi-method approach to research that included a range of qualitative methods, as well as encompassing somewhat different definitions of the goals of research, and researcher and participant roles.

10 Psychology today is a methodologically diverse discipline that draws on an eclectic range of methods and approaches in its quest for insights into the causes of human behaviour and experience.

● FURTHER READING ●

Leahy, T. H. (1992). *A history of psychology*, 3rd edn. Englewood Cliffs, NJ: Prentice Hall.
Viney, W. (1993). *A history of psychology: Ideas and context*. London: Allyn and Bacon.

Part I
METHODS OF RESEARCH

2
INTERVIEWS

CHAPTER MAP

Introduction

Types of Interviews

Structured and unstructured interviews
Exploratory and group interviews

Planning an Interview

When to interview?
Developing an interview schedule
Types of questions

Interviewing

First tasks
The interview environment
Recording the interview
Closing the interview

Psychological Processes in Interviewing

Self-presentation
Social desirability effect and response bias
Rapport
Interviewee motivation

Ethical Issues

Confidentiality
The right to withdraw from an interview

Extension Activities

Chapter Summary

Further Reading

THIS CHAPTER

- *Asks how an interview differs from ordinary conversation.*
- *Considers the different kinds of interview that can be employed.*
- *Provides guidance on how to develop a schedule of questions and identifies a range of question types.*
- *Describes the key tasks to be completed in planning, carrying out, and closing an interview.*
- *Considers some psychological processes in interviewing, such as the development of rapport and self-presentation by the interviewer.*
- *Offers guidance on how the ethics of confidentiality and the respondent's right of withdrawal should be applied in the interview.*

KEY CONCEPTS

Structured, unstructured and semi-structured interviews, exploratory interviews
rapport
self-presentation

themes
faking good acquiescent response set
open, closed, descriptive, structural questions
double-barrelled and leading questions

● INTRODUCTION ●

The interview is probably the most frequently used method of gathering information, both within and outside the social sciences. Most people have had at least one experience of being interviewed, whether at school, college or for a job, and know (possibly all too well!) what it is like to have been on the receiving end of questioning in a semi-formal setting. Thanks to television and radio nearly everyone has extensive second-hand experience of many other kinds of interview, both real and simulated, ranging from police interrogations to bantering conversation between guest and host on a TV chat-show. Clearly, we all have some knowledge, whether at first or second hand, of what typically happens in these kinds of interviews.

Does this help us understand the nature of the research interview? On the surface, it may seem that it does. It seems fairly obvious that having been an interviewee in the past helps you understand what another interviewee might feel like – and this could help you become a more sensitive interviewer. However, there are some hidden aspects of interviewing that usually don't occur to an observer, or even to an interviewee.

From the outside, research interviews might appear to consist of 'just asking questions' in order to achieve the transmission of information between the individuals concerned, but they have their own characteristic approach to the task. A research interview aims to elicit significant personal information in depth (quite unlike, say, a TV celebrity interview) and is generally based on careful preparatory work that identifies the topics to be explored, and places them within an overall structure. The interviewer also works within strict ethical guidelines that help protect the respondent against exploitative or psychologically damaging experiences.

Examples of transcripts of research interviews can be found in sources such as Burman (1994a) and on the internet. For an example, and an interesting discussion of the issues arising in the analysis of such transcripts, see Antaki (2002). A reading of any interview transcript usually reveals that its purpose of transferring information from interviewee to interviewer affects the interaction between interviewer and interviewed in the following ways.

- It appears that the respondent is more knowledgeable on the topic than the interviewer. The interviewer talks much less than the respondent so that the transfer of information occurs largely in one direction.
- Like a conversation, the interaction is governed by turn taking, but the interviewer uses her turn to speak to help move the interview forward (by expressing understanding of what is being said) rather than by expressing her own ideas.
- The respondent has voluntarily passed most of the control of the interview over to the interviewer. It is the interviewer who has decided the topic, who initiates a particular issue within that topic, and who, once an answer has been received, decides whether, and when, the interview will move on to other matters.
- The respondent is allowed to express ideas at her own pace. Much of the interviewer's speech is intended to encourage the respondent's thinking about the topic and provide space to allow ideas to emerge naturally.

The control aspect of the interview – that is, the process of managing the questioning process so that the interview moves forward – requires skill and the personal qualities to achieve a degree of control without antagonizing the informant. (See below when the issue of rapport is discussed.) Most people can acquire the skills needed to interview well but if it is to be successful, the interview also requires careful planning and an appreciation of the issues involved in using this method of research. We begin by looking at what needs to be considered when you first approach the task of carrying out a research interview.

● TYPES OF INTERVIEWS ●

Interviews differ most fundamentally in terms of the extent to which the process is structured and planned in advance.

Structured interviews

A structured interview (also called the standardized interview) is one in which the form and direction of the questioning is largely decided in advance. At the extreme this involves no more than the interviewer reading through a prepared list of questions: the verbal administration of a questionnaire. It therefore lends itself particularly to telephone interviewing when a relatively simple selection of verbal responses is required. Structured interviews give the interviewer a high degree of control over the questioning process, a feature which may be desirable in certain circumstances, for example, if the aim is to compare individual responses and/or apply quantitative techniques of data analysis. On the negative side, because questions are decided in advance, the interviewer is largely prevented from pursuing lines of inquiry that have not been anticipated.

Unstructured interviews

An unstructured interview, by contrast, is more like a dialogue in which the interviewer is not pursuing a minutely predetermined set of questions but, rather, sets off to follow a general topic, and allows the content of the respondent's answers to guide the questioning process, much like a normal conversation. Unstructured interviews thus offer a much more fluid and flexible approach in which much of the control of the direction taken by the interview is handed over to the respondent with the interviewer reacting to the respondent rather than vice versa. The unstructured approach requires considerable skill, not least because continual attention must be given to the informant's replies while the interview is in progress.

Semi-structured interviews

It is possible to combine these two approaches in interviews with a semi-structured format. In this, the general direction of the interview may be mapped out in advance as a series of topics (the interview schedule or guide) but as the interview proceeds, the questioning process is guided by the content in the respondent's answers. The guide acts as a checklist to ensure all the required topics are covered, but there are no standardized questions prepared in detail in advance. This flexible approach balances the need to allow the interviewer to retain some control over the interview, while at the same time, by allowing the respondent to initiate new topics or to direct the interviewer's attention to specific areas, it recognizes that she has unique knowledge of the research topic.

In the rest of this chapter we will have the semi-structured interview specifically in mind although much of what will be said applies also to both the structured and unstructured forms.

Exploratory interviews

An interview need not be the primary method of data collection in a research project. Because of its flexibility, and closeness to data sources, it is also ideally suited as a method for conducting the preliminary exploration of a topic before the main research effort begins. Such exploratory research may be undertaken to identify the key questions and issues in the project, to test preliminary hypotheses about relationships, or simply to locate the eventual boundaries for the subsequent inquiry. One approach to research that uses exploratory interviewing is the 'grounded theory' method (Glaser and Strauss, 1967). This technique employs extensive exploratory work as an essential part of a process whose goal is to allow theory to emerge naturally from data, rather than having data collection driven by theory (see chapter 6).

Group interviews

Interviews are not inevitably conducted by a single interviewer with a single respondent. It is also possible to conduct interviews with a number of people in the structured situation of a focus group. See Vaughn, Schumm and Sinagub (1996) for a detailed introduction to this form of interview.

● PLANNING AN INTERVIEW ●

Among the key skills required to produce good interview data is the ability to plan the questions to which the interviewee can respond. This section looks in detail at how questions may be generated and organized into an interview schedule.

When to interview?

Although it offers an extremely flexible method of research, it is clearly not appropriate to use the interview on all research questions. The main indicators are as follows.

When the wish is to obtain more or less detailed qualitative information about some aspect of individual experience or behaviour. Interviewing allows reports of perceptions, actions, emotional states, and the like, to be expressed in the respondent's own words with a minimum of intervention or editing by the interviewer. It is most effective when the researcher wishes to obtain access to the subjective world of a respondent in a particularly direct way. It may be employed alone or in tandem with other methods such as observation or a survey.

A checklist setting out the main tasks that should be considered when planning interview-based research can be found below in box 2.4.

Developing an interview schedule

Once an appropriate research problem has been found, the next task is to think about the questions to be asked and to develop them into an interview schedule.

This needs to be done carefully, since the value of an interview (from the interviewer's perspective) may hang on getting the questions right. It is important to make sure that the interview has a clear direction consisting of questions that are pertinent to the main research problem. Otherwise the questions will seem disjointed and random and the interview itself may not run smoothly.

One way of achieving this is to use a structured approach to generating questions. This might involve the following steps.

1   Write a problem statement.
2   From the problem statement identify the key themes or ideas that direct attention to different issues.
3   For each of the key themes sketch a number of specific questions that could be put directly to a respondent. These are particularly useful when a theme is being approached for the first time. (But be prepared to abandon them in the interview, if necessary.)
4   Revise the results of step 3 until you are satisfied.

By this means, a researcher can obtain a collection of possible questions focused on the issues of the research. They can then be used in an interview as required, while not necessarily restricting the respondent's replies in any way.

To see how this might look in practice, consider how a social psychologist with an interest in relationships might plan to interview young couples on the linked questions of how their relationship seems to have progressed in the past and how it might develop in the future.

The problem statement

The purpose in writing the problem statement is to help fix in your mind the precise area to be covered by the research and to say something about how it will be approached. The statement should aim to specify, as clearly as possible, the problem to be researched, the limits of the inquiry. It could also mention the areas that the research will *not* cover. The problem statement for interviews on relationship development might look like this. For example:

> The aim of the research is to investigate the process of relationship formation by means of semi-structured interviews of young couples who have recently begun dating each other. In general the interviews will focus on their recent experience of becoming a couple and their ideas about the future development of the relationship; each member of a pair will be interviewed separately.
>
> One theory of relationship formation (Thibaut and Kelley, 1959) suggests that the early development of relationships is conducted through a process of negotiation; the interviews will explore this possibility and try to identify some of its key features as well as any issues or problems that it raises for the participants. The interview sample will consist of heterosexual couples who have been exclusively dating each other for at least 2 months and no more than 6 months and who expect their relationship to continue at its present level of intensity for at least another 6 months.

Themes

The next step is to identify the themes or general topics to be explored in the interviews. These can be quite general since they are only intended to serve as pegs on which strings of questions can be hung. In the examples below the themes have been expanded towards finished questions in order to clarify the process.

Theme 1: the beginning of the relationship

How did dating begin – what was the context in terms of existing relationships? How did the relationship progress in the early days? What were the issues and problems? What were the attitudes of parents and friends? How have things changed in the relationship since those early days? What now are the feelings about this period?

Theme 2: the relationship in the present

What are their current self-perceptions? How do they see themselves and their relationship now? What are the main characteristics or features of their relationship as they see it now? How do they feel about this? How do they think parents or friends see them? How have relations with these others changed (if at all)? What is currently most important to them in the relationship?

Theme 3: negotiation processes in the relationship

What arc the sources of disagreement or conflicts in the relationship? How intense are these? How are they managed and with what results. Is it possible to provide examples? Are they aware of negotiating with each other? What issues are negotiable and what not?

Theme 4: expectations for the future

How would they like the relationship to continue? Do they expect any changes to it over the next 6 months or so? Why? How? How are any changes likely to come about?

Clearly, this is not a definitive list of all the possible themes and questions that could be explored, but it offers an indication of how an interview might begin to take shape as a set of areas for exploration in the interview itself.

Some specific questions

The themes offer a starting point and a framework for thinking about the specific questions that might be used within an interview. In the following examples the questions are all drawn from theme 1 above and consist of a number of lead questions supplemented by several (optional) prompts – reminders to the interviewer to probe the initial answer more deeply, if necessary. Depending on how an interviewee responds these might or might not be needed, and you could end up using all of them, some of them or none of them in an actual interview.

Q1:   Did you know each other before you started dating?
      Prompt if answer is yes:
            Where, when, what context?
            Can you tell me a bit about that?
            What did you think of your current partner at that point?
            Why do you think you felt that?

Q2:   Were you dating anyone else at that point?
      Prompt if answer is yes
            How long had you been dating?
            Tell me how that relationship had been.

Q3:   How did you come to start dating your present partner?
      Prompts:
            When was this?
            Where was this?
            How did it happen?

Q4:   How did you feel when that happened?
      Prompts:
            Happy?
            Apprehensive?
            Can you tell me a bit more about how you felt?

Q5:   How do you think your partner felt about you at that time?
      Prompts:
            How could you tell?
            What did he say about it?

This could be continued through the remaining themes until the entire interview has been mapped out in detail. Not all interviewers will necessarily find this level of structured preparation necessary, and some will prefer to go into an interview with no more than a list of themes to be explored. However, when one is learning the skills of interviewing, the approach outlined above will probably be preferred. It does have the merit of providing a range of prepared questions on each topic, thus ensuring that all the themes of interest are likely to be thoroughly covered in the interview.

Revision of the questions

After a couple of days take another look at the question schedule. Do the questions really cover all the angles you identified in the themes? If not what do you have to do to make sure they are covered. Similarly, if there are any redundant or mis-directed questions get rid of them or re-write them. Finally, try to see the questions from a respondent's point of view. How do you think you would respond to those questions if your roles were reversed?

The interview schedule is a working document that is used to run the interview. It consists of the themes and related questions that the interviewer anticipates it will be helpful to have to hand in the research and these should form a logical progression so that, at the planning stage at least, the interview has a clear shape. Usually, more general (or the easiest) questions should be asked before specific (difficult) ones. Ask questions about the informant's mental state as often as questions about behaviour. Try to find out how the informant responded to, or made sense of particular events and experiences. And periodically use questions that restate an earlier answer in different terms to enable you to check that you have understood what has been meant, as well as what was said.

Before embarking on the main interviews it is a good idea to pilot the interview schedule with one or two preliminary interviews in order to check whether the questions are generally comprehensible to the informant and have *the meaning you intend*. Some degree of modification to the schedule is usual at this stage, although this may involve no more than a general 'tightening up' of the questions. Piloting will also give an idea how long an interview is likely to take and allow you to practise your preferred approach to self-presentation.

Most interviews will require more than one type of question. Box 2.1 lists the main questions forms that may be used, and also lists some styles of questioning that should be avoided.

BOX 2.1   Types of question used in interviews

Different kinds of questions allow different aspects of the problem to be explored and allow a researcher to obtain a full picture from a respondent.

Closed questions invite a specific and limited kind of response, e.g. 'How many children do you have?' or 'Do you know what is meant by the term "gender identity"?'

Open-ended questions are questions that invite the respondent to reply in any way they think appropriate, e.g. 'What do you think is meant by the term "gender identity"?'

A number of different types of open-ended questions can be distinguished, for example:

Descriptive questions are those which ask for straightforward descriptions of events or processes, e.g. 'What did your mother say when she saw you helping your father work on the car in your best dress?'

Structural questions are questions about relationships between different parts (structures) of a person's experience, e.g. 'How did your behaviour at school differ from what it was like at home?'

Hypothetical questions are questions that pose a possible situation and invite a response, e.g. 'What would your mother have said if she'd seen you taking the money . . . ?' One can use hypothetical questions in order to test ideas about what might have happened under other circumstances.

General questions are questions which invite the informant to make general statements, e.g. 'Do you think that boys today identify with their fathers as strongly as they did thirty years ago?'

Types of question to avoid

Some types of question should be carefully avoided because of their capacity to confuse or mislead a respondent.

- Complex questions are too long and too wordy to be easily absorbed in one attempt. If a respondent asks for a question to be repeated it may be an indication that the question has been presented in a way that is too complicated to be easily understood.
- Double-barrelled questions are those that try to combine two questions in one sentence, e.g. 'Were you ever punished for your behaviour at school, or did you have good relations with the teachers?' Contains two distinct questions linked by the interviewer's (unsound) assumption that the answers must be mutually exclusive.
- Leading questions state a position in the guise of a question and invite agreement, e.g. 'Do you agree that children need to be given clear guidelines on acceptable behaviour?' 'Isn't it true that gender is a matter of nature rather than nurture?'

● INTERVIEWING ●

Once the question schedule has been prepared further work is necessary to plan the interview itself. This becomes relatively straightforward if you think of the interview as having three sections, a beginning, a middle and an end, each having specific necessary tasks.

First tasks

Successful interviewing depends crucially on building a good working relationship with a respondent (see box 2.2). It is good practice to let a respondent have a written statement of the aims and scope of your research project, and a note of the specific topics you would like to talk about when you first make an approach. Your informant can then consider at leisure, and begin to make an informed decision about whether she wishes to be interviewed. Respondents will also need to know from the beginning both that you will preserve confidentiality and that they will be able to remove any remarks they wish from the final record.

If it can be arranged, a pre-interview meeting held a few days before the main interview is also useful. This can be used to establish the general range of questions to be explored, and to answer any questions that the respondent may have about the process in general. One important point to establish in the preliminary meeting is how long the interview session will last. Complex topics requiring many questions may be better broken down into sub-topics and spread over a number of interview sessions if you have time, and the respondent agrees, rather than rushed through in a single session.

The interview environment

The basic requirement is for a space where you can both relax and be free of distractions or interruptions by others. A meeting on neutral territory has both pros and cons. On the one hand, you may have more control over the conditions under which the interview is conducted, but on the other hand, your informant may feel less relaxed than if you agree to hold

BOX 2.2   A summary of interviewing skills

Successful interviewing is a complex skill that can only be learned over time through practice and attention to the feedback obtained from interviewees. The following lists point towards some of the important characteristics of good interviewing.

When interviewing, try to avoid

- Asking questions to satisfy your own curiosity.
- Showing impatience, criticism or indifference.
- Staring or looking preoccupied.
- Asking questions that the respondent finds difficult to understand.
- Wanting to fill any short silences with a question.
- Looking away from the speaker.
- Interrupting what is being said.
- Planning what to say next while listening.
- Making judgements about the other person, or what they have to say.
- Feeling you want to control what is going on.
- Getting into a disagreement.
- Rushing the interview.

Try to make sure you

- Attend fully to your informant all the time.
- Give good eye contact, without staring down.
- Read your informant's body language for clues to attitudes and feelings.
- Use your posture and facial expression to show interest and a sympathetic attitude.
- Leave plenty of spaces in the flow of question and answer in which your informant can think about what to say.
- Spend less time talking than your informant.
- Adopt a neutral attitude to everything that is said, even if your opinion is asked for.
- Try to remember as much as possible, not only what was said, but how it was expressed.
- Only ask the questions that are needed
- Watch for inconsistencies in answers and repeat questions if necessary.
- Are alert to changes in the interviewee's body language that may signal an unwillingness to continue.

the interview on his or her home territory. If the interview takes place in the informant's living room you just have to accept the situation as you find it. It is not a good idea to allow anyone else to be present unless you are interviewing them as a couple.

The seating arrangements can also make a difference to the success of an interview, and you should try to get the seating arranged so you both sit on the same level, or if this is not possible, that you, as interviewer sit at a lower level than your informant. Height is a powerful indicator of status, and to be seated with an informant at a lower level sends an inhibiting message. If possible, also have the seating arranged so that you are sitting at an angle to your informant. This makes it easy to maintain eye contact without seeming to dominate or appear adversarial.

The beginning phase of an interview besides the initial greeting, and any small talk (important to the development of rapport) should be directed towards the following points.

1 Restate the purpose and scope of the interview in case the informant has forgotten, or misunderstood (essential with some older respondents).
2 Check that these are understood.
3 Obtain once again your informant's consent to be interviewed and restate the right to withdraw at any time.
4 Collect any personal details such as name, age or marital status. This starts to get the respondent accustomed to being in the interviewee role and to your style of asking questions.

Recording the interview

The information generated by an interview has to be recorded in some way so that it can be examined and analysed later. This in turn raises the issue of how you manage the recording process. Essentially the choice lies between written notes and some form of electronic recording. Whichever method is selected, obtaining an informant's permission is essential.

In principle, written notes may range from a verbatim record to brief notes. However, in practice, verbatim recording in handwriting always takes too long and very brief notes make problems when they eventually come to be reconstructed. It is therefore necessary to pitch the note-taking somewhere between the two extremes and only experience, or a few trial runs will show the best solution for you.

An alternative to the difficulties of taking written notes is to use electronic recording – either audio alone or with video. These have the advantage of producing a verbatim record that can be transcribed later, thus allowing you to concentrate on listening to what your informant is saying and considering your next question. If possible, run a preliminary test to make sure that you can obtain a clear recording from where the interview is to take place – it may be acoustically poor, with lots of echo or intrusive noise. It also goes without saying that you need to be totally sure of the reliability of the equipment that you will be using, and to take along spare tapes and batteries.

Some ways of analysing the transcripts resulting from an interview are discussed separately in chapter 6.

Closing the interview

Once you have asked all the questions on your schedule and/or are satisfied that the information gathering is as complete as you can make it on this occasion, begin to close down the interview. The key elements of this are:

• Check, using open-ended questions such as, 'Is there anything else you would like to say about X?' or 'Do you think we have left out anything on this subject?', that you have covered the intended ground as thoroughly as possible.
• Check your informant's feelings. It is important to do this conscientiously if you think that your questions have touched on anything painful, but it is also good practice to do

it anyway. Try to help your informant deal with any painful emotions she may have as a result of participating in the interview, and be ready to seek the advice of a more experienced researcher if necessary.

• Give your interviewee some 'positive strokes', for example, by commenting on anything you found interesting or especially helpful to your project. Your aim should be to leave her feeling good about participating in the research.

• Finally you need to manage the return from interview mode to a more normal style of interaction with your informant. Comments such as 'You must be tired after answering so many questions', or 'I can see I was worrying unnecessarily about doing this interview' are good for helping the transition to normal conversation and can merge quite naturally into general leave-taking remarks. Before you finally part, confirm that a transcript of the interview will be provided later.

After the interview a brief letter of thanks to the informant will be appreciated. Later on, send the transcript, at the same time reminding the respondent of her right to have removed any section of it that she now wishes to withdraw. If there is no reply after a reasonable interval you should make a further effort to make contact, but are probably safe to assume that there is no objection to your use of the transcript. Seek advice from an experienced researcher on this point if necessary.

● PSYCHOLOGICAL PROCESSES IN INTERVIEWING ●

Given that it involves two people interacting for an extended period of time, sometimes on topics of high personal significance, it is hardly surprising that an interview may be psychologically complex. In the following section we review some of the influences present in all interviews.

Self-presentation

In an interview your 'performance' as an interviewer is under scrutiny as the respondent, often without much consciousness of the process, forms a judgement about you. As happens in all social encounters, the parties are rapidly evaluating each other and drawing conclusions. This may include decisions about your credibility, trustworthiness, efficiency, level of knowledge, and much else besides. Clearly it is necessary to think about what the respondent is likely to make of you and your research during the interview.

The way in which you present yourself will play an important part in deciding her general willingness to help, how she responds to particular themes or questions, and thus, ultimately, the success of the interview. Smiling, for example, is usually interpreted by others as indicating a relaxed state and a liking for the other person, so it is a good idea to smile. However, smiling that the respondent feels is inappropriate (perhaps because it occurs too frequently, or too intensely) can also be interpreted as indicating a lack of confidence, an over-eagerness to please or even as threat and may therefore unsettle an informant and reduce her willingness to co-operate in the interview. Paying attention to how your informant seems to be 'reading' you is therefore essential.

The goal is to try to present yourself in a way that both feels natural and also allows you to demonstrate that you possess a key cluster of attributes and skills. The ability to ask questions clearly and concisely, to keep track of progress, and to have a warm and friendly, but not overbearing, demeanour are essential if you are to put a respondent at ease and conduct a successful interview.

An interviewee's answers will invariably be affected by a complicated mix of factors such as the perceived age, sex, social class, and ethnicity of the interviewer, especially when these are different from her own. It is impossible to predict how these influences will work in individual cases, but clearly it is necessary to consider their possible impact, not least because they may make it very difficult to elicit information. It has, for example, been shown that working-class interviewees provide much fuller information in response to questioning if the interviewer is also perceived to be working-class, than if she is perceived to be middle-class.

Dress is one key indicator of social status that can be easily 'read' by almost everyone. The greater the perceived difference in status, the less likely it is that informants will relax and speak easily. Therefore, you should consider how the clothes you intend to wear may be 'read' by your informant in the light of the information provided by other sources such as your accent or your ethnicity. 'Dressing down' to interview working-class respondents is not likely to neutralize the status differences if you also have an extremely 'posh' accent. Nor will 'dressing up' be helpful if it creates suspicions about your motives or background.

Social desirability effect and response bias

This is also known as 'evaluation apprehension' or, more plainly, as 'faking good'. In an interview the respondent may feel uncomfortable with some of the questions, usually because of their content. The normal, socially learned, response to this feeling is to answer evasively in the way most likely to place oneself in a favourable light, or to be socially acceptable. For example, respondents asked whether they have ever stolen anything may deny it vehemently, or people questioned about their relationships may tone down outright hatred to expressions of mild dislike.

Social desirability clearly affects the trustworthiness of the data, and if an interview covers matters on which it seems likely to operate, one obviously has to treat a respondent's answers with caution. However, the possibility of social desirability effect can also be reduced to some extent by taking care to develop rapport with a respondent.

Even where the social desirability effect seems unlikely, respondents can still show unconscious bias in their answers to questions in the form of an 'acquiescent response set'. This is the tendency to agree to questions that offer a choice of a 'yes' or 'no' answer. The root cause of this form of bias is probably similar to the social desirability effect mentioned above. Respondents may unconsciously regard negative answers as unhelpful, and therefore tend to produce positive (socially desirable) answers when they have the choice. Their need to feel that they have assisted the researcher outweighs their need to tell the strict truth.

Rapport

An interviewer should also aim to build a good sense of rapport with the person they are interviewing. Essentially, this means trying to develop a relationship with the other person in

BOX 2.3 Developing rapport with an informant

The development of a sense of rapport – implying mutual trust and open communication between interviewer and interviewee – clearly depends to some extent on the personalities involved. However, an interviewer can also foster rapport through her own behaviour.

- Honest and open communication is vital. Any hint of evasiveness may be seen as confirming suspicions about the researcher's motives, or integrity.
- Demonstrate respect for the respondent. The researcher should endeavour to demonstrate that the research will be conducted with integrity and consideration for other people.
- Show you are aware of what it feels like to be interviewed. The researcher should reassure the respondent that they are aware of what they may be experiencing through participation in the interview, even though they can't fully share the feelings.

which both of you feel you are 'on the same wavelength', and are able to communicate clearly and honestly with each other. Rapport can be thought of as occurring in three phases in an interview.

Initially, of course, rapport will be low because an informant may be wary, even mistrustful of the interviewer. At this stage you don't know each other at all, so sensitive information is likely to be held back, or heavily censored.

As the interview progresses and rapport starts to build up, there is a greater willingness to reveal personal details, and to make self-disclosing statements. The way in which such information is received by the interviewer is important for the further development of rapport.

In the third phase, the continued disclosure of personal information, and appropriate responses from the researcher enable a sense of rapport to emerge. There may be a high degree of trust between the participants. When rapport is this good, the informant may adopt the role of a collaborator in the research, using privileged knowledge to direct the interviewer's attention to particular items of information rather than simply taking a passive role.

Interviewee motivation

The most important factor in determining whether an interview is successful is the motivation of the informant (see box 2.3). Motivation – the desire to help you in your research – is, to put it crudely, what determines how hard an informant will be prepared to work for you in the interview. Talking, thinking, remembering, and similar cognitive activities all require effort, and are tiring, especially when they have to be done to order, and interviewers should try to ensure that informants are well motivated in order to maximize the work that they are prepared to put in to the interview. This is particularly true of interviews asking for very detailed explorations of behaviour or experience.

The ideal is an informant who is just as interested in and committed to your research goals as you are yourself (and people can be extraordinarily tolerant of a researcher's demands). The following points can help them do their best to help you.

- Tell informants, from the first contact, how grateful you are, and how useful their information will be to you, even if you're not sure.
- Take the time to explain the aims and background of your research project in understandable terms. Be particularly careful to say why you want them to help you (otherwise they may be left wondering 'why me?').
- Explain what will happen to the information (both raw data and the final report) once it is in your care, and make it clear that all information is protected by a confidentiality rule (see below). Give, and respect, any further assurances about confidentiality that are demanded. Uncertainty about any aspect of the interview reduces motivation, and this is particularly true of doubts about the eventual uses of the information.

● ETHICAL ISSUES ●

As with all research in social science, interviews should be planned and executed with ethical issues at the forefront of a researcher's mind. A summary of the British Psychological Society guidelines can be found in appendix 1, but two issues in particular should be considered particularly carefully when considering interview-based research.

Confidentiality

Qualitative data is highly accessible – it consists of verbal descriptions which can easily be read by anyone – so it is essential to take care to maintain confidentiality. This is particularly necessary given that informants may reveal more than they intend when a good rapport has been established with an interviewer.

Confidentiality requires that all records – interview notes, as well as subsequent re-writings – should be organized so that the source of the information cannot be identified. This can be achieved by using a code number or a fictitious name to identify a respondent. Similarly, all personal information, such as place of residence, or occupation, which could lead to identification should be either removed from the transcript or disguised. If it is necessary to have a record of an informant's personal details, this should be kept entirely separate from the interview data, so that the two cannot be connected. This rule should be regarded as absolute even if informants give permission for real names to be used.

The right to withdraw from an interview

The right of every informant to withdraw from the interview, at any point and without giving a reason, should be clearly stated at the beginning of the meeting and repeated, if necessary, at intervals.

The nature of the interview means that there is always the possibility that an informant will want to withdraw after it has begun, especially if the questioning approaches matters of deep

BOX 2.4   A checklist for interview planning

Preliminaries

Have you:

- Clearly described the research problem?
- Stated the aim of the interview?
- Identified the general categories/areas of information you are interested in?

Themes and questions

Have you:

- Generated an appropriate set of themes and questions?
- Planned the order in which the questions should be presented?
- Considered the balance you want between structured and unstructured interviewing?

The interview procedure

Have you:

- Considered issues of self-presentation?
- Identified and approached potential respondents?
- Planned the pre-interview meeting?
- Planned the post-interview debriefing?
- Decided how the information is to be recorded in the interview?
- Considered the ethical issues raised by the proposed research and sought advice if necessary?

---

personal significance such as bereavement, or divorce. A change in an informant's willingness to continue with an interview can be signalled in a number of ways – by sudden restlessness, changes to tone of voice, or by a shift from self-disclosing to self-defensive replies, as well as by simply asking for the session to end. The interviewer should be alert to the possibility of withdrawal and offer to end the interview any time the informant's willingness to continue appears to change. Sometimes simply switching to a new topic will be enough to make the interviewee feel more comfortable. However, it is always better to have an interview cut short than to subject an informant to questioning with which they are uncomfortable.

If, at the planning stage (see box 2.4) you feel that your proposed interview could lead you to touch on topics that evoke painful responses in your interviewee, it is important to seek the advice of a more experienced researcher, and to consider carefully whether training will help you conduct interviews on sensitive topics.

The right to withdraw also extends to the information given in the interview. As already noted, the respondent must be allowed to see the interview transcript before it is communicated to others and withdraw any section if desired.

EXTENSION ACTIVITIES

Activity 1

Using the information in this chapter as a guide, develop a question statement, and some themes and specific questions that you might wish to use in a research interview with another person on one or more of the following topics.

- People I find attractive
- Inter-generational relationships
- The experience of being step-parent/step-child
- Experiencing difficult people
- My family
- Coping with negative experiences (loneliness, rejection, depression etc.)
- School days

Activity 2

Take one or more of the themes from the examples earlier in the chapter and develop a set (about ten minutes' worth) of questions for use in an interview. Try them out by interviewing a friend or relative. Afterwards, try to answer the following questions.

- What went well in the interview and what, if anything, went less well?
- How did you feel while you were doing the interview?
- How do you think the interview might be improved?
- How did it feel to your respondent to be interviewed by you? Ask for some honest feedback. Compare your own perceptions with those of your respondent.

Repeat the process with a different respondent, making whatever changes to your approach and/or questioning that you feel are needed, and try to obtain an interview that is more satisfying to you both.

Activity 3

Try to find a 'real' interview on TV (i.e. one that is not part of a drama or chat-show). Video it if possible so you can watch it more than once. Consider the following questions.

1   How does the interviewer manage the situation? Is the interviewee relaxed and giving his best? How can you tell?
2   How would you describe the interviewer's goal in conducting the interview?
3   Listen to the questions being asked. What types of question are used? Are they the types you would use if you were interviewing that person?
4   Now listen to the answers. If you were interviewing that person how would you respond to hearing those answers? How would that influence your questions?
5   Is any emotion displayed in the interview? What do you think is its meaning?

Chapter Summary

1   The similarity between an interview and an ordinary conversation is misleading. Interviews are designed to facilitate the passing of information between interviewer and interviewee and are therefore more structured, more disciplined and more one-sided than a conversation.

2   Interviews differ in terms of the amount of structure in the questioning. In structured interviewing, the interview is based on a schedule of questions which have been worked out in advance. In unstructured interviewing there may be little or no pre-planning of the questions. For general research purposes, some combination of these types will often be used.

3   Some planning of the interview is, however, usually essential, and a structured approach to question generating is advocated that begins with a statement of the problem, and moves through the identification of themes, to the production of a more detailed set of questions. This ensures their pertinence to the research aims and also reassures the less experienced interviewer that all topics of interest will be thoroughly explored.

4   An interview is a complex psychological environment in which a number of factors may affect the outcome. These include, but are not limited to, the effects of self-presentation by the interviewer, variability in the respondent's motivation, the existence of faking good or an acquiescent response set, and the development (or not) of rapport with the interviewer.

5   Interviews are, of course, subject to the general ethical principles that govern all psychological research. However, the issues of confidentiality of data and right of a respondent to withdraw from an interview should be given particular attention.

● FURTHER READING ●

Banister, P., Burman, E., Parker, I., Taylor, M. and Tindall, C. (1994). *Qualitative methods in psychology.* Buckingham: Open University Press.

Foster, J. and Parker, I (1995). *Carrying out investigations in psychology.* Leicester: B. P. S. Books.

Hayes, N. (1997). *Doing qualitative research in psychology.* Hove: Lawrence Erlbaum.

Robson, C. (2002). *Real-world research*, 2nd edn. Oxford: Blackwell.

3

SURVEYS, SAMPLING AND QUESTIONNAIRES

CHAPTER MAP

Introduction

Survey Architecture

Descriptive surveys
Explanatory surveys
Complex designs

Populations, Samples and Sampling

Populations
Samples
Sampling error
Sample size
Sampling techniques
Probabilistic sampling methods
Non-probabilistic sampling methods

Data Collection by Questionnaire

Developing a questionnaire
Common question formats
Some pitfalls in questionnaire design
Organizing the questionnaire
Testing the questionnaire
Questionnaire distribution
Evaluating a questionnaire

Extension Activities

Chapter Summary

Further Reading

THIS CHAPTER

- *Introduces the survey as a method of data collection involving the three elements of overall design, sampling method and data collection.*
- *Reviews some of the main types of survey architecture.*
- *Introduces the role of sampling in survey research and provides an overview of some essential methods of sampling.*
- *Outlines some basic types of questionnaire item and provides guidance on assembling and testing the questionnaire.*

KEY CONCEPTS

Descriptive, explanatory, longitudinal, cross-sectional, one-shot, before–after, two-groups, longitudinal, cross-sectional designs
Population, sample, representative sample, sampling error, probabilistic sampling, purposive sampling, sampling frame, random sample
Open and closed questions, contingent questions, graded response questions, biased questions

● INTRODUCTION ●

The survey can claim to be the most widely used way of collecting data, both within and outside social science, no doubt partly because it provides a flexible, and economical method of data collection that can be used for virtually any kind of inquiry. Virtually everyone reading this is likely to have experience of survey research as a participant – perhaps by voting in an election or by enduring an encounter with a market researcher in the street, or by mailing back a customer-service questionnaire to a retailer. Arguably, though, the chief reason for its popularity as a method of gathering information is that it offers a way of dealing with a basic problem in research: how to collect data from respondents who are either too numerous, or too widely dispersed to be easily accessible as a whole. In essence, a survey is a way of organizing the collection of data in such circumstances.

For the purpose of describing it in more detail, the survey can be divided into three components – the survey architecture, the sampling method and the data-collection instrument.

Survey architecture

The architecture, or general design, of the survey decides the number and timing of data collections and is largely determined by the kind of question, whether description or explanation, that the survey is trying to answer. A descriptive approach is where the purpose of the survey is to establish the characteristics of a particular group or describe an existing state of affairs. The explanatory approach, in contrast, is where the survey is used to try to uncover the cause of some phenomenon by identifying a possible cause-and-effect relationship between variables. Explanatory surveys are difficult to carry out successfully because of the problem of excluding all possible alternative explanations for the data other than the presumed cause. They are thus more complicated to design and implement than the descriptive type.

Sampling

The sampling method is the process that allows a sub-group (the sample) to be drawn from a much larger group (known as the population, or universe) with the intention of obtaining an accurate representation of the characteristics of interest in the population within the sample. Through sampling, the problem posed by the need to collect data from a large and inaccessible group becomes much more tractable in research terms, because, if sampling is effective, valid inferences can be drawn about the population.

Data collection

Some form of instrument for collecting data from the individual members of a sample is also required. Typically, this is likely to be a questionnaire, but, as Fife-Schaw (2000a) points out, it need not be. There are other techniques of data collection such as interviews, psychometric tests, or indeed some form of observation, that can equally well be used.

Planning for a survey involves decisions in each of these three areas: the remainder of this chapter deals in more detail with each in turn.

● SURVEY ARCHITECTURE ●

Descriptive surveys

The one-shot survey

The simplest and probably the most frequently used survey is the 'one-shot' type, in which the data are collected from a single sample drawn from the population of interest. If an appropriate sampling method is used the sample may accurately reflect the population and allow valid conclusions to be drawn about its characteristics.

However, because it presents a single 'snapshot' of data this design permits only descriptive research to be pursued. There is no provision for the collection and comparison of different sets of data that would be required if causal inferences are be made.

In an example of the one-shot approach, Rees (1972) tried to establish the frequency of post-bereavement hallucinations among people who had recently lost a close relative. Using a semi-structured interview based on a standard questionnaire he collected information on the extent to which the experience of hallucinations (if any) co-varied with other variables such as age, duration of marriage, and age at widowhood.

Rees did find that his sample suffered from post-bereavement hallucinations, but as he did not investigate the incidence of hallucinations among an equivalent group of the non-bereaved he was unable to draw any further conclusions. While it was possible that bereavement may have caused the hallucinations, most of the sample were elderly, and some were unwell, so the reported hallucinations could equally well have been caused by age, illness, or the effects of medication.

The two-groups controlled comparison

An alternative to the one-shot approach is the two-groups controlled comparison design. In the simple version, data are collected contemporaneously from two separate samples that are regarded as having been treated in different ways because they represent different levels of a 'grouping' variable such as age, sex or marital status. This approach can be used to look to see whether and to what extent the variable that defines each group covaries with the variable measured by the survey. This approach closely resembles the 'non-experimental' design discussed in chapter 5.

The results from applying this approach should be interpreted with care. Although the two samples may be considered to be significantly different, it is their acquired or inherited characteristics rather than the decision of the researcher that places them in one group or the other. Consequently, they may possess all kinds of other attributes that could influence the observed correlation.

Explanatory surveys

The before – after survey

This design addresses the critical weakness in the one-shot and correlational designs, namely their inability to identify a potentially causal relationship between variables. In the before–after approach, data are collected from the members of a single sample on two occasions that are separated from each other by a period during which some treatment or event occurs (see figure 3.1). By comparing the second set of data with the first, it can be seen whether a change has occurred between the two collection points. If so, it may be possible to argue that the second set of results has been influenced by whatever event or process has happened to the sample between the two data collection points.

Essentially, this argument depends on two points of justification. The first, obvious, point is that the critical event occurred in time before the second set of data were collected. Since causes always precede effects, the intervening event qualifies as a possible cause of any observed difference between the earlier and later sets of data. The second point is that there should be some reason, ideally derived from a theory, that explains why and how the intervening event could influence the measured variables in the observed fashion. Without the presence of this explanation almost any intervening event could be invoked as a possible cause for the difference between the two sets of data.

The value of this design can be appreciated by considering again the survey conducted by Rees (1972). If the members of his sample had been contacted both before *and* after their

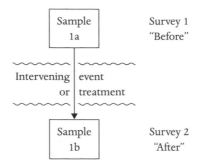

Figure 3.1   The before–after survey

partners died his research could have acquired some explanatory power. Comparing the results from the two sets of questionnaires would have indicated whether the frequency and content of any hallucinations had changed in any way after bereavement. However, one could not conclude with certainty that bereavement *caused* such change, since that would require that *only* the intervening event, *and no other*, had influenced the second set of data, although it could nevertheless be regarded as a useful indicator.

The presence of a causal relationship is particularly difficult to test for by means of a survey because it is hard to control the collection of data to the extent that is required to demonstrate a causal link conclusively. There are always other possible explanations for changes that may occur between one data collection and another. Among the possibilities are factors such as the effect of the passage of time (maturation, ageing, increased experience, learning, fatigue) the presence of one or more uncontrolled variables, and the effect of sampling the same group of individuals on two, or more occasions (the repeated measures effect).

The two-groups before–after survey

The before–after design with controls is the most powerful of the survey designs to be discussed here. It involves three stages. The first is the pre-test when data from two (or more) samples may be used to establish either the degree of difference between them, or to confirm their equivalence in some crucial respect. The second is the application of some treatment or exposure to influence that is either the same for all groups (if they are identified as different by the pre-test) or different for each (if the pre-test identifies them as equivalent). Third, all groups are subsequently re-tested by an equivalent test to the pre-test, or some other. The logic of the procedure is thus that if the groups are different and respond differently to identical treatments or are equivalent and respond differently to different treatments then it is possible to argue that the subsequent difference is caused by the conditions intervening between the two tests (see figure 3.2).

For example, this design might be used to investigate the effectiveness of relaxation training to help control the symptoms of pre-exam anxiety. Following the completion of a scale to measure initial levels of anxiety, the sample would be divided into high and low anxiety groups and both groups given identical training in relaxation techniques. The groups

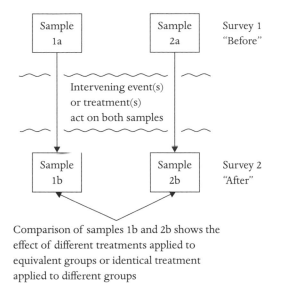

Comparison of samples 1b and 2b shows the effect of different treatments applied to equivalent groups or identical treatment applied to different groups

Figure 3.2 The two-groups before–after survey

subsequently take the same examination, and the results could be used to decide whether the level of pre-training anxiety exerted any influence on the effectiveness of the relaxation training.

Complex designs

Longitudinal surveys

Longitudinal surveys sample the same group of participants two or more times over an interval of time that may last a number of years. In principle, it allows for the effects of systematic factors associated with the passage of time, such as learning, maturation or ageing, to be assessed, while controlling for differences between the groups (see figure 3.3).

However, two difficulties weaken this design. First, unpredicted events occurring between data collections may introduce a confounding influence so that data obtained at later points reflect both the passage of time and the unpredicted event. Second (and possibly more likely) the initial sample may reduce in size as time passes because its members die or move away or are not available for other reasons. Consequently, the character of the sample may change significantly and compromise the comparability of earlier and later results.

Cross-sectional surveys

When the effect of the passage of time is to be studied without either risk of attrition to the sample or other uncontrollable changes due to the passage of time, the cross-sectional design may be chosen. This requires the collection of data at the same point in time from a single

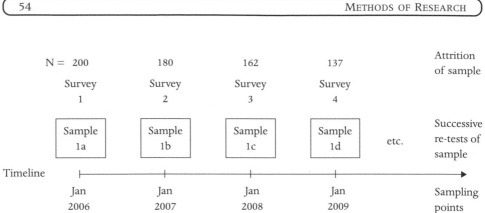

Figure 3.3 The longitudinal survey

Survey date: January 2006		
Sample 1	**Age of units in sub-samples (y:m)**	Any differences observed between sub-samples may be due to differential exposure to the passage of time of up to six years in duration.
Sub-sample 1.1	10:00 to 10:11	
Sub-sample 1.2	12:00 to 12:11	
Sub-sample 1.3	14:00 to 14:11	
Sub-sample 1.4	16:00 to 16:11	

Figure 3.4 A cross-sectional survey

sample consisting of a number of sub-groups that have experienced different degrees of expo-sure to the passage of time before the survey takes place. For example, the sample might consist of people who have been working for a firm for different lengths of time (say, 1, 3, 5 and 7 years) with each sub-group containing individuals with the same length of service (see figure 3.4).

Because the data will all be collected at the same point in time, there is no likelihood of losing sample members between survey points in this design. However, unless care is taken in forming the sub-groups any differences that may be observed to exist between the groups could result from the confounding of two separate influences – the fact that each group holds different individuals, and the fact that those individuals have been exposed to a particular factor for different lengths of time. A solution is to screen sample members on known criti-cal variables in order to ensure that each sub-group is as homogeneous as possible. It is also possible for data obtained from the cross-sectional design to be influenced by a 'time of measurement effect' in which historical or similar events occurring concurrently with the data collection unexpectedly influence results, and this may or may not affect all subgroups equally.

The cross-sectional design can be extended to form a 'time series' by taking a run of equivalent samples over a period of time to reveal the effects of time on the measured variable(s). However, for this to be effective one must be confident that each sample group is equal to the others in the crucial respects. Further combinations of the basic longitudinal and cross-sectional types are also possible (e.g. the 'longitudinal cohort sequential design'; Fife-Schaw, 2000a).

● POPULATIONS, SAMPLES AND SAMPLING ●

Sampling is the key technique in survey research. As noted earlier, it turns the problem of collecting data from a large and widely dispersed set of individuals (a population) into one of accessing a much smaller subset of the same large group (a sample). Ideally, this is done in a way that allows valid conclusions to be drawn about the former from the data obtained from the latter.

> In sampling terms a population is any set of individuals who share a given set of characteristics. People who are amibidextrous, the patients in a particular hospital, or people who use the same supermarket are equally populations in this sense.
>
> A sample is a sub-group of any size drawn from a defined population.

Populations

It is usual to distinguish between two types or levels of a population of interest (Smith, 1975). The 'general universe' is the abstract, or theoretical, population in any particular case. For example, one such might be defined as the set of people who are customers at a particular supermarket. The general universe is a theoretical construct in the sense that it requires operationalization before it can be applied in research. Why? Because the theoretical population of customers of supermarket X includes everyone who has ever shopped there. It thus includes both regular and occasional shoppers and people who have since changed their shopping allegiance to supermarket Y. Most of these individuals are likely to be hard to reach for sampling purposes.

The operationalization of the general universe is called the 'working universe or working population', and its purpose is to define the effective (i.e. reachable) subset of the general universe or population. To pursue the example, the working universe of customers of supermarket X could be defined as consisting of those individuals who at the time of the survey are actively shopping in branches of supermarket X. Other definitions for other surveys are, of course, equally possible.

Samples

As may be appreciated from the example above, a working universe still contains a large number of individuals, and is usually difficult to access in its entirety. The usual means of collecting data from a working universe, therefore, is to sample from it. The sample is the set

---

BOX 3.1   Representativeness

Representativeness is a characteristic of a sample in relation to the working universe from which it was taken. A sample is said to be representative if the characteristics of the sample match the characteristics of the working universe in those respects thought to be relevant to the inquiry.

Obtaining a representative sample depends first on obtaining the right-sized sample and second on only including those individuals within the sample who fully meet the sampling criteria set out in the definition of the working universe.

---

of individuals who have been selected from the working universe by some procedure so that they can contribute data to an inquiry. However, the real focus of interest in sampling remains the general universe: the aim is always to draw conclusions about the theoretical population from the data obtained from the sample. This depends on two factors. The first is whether the working universe represents a valid operationalization of the theoretical universe and the second is the extent to which a sample is representative of the working universe (see box 3.1).

Sampling error

No matter how carefully sampling is carried out, or how closely the sample matches the working universe, the data obtained from a sample are invariably different from what *would* have been obtained had the whole working universe been tested. This difference is due to sampling error. It arises from two sources. One is inevitable since it lies in the nature of samples themselves, while the other is more preventable since it follows from any failure to contribute data by some sample members.

> Sampling error is the difference between the picture presented by the data from the sample and the picture that *would* have been obtained if data had been collected from the whole working universe.

Error caused by sampling

Error arising from the act of sampling is not preventable. This is because whenever the sample size is below 100% of the working universe, any sampling method generates data that deviate to some degree from the data values in the working universe. This is true even when random sampling is employed. In fact, the major virtue of random sampling lies not in its ability to produce a more representative sample but in the fact that the magnitude of sampling error can be quantified. (See box 3.2 for more information on how this can be done.)

Error due to non-response

The second, and somewhat more tractable, source of sampling error is non-response by some sample members. This occurs because not everyone intended for a sample may be able to be

BOX 3.2 Quantifying sampling error

When non-probabilistic sampling methods have been used, or the data are qualitative, the size of sampling error can never be more than guesswork. However, if quantitative data have been collected and sampling has been random it is possible to identify the range of values – called the confidence interval – within which a population parameter, such as a mean, would be likely to lie. (A closely related concept is margin of error which is the proportion by which an estimate is likely to deviate from the value of the parameter in question.) These values are attached to an assessment of probability called the confidence level. By using these concepts, the likely difference between sample and population can be characterized quite precisely.

More information on the how these concepts are applied can be found in the section on parameter estimation in chapter 8.

BOX 3.3 Strategies for reducing non-response

Some proportion of non-responding is inevitable, but persuasion, persistence in re-contacting sample members and the collection of questionnaires in person can be effective counter-measures against random non-response. There may be some reason why non-responding is occurring systematically within a sample, such as mothers with young children being less likely to return questionnaires. If this can be discovered, by sampling non-responders, postcode analysis or some other method, then there are statistical techniques to allow the sample data to be corrected to allow for non-response.

contacted or wish to participate. So even if efforts are made to include all intended members, some degree of non-response can always be expected. The dataset obtained from such an incomplete sample will obviously differ from what would have been obtained if the whole sample had contributed as planned.

To some extent, the problem can be corrected by taking a larger sample to allow for whatever level of non-response is expected. However, this does little to address the fundamental problem. Even if a sample of the desired size is obtained by using the compensating procedure, the data will still vary from what would have been obtained from the original sample with no non-responses. In fact, over-sampling compounds the problem by ensuring a larger group of responding individuals, rather than a smaller group of non-responders. This carries important implications since the greater the extent of non-response, the more likely that the sample will differ from the working universe. Box 3.3 suggests some strategies for coping with non-response in a survey.

Sample size

In sampling, bigger generally means better. If one is sampling from a reasonably homogeneous population the greater the sample size the greater the likelihood that it will reflect the working universe (although this also depends on the sampling method used). In statistical terms, the estimate of a population parameter that is provided by a single sample grows more accurate as sample size increases. The reason for this is that every natural population contains a number of people who, if included, contribute extreme responses to the dataset. In a large sample, the effect of these is buried within the mass of more moderate scores but in a small sample any extreme responses obviously exert greater influence.

> A homogeneous population is one in which all the individuals (sampling units) are essentially the same, at least as regards the variable(s) of interest.
>
> A heterogeneous population is one in which the sampling units differ from one another, especially in ways that may influence the variable(s) of interest.

If the working universe is not homogeneous, perhaps because it contains a number of subgroups of different sizes, then taking a large sample increases the likelihood that all subgroups will be represented in the sample.

Determining sample size

It is possible to determine the sample size that will be needed, providing the sample is to be a random one. Special tables exist that give, for any size of population, the size of sample needed to achieve a given level of sampling error for a range of confidence levels (e.g. Slonim, 1960). Online calculators of required sample size are also available on websites, such as that of Creative Research Systems (2003). These allow a desired confidence level, margin of error and the size of the population to be sampled (if known) to be input and return the sample size that would be required by simple random sampling. For an example, see box 3.4.

> Statistical power is the probability that a false null hypothesis will be correctly rejected. Effect size is the difference between the population mean predicted by a null hypothesis and that predicted by its alternate hypothesis. Thus, it is a measure of the extent to which a null hypothesis is false.

Sample size is also critical to two important statistical considerations, namely, power and effect size. Essentially, both the power of a statistical test and effect size increase as the sample size increases. It is, therefore, particularly desirable to obtain as large a sample as practicable if the statistical analysis of survey data is contemplated. More information on the relationship between sample size, power and effect size can be found in Howell (1997). See also chapter 8 for more information on statistical hypothesis testing.

Sampling techniques

Although there are well over 20 different ways of constructing a sample (for the full collection, see Smith, 1975) a much smaller set of techniques will suffice for most tasks. The two fundamental types of sample are the probability sample and the purposive sample.

BOX 3.4 An example of a calculation of sample size

What size sample would one need if one is sampling from a working universe of unknown size? The CRS online calculator, mentioned above, indicates that in these circumstances a random sample of 666 is required in order to yield a margin of error of no more than 5% at the 99% confidence interval. In plain English this means that if one were to take 100 random samples of 666 individuals from that population, one could be confident that in 99 of the samples the results will be within ± 5% of the results that would have been obtained if data had been collected from the entire working universe. Table 3.1 illustrates the way that the sample size changes as population size increases (data from the same source).

Table 3.1 The required sample size at the 5% margin of error and 99% confidence level for a range of population sizes

Population	Sample required	Sample as % of population
100	87	87
200	154	77
400	250	62.5
800	364	45.5
1500	461	30.73
3000	545	18.17
6000	599	9.98
12000	631	5.26
unknown	666	?

Source: Output from Creative Research Systems, 2003.

A probability sample is one constructed so that there is a known probability that any individual in the working universe will be included in the sample. The representative nature of such samples can be judged because they bear a known relationship to the working universe. Samples of this type require equal access to all members of the population and are based on an exhaustive sampling frame that lists all the individuals in the working universe (see box 3.5). These may not always exist, so in planning a survey some consideration should also be given to whether it is essential to be able to use a probability sample. In some cases it may be that a purposive sampling technique can nevertheless deliver a representative sample.

A purposive sample is a sample obtained without the use of a sampling frame where the probability that any given individual in the working universe will be included in the sample is unknown. This approach may be used when a sampling frame is not available and/or a probabilistic sample is not required.

BOX 3.5   Sampling frames

A sampling frame is the list of all the units in the working universe from which a sample will be drawn, and its function is to identify all the individuals who potentially may be included in the eventual sample. A working universe may be defined in such a way as to make use of any list that exists. The membership list of a club, for example, could provide the sampling frame if that were the universe to be sampled. Sometimes, official or commercially compiled lists, such as the electoral register, can be used as a sampling frame, but it should be borne in mind that they have been compiled for other purposes and are not necessarily completely accurate.

If no sampling frame can be found one must be constructed before sampling can proceed. For example, a researcher might want a sample of people in the UK who were identified by a 'speed camera' as exceeding a speed limit within the past year. A sampling frame for this purpose would require to list all people currently living in the UK (and not otherwise inaccessible) who meet those particular criteria. However, it is unlikely that such a list exists as each local council manages its own cameras. So, each council would need to be approached and, if possible, a sampling frame constructed from their records.

Probabilistic sampling methods

The simple random sample

The most desirable of all methods of sampling, this procedure provides a sample that stands in a known relationship to the population, and it thus provides the 'gold standard' against which other procedures can be compared. As discussed in chapter 8, it also provides the essential basis to inferential statistics. Taking a random sample normally requires that the variable of interest is known, or assumed, to be reasonably evenly distributed throughout the population since if the distribution of origin is biased it may contribute significantly to the sampling error. In such cases there are correction procedures that can be applied to the data.

In addition to the requirement of an exhaustive sampling frame, constructing a random sample also requires a procedure for selecting individual units in accordance with the definition. Two common ways of doing this are the 'tombola' method of putting into a container the names or numbers that identify all individuals in the sampling frame and drawing them one at a time, and numbering the individuals in the sampling frame and using a table of random numbers to select the sample. These methods produce 'sampling without replacement' – the normal practice in random sampling.

A random sample is defined as a one in which each sampling event is wholly independent of every other when all units in the working population have equal probability of being selected.

Sampling without replacement occurs when, once an individual is selected into the sample, he is counted as removed from the working universe and so cannot be selected again.

The advantage of using simple random sampling is that, depending on whether the variables of interest are homogeneously distributed through the population, it may produce a sample that is less subject to sampling error than any other method. It also allows quantified estimate of the closeness of the sample data to the data in the universe to be produced. (See the above discussion of sample size and chapter 8.) Its main disadvantage (apart from the need for an exhaustive sampling frame) is the practical difficulty of constructing a truly random sample from a widely dispersed population.

The systematic sample

Systematic sampling is a quasi-random procedure that offers an acceptable alternative to random sampling. It gives results that in many cases are not distinguishable from a random sample as long as two conditions can be met. These are, first, that the variable of interest is homogeneously distributed throughout the population and, second, that there are no recurring patterns in the sampling frame that could give a biased sample. (However, this latter possibility can be prevented if the contents of the sampling frame are randomized before the systematic sample is taken.)

Like the random sample it also requires an exhaustive sampling frame, but the procedure involves drawing individuals at regular intervals rather than sampling at random. An example will make this clear. To take a 20% (1/5) sample from a population by this method, first inspect the sampling frame for obvious regularities, for example alternate male and female names or names grouped by family. If there are regularities randomize the list to remove any possibility of bias. Next, determine a starting point in the list. This will be n places from the head of the list where n is a whole number below the larger term in the sampling ratio. In this case, n must be less than 5, and can be determined by reading the first value in the appropriate range from a table of random numbers. Beginning then with (say) the third name on the list, take every fifth name in the list to form a systematic sample.

The stratified random sample

The random and systematic sampling methods are most useful when the universe to be sampled is a relatively homogeneous one as far as the variables capable of influencing the results of a survey are concerned. However, sometimes it may be necessary to sample from a non-homogeneous population, in which the individuals making up the population differ systematically from each other in ways that influence the data. For example, a survey planned to find out more about people's attitudes to money will need to consider that men and women are likely to have different patterns of spending, and different amounts of disposable income, and also that spending patterns vary with age. Stratified sampling gives a sample that is as close as possible to such a heterogeneous universe.

This approach also requires an exhaustive sampling frame that has been organized into groups corresponding to each level of the variables that have been identified as potentially influential. Thus, to follow the above example, one would group the elements in the sampling frame first by sex, then by age. Each subdivision of the universe obtained in this way is a different stratum of the population (see tables 3.2 and 3.3). Finally, a random sample is

Table 3.2   A 10% sample stratified by age and sex

Sex	Age	N	Sampling units
Males	21–30	262	1–262
	31–40	170	263–432
	41–50	443	433–875
	51–60	301	876–1176
Females	21–30	276	1177–1452
	31–40	150	1453–1602
	41–50	300	1603–1902
	51–60	292	1903–2194

Summary of a sampling frame (N = 2194) organized by age and sex
showing the numbers in each stratum.

Table 3.3   A plan for a 10% random sample from the sampling
frame in table 3.2

Sex	Age	N	Units included in sample
Males	21–30	36	17, 188, 263, . . .
	31–40	17	399, 404, 430, . . .
	41–50	44	490, 574, 663, . . .
	51–60	30	905, 1063, 1105, . . .
Females	21–30	28	1273, 1384, 1401, . . .
	31–40	15	1487, 1541, 1585, . . .
	41–50	30	1666, 1792, 1842, . . .
	51–60	29	1937, 2057, 2138, . . .

taken from each of the strata, using the same sampling fraction in each case. This preserves the relative proportions of the different groups in the population into the sample.

The value of this approach lies in the fact that it maximizes the probability that all groups of interest in the working universe will be adequately represented in the sample, although clearly it depends on the possibility of identifying all individuals who match the strata criteria.

The multistage cluster sample

Multistage cluster sampling enables a representative sample to be generated when a complete sampling frame is not available, but the universe to be sampled is capable of being organized hierarchically, with each higher level including all the lower levels. It is also useful when a population is very large or dispersed geographically. The technique is to form one or more random samples from the top-level unit, then to sample in turn from each of those samples until the level of individual sampling units is reached. Cluster sampling thus dispenses with the need for an exhaustive sampling frame containing the entire population (which may not exist). All that is needed is a sampling frame for each level or cluster (see box 3.6).

> # BOX 3.6 The multistage cluster approach used to obtain a sample of 11- to 16-year-old school students
>
> - *Universe*: School students in years 7 to 11 within the state system in England and Wales.
> - *Stage 1 sampling frame*: A list of all local education authorities. A random sample of LEAs is constructed from this list.
> - *Stage 2 sampling frame*: A list of all the schools managed by those LEAs selected at stage 1.
>
> Select a random sample of schools from this list.
>
> - *Stage 3 sampling frame*: A list of all the classes containing students up to year 11 in those schools appearing in the sample at stage 2. Select a random sample of classes from this list.
> - *Stage 4 sampling frame*: A (randomized) list of all the students on the registers of the classes selected into the sample at stage 3.
>
> Select a final random sample of students from this list.

An important decision in cluster sampling concerns the number of elements to sample at each stage of the process to ensure that the result is representative. If too large, the final sample may be unmanageable, while if too small, its claim to be representative may be compromised. The best chance of obtaining a final sample that is both the desired size and adequately representative is to make the early ones as large as possible, and reduce them in size as the final stage is approached.

Non-probabilistic sampling methods

Non-probabilistic forms of sampling can be attractive because they avoid the difficulty posed by a lack of an exhaustive sampling frame. However, with the exception of quota sampling, they are all weaker methods than those discussed above in the sense that they are unlikely to produce a representative sample. Despite this drawback they are often used because there is no alternative.

Quota sampling

Quota sampling is a technique that can be used to sample from a heterogeneous population for which no exhaustive sampling frame exists. The basic idea is that a representative sample may be obtained without the need for an exhaustive sampling frame as long as the population can be subdivided on one or more variables in known proportions, and if those relationships are subsequently preserved within the sample taken from each subdivision. Quota sampling is non-probabilistic because the sample consists of a fixed number of individuals (the quota) who are included in the sample because they possess certain characteristics rather than on the basis of a standard procedure, as in probabilistic sampling.

For example, if a population is known to contain 55% females and 45% males, then the 'quota' for the proportions of males and females in the sample is also 55% and 45%. Sampling to obtain quotas simply requires that, once the final sample size has been decided, individuals are selected from the population using one of the other non-probabilistic procedures but are accepted into the sample only on the basis of their biological sex. Once the numbers required to fill the both the male and female quotas are reached, sampling ends.

This procedure can give a sample that is close to the working universe on the characteristics selected, but it is also vulnerable to bias, particularly from the fact that some quotas may be easier to fill than others.

Judgemental sampling

Judgemental sampling involves the researcher using her judgement and knowledge to decide which members of a population should be taken into the sample. For example, to form a sample of 11- to 16-year-olds, by the judgemental sampling method would require guessing or estimating the age of each candidate for inclusion rather than checking birth certificates or similar official records. Whether the sample obtained is adequately representative therefore depends on how accurately the researcher's judgement is exercised.

Opportunity sampling

An opportunity sample consists of those individuals who are willing to take part in the research at the time. The usual method of putting together an opportunity sample is simply to ask members of the population whether they would like to participate in the research. This form of sampling is much used in psychology because it is argued that, for most purposes, more structured techniques of sampling, such as random sampling, would be unlikely to generate a more representative sample.

Volunteer sampling

Volunteer sampling is the form of sampling that occurs when those individuals who have volunteered in response to an advertisement or a similar invitation are accepted into the sample. The key feature of a volunteer sample is that its members are all self-selected and for this reason it is generally accepted that they differ in various ways from the general population.

Theoretical sampling

A theoretical sample is one created from a working universe whose members are defined in terms of particular characteristics of theoretical interest. For example, if research is concerned with the deleterious effects to emotional attachments of being in hospital as a child, a theoretical sample would be one that draws from the working universe of children who actually show evidence of disrupted attachments following a stay in hospital rather than from one defined more generally.

● DATA COLLECTION BY QUESTIONNAIRE ●

The last element required for a survey is an instrument to collect data. As noted already, this is frequently a questionnaire, the basic tool of survey research, because it can be tailored to meet the needs of almost any inquiry.

At its simplest a questionnaire need be no more than a list of questions. However, to reduce the possibility of misunderstandings to a minimum, and to enable data to be compared across a sample, the questions are normally presented in a very structured way. A notable feature of survey research is that, unlike an experiment or interview, there is usually only one opportunity to collect data from each informant. It is therefore important to make the questionnaire as clear and effective as possible.

Questionnaire research is probably most effective when used to obtain clearly defined information on a restricted range of topics or issues. It is better to ask quite detailed questions about a few issues than the same number of questions on lots of topics, or, worst of all, a very large number of questions on a very wide range of topics.

Developing a questionnaire

The early stages of developing a questionnaire are identical to the preparation of a schedule of questions for a semi-structured interview, given in chapter 2. Box 3.7 gives an overview of

---

BOX 3.7   The stages of questionnaire design

- Write a problem statement.
- Generate a preliminary set of ideas or topics.
- Conduct a literature search to see whether a similar scale has already been developed.
- Turn the ideas into raw questions.
- Refine the raw questions into questionnaire items.
- Organize the items into an appropriate sequence to form the questionnaire.
- Test the questionnaire informally by asking people to read it through and 'think aloud' about the form and meaning of the items and the overall structure of the questionnaire.
- Pilot the questionnaire on a subgroup of sample members and carry out an item analysis on the results.

the steps involved. The account below takes up discussion of the process at the point where raw questions are refined into questionnaire items.

Having identified a body of raw questions, turning them into a set of finished questionnaire items begins with identifying an appropriate format for each one. This depends partly on the content of the question, and partly on the kind of sample on which it is to be used. Some frequently used question formats are outlined below.

Common question formats

Closed questions

Closed questions are those where the range of possible answers is completely determined by the researcher and respondents are required to select one.

Q: How old are you? (Tick to indicate):   20–29 years
30–39 years
40–49 years
50–59 years
60 years or older

Closed questions are straightforward, quick to answer, and lie within the intellectual reach of the majority of the population. The answers are easily turned into quantitative data that can be analysed statistically and this facilitates the comparison among different respondents and the aggregation of answers to present an overall picture of the sample.

Questions of this type are used when the aim is to obtain simple, largely factual, information from respondents, hence their use in opinion polling. They can also be used as contingent questions to structure the questionnaire by establishing basic information that later items can go on to explore in more detail (box 3.8).

Types of closed questions

Checklists

A checklist presents a range of possible answers, but instead of requiring the selection of a single answer the respondent can choose as many of the options as may apply.

Q 3: The following is a list of common leisure-time pursuits. Place a tick against any that you have carried out alone or with your partner during the past week.

Gardening or DIY	Watching TV	Reading
Visiting friends	Going for a drive	Entertaining people at home
Participating in sport or fitness activity		Shopping
Going to pub or restaurant		

BOX 3.8   Contingent questions

Contingent questions are those that must only be answered by members of the sample who identify themselves as having certain characteristics. This allows a specific inquiry to be targeted on different subgroups within the sample. As an example of the initial structuring question and the contingent instructions that might be used to set up three different routes through the questionnaire, consider,

Q 1: How do you believe that your relationship has been over the past year? (Tick one):

Has it   Grown more satisfying
Grown less satisfying
Stayed about the same

If you answered 'Grown more satisfying' to this question continue with Q2 below; if you answered 'Grown less satisfying' go on to Q3; otherwise go to Q4.

Rankings

Questions of this type extend the checklist by asking the options to be placed in rank order in terms of preference, frequency, or some other variable.

Q 4: Here is a list of some possible causes of disagreements in a close relationship. Place a 1 against whichever seems to you to be the most frequent cause of your disagreements, a 2 against the next most frequent, and so on. If you feel that two (or more) of the items are equally frequent, give them the same number. Please make sure that you number all the possibilities in the list.

Sexual matters; money; in laws; holidays; housework; food; friends; work outside the home; shopping; political or religious beliefs; possessions; personal habits.

Graded response questions

Graded response questions allow respondents to express degrees of magnitude in their answers. There are several types, including attitude statement questions that provide a statement reflecting an attitude to a particular issue. The respondent is invited to indicate the degree of agreement by choosing the statement on a continuum of response that most closely matches their attitude.

Q 5: Here is a belief that some people hold about relationships. Read it and choose the answer that most closely matches your response to the statement.

'In a relationship both partners should work equally hard to avoid serious disagreements.' Do you:

Strongly agree
Agree   (tick one only)
Neither agree nor disagree
Disagree
Strongly disagree

Likert-type questions are very similar to attitude statement questions except that the response is expressed as a numerical value. Questionnaire items such as this can have either an odd (typically 3, 5, 7 or 9) or an even number of divisions. Scales with an even number of scale points provide a 'forced choice' between the two halves of the scale that may be desirable in some circumstances.

Q 6: How emotionally close would you say you are to your partner? Indicate how close you feel you are now by placing an x on the scale below. 1 indicates 'hardly close at all' and 5 indicates 'extremely close'

1 2 3 4 5

Semantic differential questions are based on the work of Osgood (Osgood et al., 1957) and offer a way of quantifying feelings, emotions, and other subjective experiences that may otherwise be difficult to capture. They represent the target variable as one or more pairs of bipolar adjectives and informants are asked to identify the position on each scale that best describes the feelings in question.

Q 7: Place an X on the scale to indicate how you would describe your relationship with your partner as it is at this moment.

Undemanding |......|......|......|......|......|......|......| Demanding

Open-ended questions

Open-ended questions provide a respondent with space in which to reply to the question in her own words, thus inviting a more precise and personal response than questions of the closed type. However, the inevitable difference between individual responses may cause difficulties when the time comes to analyse the data, and this type of question makes an obvious (and possibly unjustified) assumption about the respondents' ability to express themselves in writing.

Some pitfalls in questionnaire design

Three types of poorly-constructed questions should always be removed from a draft questionnaire. They can easily be prevented from appearing by thoroughly proof-reading the questionnaire before it is used.

- Double-barrelled questions ask about two entirely different topics at the same time. This causes confusion, and the question may consequently remain unanswered.

Q 8: Do you think that families are more democratic in their decision-making these days, or do you feel that young people need to be given more say in what is decided?

The solution is to split the question into two.

- Questions containing negatives can similarly result in confusion and an erroneous response.

Q 9: Do you not agree that young people do not have as many pressures to contend with as previous generations?

Here the best solution is to cast the question into the positive form, thus

Q 10: Do you agree that young people have fewer pressures to contend with than in previous generations?

- Biased, or leading questions are questions of the 'Have you stopped beating your wife?' variety. They require their assumptions to be accepted before an answer can be given. Sometimes the assumptions on which a question is based can be quite well disguised, but a crude example of this type of pitfall is as follows.

Q 11: Given that the police always do their best to catch criminals, what do you think is the best way to tackle the increasing level of crime in society?

This problem can be effectively removed if all questions are carefully proofread (see below).

Organizing the questionnaire

The next stage in developing a questionnaire is to organize the questions and other necessary information in an appropriate way. Once it has been constructed in draft form it should then be carefully proof-read, ideally by another person, to catch spelling, punctuation or other errors. Box 3.9 offers some suggestions about the design and layout of the material on the page.

The introduction

The function of the first section of the questionnaire is to introduce the research to each respondent and for obvious reasons it is important to get this initial approach right. Among the pieces of information that one would expect to find in this section are:

- The name of the questionnaire (such as 'Marital Stability Questionnaire')
- A brief paragraph to explain the purpose of the research
- A request for the respondent's help in the research by completing the questionnaire fully and candidly

---

BOX 3.9   Questionnaire design

A well laid out appearance can contribute to a good response rate, so it is worth spending time adjusting the layout of the questions on the page.

- Avoid cramming the questions together: respondents are likely to lose motivation if it is difficult to tell where the answers are supposed to be written.
- On the other hand, if questions are spaced too generously the white space can be intimidating, and it increases the number of pages in the questionnaire.
- Print the questionnaire on only one side of the paper – if both sides are used a respondent may not notice and consequently fail to answer some questions.
- Leave sufficient space for the answers to all the open-ended questions – up to half a page may be necessary if lengthy responses are anticipated or wanted.
- List alternative answers down the page rather than across. Listing across makes it harder for informants to pick them out as alternatives.

- Broad indications of what issues the questionnaire will cover, and how long it may take to complete
- The researcher's name and institution and a contact phone number
- An assurance that anonymity will be preserved and data held in confidence.

The middle section

The central part of the questionnaire contains the questions themselves. The following points and the suggestions given in box 3.9 may help construction of this section.

- It is a good idea to make the early questions as factual and as undemanding as possible. Try to ensure that they are clearly relevant to the research topic as described in the introduction so as to strengthen face validity.
- Organize the questions to run from straightforward ones early in the questionnaire to more demanding ones later. If possible place open-ended questions towards the middle of the questionnaire.
- Try to ensure that there is a sense of connectedness between the different questions so that one question leads smoothly into another. Avoid jumping backwards and forwards between topics. If you need to introduce questions on different topics signal that this is about to happen, either by dividing the questionnaire into sections each with a heading that clearly identifies the topic of the section, or alternatively, by inserting a verbal 'signpost', such as:

'Turning now to your relationships with your partner's relatives will you please now answer the following questions?'

- Place questions on demographic matters, such as age, sex, and marital status at the very end of the questionnaire.
- Use as wide a variety of question formats as is appropriate to the research topic, but don't include too many open-ended questions. Be aware that informants may find these fatiguing and difficult and may fail to complete them.

- Check the length. This will depend on the topic and the nature of the target population, but questionnaires of 30 to 50 items are generally found to be adequate for most purposes. If a longer questionnaire seems necessary consider first whether all the questions are really necessary. If so, dividing the questionnaire into two separate instruments may be an option.

The conclusion

The last section of the questionnaire can be used to present some essential information such as:

- A request that respondents check that they have answered all the questions
- An expression of thanks for the help in completing the questionnaire
- An offer to answer questions about the research via the contact number
- Explanation about how the results of the survey can be obtained
- A reiteration of the confidentiality of the data.

Testing the questionnaire

Once a draft version of the questionnaire has been produced and proof-read it should be evaluated before it is used. It is unsafe to assume that because it looks right it will collect the intended data and prove to be a valid and reliable instrument. Two methods are used for checking critical issues – that the questions are comprehensible and also carry the meaning intended by their constructor. These are, the read-through test and the pilot survey.

The read-through test involves asking several people to read through and 'think aloud' about such matters as the form and meaning of the items and the overall structure of the questionnaire. Their responses may help identify any overlooked defects such as ill-formed, ambiguous or unclear questions, errors in constructing contingent questions, or other weaknesses of logical structure, as well as any spelling or punctuation errors that may have slipped through the proof-reading.

A pilot survey involves administering the questionnaire to individuals drawn from the working universe by the same sampling technique as the main sample and carrying out an item analysis on the subsequent data. The item analysis allows the following matters to be checked:

- That responses are complete and appropriate.
- Whether there is evidence of response bias.
- Whether the same individual gives different answers to similar questions, which may suggest either misunderstanding or an attempt to mislead.
- Whether the responses of high and low-scoring groups differ sufficiently.

It is also good practice to arrange debriefing interviews with some of the members of the pilot group to check that the overall 'feel' of the questionnaire is acceptable: for example, that questions on sensitive matters have been posed in an acceptable way. The debrief should also reveal whether the overall design is clear, such that respondents find it easy to navigate through any contingent questions. The questionnaire should obviously be amended in the light of any comments from the pilot sample before it is given to the main sample.

Questionnaire distribution

Once a fully tested questionnaire is to hand, the next task is to distribute it to the members of the sample, and have it returned, so that the responses can be analysed. The aim is always to have as many fully completed questionnaires returned as possible. As regards distribution, the main options that exist are as follows:

- Mailshot
- Personal distribution
- Collection by respondents from a central point
- Assisted completion
- Telephone survey
- Online access.

The method chosen will depend on a number of factors, such as the nature of the population, the sampling strategy and also the extent to which a researcher is prepared to accept a low response rate.

Mailshot

In a mailshot, the delivery of a questionnaire is carried out by the Post Office or an internal mail system. This is convenient, and relatively easy, but the response rate (i.e. the proportion of fully completed questionnaires received back) will be low, especially if completed questionnaires are to be returned by the same method.

Personal distribution

An alternative approach is to distribute the questionnaire personally to members of the sample. This offers the advantage that the researcher makes direct contact with each individual and can give more information about the research than can be provided in the questionnaire itself. Personal contact such as this may well be an important factor in motivating respondents to complete and return the questionnaire. However, this is obviously only a feasible strategy when the sample members are easily contacted.

Collection from a central point

The third approach, which can be used if a volunteer sample is required, is to allow respondents to collect a questionnaire from a distribution point (such as health centre waiting rooms) and return them when completed. This only requires a supply of questionnaires to be placed at the distribution point, and a subsequent trip back to collect them. However, unless there is good point-of-distribution publicity, the questionnaires may be overlooked.

Assisted completion

A solution to the problem of low response rates is for the questionnaire to be directly administered by the researcher, who reads out each question and records the answers. Alternatively, the researcher may give the questionnaire to the respondent to complete, but remain in the vicinity to keep an eye on things and deal with any questions.

There are clearly advantages to both these strategies: they enable the researcher to deal at once with any queries which may arise from any lack of clarity in the questions, and also provide an opportunity to spot any misunderstandings at the time they occur. On the other hand, reading the questions may exert influence on the respondent's answers by unconsciously stressing certain words in the question. Both make the anonymous completion of the questionnaire impossible, and this may in turn influence the answers produced.

Telephone survey

If the telephone numbers of sample members are available, then conducting the survey by telephone may be an option. This simply involves using the telephone to contact each individual and reading out the questions as in the face-to-face version of assisted completion. This may work well if the questionnaire is a fairly short and simple one that focuses mainly on factual matters. However, longer questionnaires, or those dealing with complex or sensitive issues may be less easy to administer by telephone, and the inability to read a respondent's body language may prevent the researcher from identifying any lack of comprehension when it occurs.

Online access

It is now a relatively straightforward matter to use computer technology to distribute a questionnaire either by creating an online version that can be accessed on a website or by sending it to potential respondents as an email attachment.

The former approach may be attractive since, once the questionnaire has been designed and uploaded to a website, no further effort is needed to collect the data, no matter how large the sample. The perceived anonymity of online access may also encourage people to respond. However, the sample will obviously be limited to those individuals who have internet access, and have visited the website, and chosen to respond to the questionnaire. This may limit the usefulness of the data obtained.

The latter method obviously requires that the email addresses of the sample are known to the researcher, which may pose an obstacle. If a survey is to be conducted within a large organization, such as a university, it may be possible to selectively email groups of users of its computer network by means of a group ID such as 'staff' or 'students'.

Evaluating a questionnaire

When a new questionnaire has been constructed, it is desirable to be able to show that the information it provides is both accurate and consistent. The concepts of validity and reliability are used to assess these aspects of research instruments – validity deals with whether the questionnaire can provide the information that it claims to provide and reliability deals with whether it provides accurate and consistent data (see box 3.10).

Validity

- Criterion-related validity is established by comparing a prediction made on the basis of the test instrument to some external criterion. For example, if a questionnaire claimed to assess friendliness it would be valid in terms of criterion-related validity if it could successfully predict whether an individual made friends easily.
- Concurrent validity is demonstrated by comparing the results from an established test instrument that can be given to the same sample at the same time as the questionnaire.
- Content validity assesses the content of the questionnaire against its intended purpose. A questionnaire intended to assess the stability of friendships will not have validity as an indicator of (say) educational experience, because the kinds of questions that need to be asked in each case are quite different. The content validity of a questionnaire or scale is established by checking that its content reflects the issues or topics being investigated.
- Construct validity offers a more refined approach to content validity. Constructs are ideas or concepts, and a questionnaire possessing construct validity is one that has been closely based on a particular theoretical concept. If a questionnaire is intended to measure, say, the concept of learned helplessness (Seligman and Maier, 1967) it may be said to be valid if it measures those variables that were identified as important by these researchers.
- Face validity is a form of content validity that is concerned with the appearance of the questionnaire and asks whether it seems appropriate for its purpose from the perspective of research participants. This is not a trivial issue because respondents' expectations of and reactions to the questionnaire can determine whether or not they take it seriously.

Reliability

A reliable questionnaire is one that produces the same result when given to the same individuals on different occasions. A judgement of reliability therefore rests on the extent to which it resists effects that are related to the passage of time, such as learning, fatigue, or changes to motivation. Reliability is assessed by means of the following indicators.

- Test–retest reliability is concerned with whether a questionnaire produces consistent results over time. This is assessed by having the instrument completed by the members of the same sample on two different occasions (preferably with a long enough interval between administrations to prevent remembering from influencing the results). A reliable questionnaire, on this measure, will be one in which the same answers are produced on

BOX 3.10 A checklist of survey design tasks

This checklist lists the key tasks involved in planning for a questionnaire survey.

Preliminaries

- Describe the research problem
- State the aim of the survey
- Develop an explanation that either links the proposed survey to a theory, or says why the survey should be carried out
- Decide whether a descriptive or explanatory survey is required
- If appropriate, state the hypothesis to be tested
- Identify the theoretical and working populations (universes).

Survey design and sampling

- Decide which survey design to use
- Determine whether an exhaustive sampling frame is available
- Decide whether probabilistic or non-probabilistic sampling is required
- Select the sampling method to be used and justify the choice
- Decide the size of the sample to be taken, and justify the decision.

The questionnaire

- Generate an appropriate set of questions
- Check that a range of question types have been used
- Check the questionnaire structure
- Review the language of the questions for clarity and emotional content
- Have the questionnaire read over by other people
- Perform a pilot study
- Incorporate the results of the read-over and pilot study
- Assess the questionnaire for reliability and validity
- Check that the research conforms to ethical guidelines.

Distribution

- Decide how the questionnaire will be distributed, and collected
- Decide how the data will be analysed
- Determine the extent of non-response and its effects on any conclusions.

both occasions. This can be expressed numerically by means of a correlation coefficient (see chapter 6).

- Internal consistency is the extent to which its items measure the same variable, and is often assessed by means of the 'split-half' or 'alternate form' procedures. To find the split-half measure, the questionnaire is divided into two halves, which are administered separately to the same sample, and the correlation coefficient of the two sets of scores is found.

A high correlation indicates that a high score on one half of the test predicts a similarly high score on the other half and therefore that the test is internally consistent. The alternate form measure requires the preparation of two equivalent questionnaires that are administered separately to the same sample on different occasions. The correlation between the two sets of scores indicates whether the two scales are likely to be measuring the same variable.

- The Cronbach's *alpha* statistic (Cronbach, 1951), which does not require the construction or administration of more than one form of the questionnaire, may also be used to obtain a conservative estimate of internal consistency. The formula, and a related discussion, are provided in Hammond (1995) and it can also be found with a number of other techniques for assessing reliability in SPSS v. 13 under **ANALYZE > Scale > Reliability Analysis**.

EXTENSION ACTIVITIES

Activity 1

Consider how you would try to obtain a representative sample of the customers at a particular supermarket branch on a specific day in the year. What sampling technique would be most appropriate and what strategies might you employ to limit non-response?

Activity 2

Construct a short questionnaire (say 15–30 items long) on any topic of your choice (politics, music, hopes for the future, personal relations) using the material in this chapter as a guide. Ask someone to conduct a detailed and critical read-through of the questionnaire and consider what you have learnt about questionnaire construction as a result.

Chapter Summary

1   The survey offers a flexible and economical way of collecting valid and reliable data from large and relatively inaccessible groups of individuals. All surveys consist of three components: the survey architecture, the sampling method and the data-collection instrument.

2   The basic distinction to be drawn among surveys is between the descriptive and explanatory forms. Among the former, the one-shot survey is probably the most widely used type, although other, more sophisticated types exist. All, however, suffer from the disadvantage that they do not support causative inferences. Explanatory surveys, such as the two types of before–after survey, are, in contrast, able to throw light on possible causal relations between variables.

3   A population in sampling terms is a set of individuals who share some common feature. Sampling is the process of constructing a subset of individuals (the sample) from this larger group (referred to as a population or a sampling universe). Two levels of population are to be distinguished: the theoretical universe and the working universe and the goal in sampling is to obtain a sample that accurately represents the critical characteristics of the working universe.

4   Sampling is always subject to error, which means that any data obtained from a sample invariably deviates to some degree from what would have been obtained from the entire working universe. If sampling has been random and data are quantitative the size of any sampling error can be accurately estimated for any given confidence level.

5   Many specific sampling methods exist. However, the basic difference among them follows the distinction between probabilistic and purposive sampling techniques. Probabilistic approaches are those which, because they are based on an exhaustive sampling frame, allow the probability to be calculated that any individual in a working universe will be included in a sample. Random sampling is the strongest form of probabilistic sampling for the reason given earlier. Purposive sampling, on the other hand, does not utilize a sampling frame and so the probability of including an individual in a sample is unknown.

6   Most survey research depends on some form of questionnaire for data collection. Questionnaire design begins with a process of question generation that is essentially the same as is used in preparing a semi-structured interview. However, the construction of questions involves using a more highly structured format than in an interview. The basic distinction lies between open and closed questions, with the latter offering a range of specific formats for different purposes.

7   The construction of a draft questionnaire involves organizing questions into an appropriate structure. All questionnaires produced for research purposes should begin with an introduction that sets their purpose and other essential information. The questions themselves should be arranged logically in the middle section and there should be a concluding section that effectively terminates the questioning process.

8   Once a draft questionnaire has been constructed and proof-read it should be tested by means of a 'read-through' exercise and a pilot study. The latter should use a pilot sample taken from the working universe by the same sampling method as will be used to obtain the main sample. The purpose here is to provide data for an item analysis and to check that the questionnaire is fit for purpose.

9   Finally, the researcher must address the question of how to place the questionnaire in the hands of respondents. At least five options exist here, ranging from postal distribution to online administration. No one method can be recommended, since different situations require different methods, but postal surveys are noted for suffering from low response rates.

● FURTHER READING ●

Gilbert, N. (2001). *Researching social life*, 2nd edn. London: Sage.
Robson, C. (2002). *Real-world research*, 2nd edn. Oxford: Blackwell.

4

OBSERVATIONS

CHAPTER MAP

Introduction

Types of Observation

Casual observation
Participant observation
Systematic observation

Observation Design and Planning

Where to observe?
What to observe?
How to observe?
When to observe?

Data Collection and Analysis

Validity and Reliability in Systematic Observation

Validity
Reliability
Reactivity

Observation and Research Ethics

Extension Activities

Chapter Summary

Further Reading

THIS CHAPTER

- *Introduces observation as a method of data collection and provides an overview of the casual, participant and systematic forms of observation.*
- *Reviews key issues in the planning and design of observational research with particular reference to systematic observation, under the headings of where, what, how and when to observe.*
- *Discusses the issues of reliability and validity in relation to observational research, giving particular attention to the problems of observer drift and participant reactivity.*
- *Considers briefly the ethical issues arising from both overt and covert observation.*

KEY CONCEPTS

Casual observation
participant observation
systematic observation
reactivity
observation system

continuous observation
time-based observation
observer drift
overt and covert observation

● INTRODUCTION ●

Observation, conceived as the search for patterns and regularities in the natural world, is the cornerstone of all empirical science, providing the basic method of research across the range of disciplines from astronomy to zoology. Psychology is no exception: here too observation is widely used as a method of data collection. Among the fields of psychology where classic observational studies can be found are abnormal psychology (Rosenhan, 1973); child development (Ainsworth and Bell, 1969); social psychology (Milgram, 1963); language development (Brown, Cazden and Bellugi, 1969); and biological psychology (Dement and Kleitman, 1957) to name only a handful. On this evidence alone, observation may arguably be regarded as one of the key research methods available to psychologists.

● TYPES OF OBSERVATION ●

The fundamental point about observation, considered as a method of research, is that the act of observing necessarily requires a decision to have been made about *what* to observe. Observation is *always* a directed activity involving a selection from the range of possibilities. As has frequently been pointed out, it is impossible just to instruct someone to 'observe' without prompting the question 'observe what?'.

Apart from sharing this basic feature of paying attention to the behaviour of interest the task of collecting data through observation can be approached in a variety of different ways, reflecting the influence of disciplines such as anthropology, sociology, and ethology. As a starting point, though, three main types of observation can be distinguished. These are: casual observation, participant observation, and systematic observation.

Casual observation

Casual observation (also sometimes called unstructured observation) is a form of observation that consists essentially of 'just looking'. It involves collecting information from some environment of interest (such as, say, a hospital ward) just by watching what goes on. It is, therefore, quite close to the kind of observation of the world that everyone does every day.

However, there are differences. One difference is in the extent to which it is organized by the intention to focus on a limited range of behaviour. Another is in the fact that casual observation carried out in the course of research may lead to the construction of a record of what is observed.

Depending on its purpose, the data record from a period of casual observation may be quantitative, or qualitative, ranging from a set of very brief field notes that simply capture essential points or general impressions, through to a more detailed connected narrative.

'Casual' in this context refers to the adoption of an open approach that allows data to be collected on any behaviour of interest that may be present and also to the absence of a definite sampling method to guide the collection of data. This approach contrasts most clearly with the systematic approach to observation discussed below. In casual observation, the researcher just observes and records whatever may be seen to be going on in that place.

Because it offers a very flexible approach, casual observation can be applied to a wide range of situations and research questions. It is particularly useful as a way of doing exploratory research in an unfamiliar milieu before adopting a more detailed and rigorous approach. Among other advantages, it allows an assessment to be made of the frequency of particular forms of behaviour, and it can provide essential background information to guide the formation of tentative hypotheses that can be properly tested at a later date by data obtained through systematic observation.

However, despite its genuine usefulness as a preliminary method of research, it also possesses two major weaknesses. As already mentioned, its lack of a definite sampling strategy means that there is no way of assessing whether or not behaviour is representative of a population. In addition, any observations made in this way are clearly likely to be subject to bias because they are not organized by any framework or specific intentions. The essence of the method is to define all behaviour as potentially interesting, so there is nothing to prevent an observer's attention from being diverted at any time. Inevitably, therefore, observations made using the casual approach have unknown reliability and validity.

Participant observation

Participant observation is also known as field research (in sociology) or ethnography (in anthropology) where it is generally used as way of developing a deep understanding of the everyday life of a social group from the perspective of the members of that group. By sharing the experiences of others and learning to see things through their eyes it permits a researcher to approach the understanding of a cultural insider to a degree that would otherwise be virtually impossible to achieve. This form of inquiry requires the immersion of the researcher in the research milieu over a considerable period of time, in order to obtain the full acceptance by the other participants and the degree of social invisibility that are needed to penetrate a culture fully.

The data collected through this version of participant observation may consist of field notes, interview transcripts and possibly also quantitative measures obtained through a mixture of observation, interviews and active participation in the life of the group. Hypotheses may be formed from data acquired in this way, to be tested later in a cyclical process of data collection, analysis and hypothesis formation with the aim of constructing a connected narrative that dissects and analyses the social life of the group. More information about planning and carrying out participant observation can be found in social research texts, such as May (2001) and Hammersley and Atkinson (1995).

One important benefit from this approach is that it can facilitate the collection of data that would otherwise be inaccessible, or at least very difficult to obtain, by other methods. While it can be applied to the study of any social group whose collective life is of interest, participant observation is often used as a way of collecting data in situations that are hard to access such as prisons or similar institutions (Goffman, 1961) or from marginalized groups (Humphreys, 1970).

On the other hand, it can obviously be a demanding way of doing research. It requires the roles of participant and researcher to be simultaneously sustained over an extended period of time, and this can lead to difficulties in adequately meeting both demands. The need to be accepted into the life of another social group and to participate actively in the flow of events may require a lengthy span of time that makes it a relatively costly approach. And, from the point of view of evaluating the outcome of the research, it may be difficult, even impossible, to decide whether and how the researcher has influenced the events that are reported. The demands of being a fully immersed participant observer on the ethnographic model have therefore meant that this approach has been relatively little used in psychology, although examples exist, such as Rosenhan's work in mental institutions in the USA, that has already been mentioned (Rosenhan, 1973) and more recently, Quirk and Lelliott's (2002) study of life in acute psychiatric wards in the UK

One response to these demands is to find a different point of balance between the full participation that requires continuous immersion in the situation and no participation at all. Gold (1969; see table 4.1) has identified the possible ways in which the requirement to act as a researcher may be combined with the participant role. In one of these, the researcher acts solely as an observer, but the other three represent different degrees of engagement with the participants and different levels of commitment to the role of participant as well as researcher. Box 4.1 has an example of how less-than-full participation in a social group may nevertheless be managed in a way that produces informative research.

Systematic observation

This form of observational research, sometimes referred to as formal observation or structured observation (Wilkinson, 2000) tends to be associated with the researcher as uninvolved observer. It differs from participant observation in two main ways. First, the researcher is

Table 4.1 The range of possible research roles of participants and observers

Example	A psychologist observes a child's behaviour. wholly covertly	A psychologist observes a child by sitting in a classroom and openly taking notes on behaviour	A psychologist obtains a job in an organization that involves observing and recording children's behaviour	A psychologist applies a behavioural intervention to a child client and observes the outcome
Research role	Complete observer	Observer as participant	Participant as observer	Complete participant
Probable degree of researcher's involvement with the research participants	Low			High

Source: Based on Gold, 1969.

BOX 4.1   The researcher as both observer and participant

An example of how a form of participant research can be done without using the full ethnographic version comes from Beck (1993). Although not a depressed mother herself, she participated as an observer in a support group for mothers suffering from post-natal depression, her membership of the group being explained to group members by the fact that she was a trained health worker. This group held monthly meetings, which Beck attended and observed, over a period of 18 months and the results of those observations were used to guide the individual in-depth interviews that she also subsequently conducted.

---

likely to be confined to the role of the detached observer, rather than interacting directly with those being observed. Second, the process of data collection is organized by means of an 'observation system'. This is essentially a set of descriptions and definitions, constructed before data collection begins, that specify the behaviours to be observed. An example of a very simple observation system is the one devised by Jenni and Jenni (1976) to look into a possible difference between the sexes in techniques of carrying books (table 4.2 and figure 4.1). Their system distinguished two main forms of book carrying, designated type A and type B and a third type that was simply a category into which were put those rarely observed forms that were of little interest to their study. Note that all possible ways of carrying books can be located somewhere within this scheme.

A contrast to the simplicity of the Jenni and Jenni (1976) study is Bales's Interaction Process Analysis (Bales, 1950a, 1950b) in table 4.3.

Table 4.2   Three types of book carrying

Type A	Type B	Type 'other'
One or both arms wrap around the books; the forearm, on the outside of the books, supports them. The short edges of the books rest horizontally against the body on top of the hip or in front of the body in line with or higher than the hips. When books are carried in one arm, the fingers wrap around the long edges. When they are carried in both arms, the fingers wrap around contralateral edges or grasp contralateral forearms or wrists.	Books are supported by one arm and hand at the side of the body, with the long edges approximately horizontal. The hand may be above the books, pinching them between the thumb and the fingers, or on the outside of the books with the fingers wrapped around the lower edges. When the elbow is flexed and the books are raised, the long edges sometimes rest on both the hand and the forearm or wrist.	Any book carrying not defined as type A or type B (such as resting books on the shoulder).

Source: Jenni and Jenni, 1976.

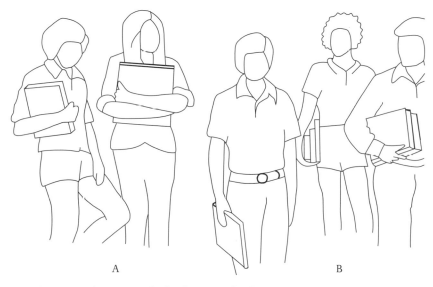

Figure 4.1   Type A and type B methods of carrying books
Source: Jenni and Jenni, 1976.

The observation system has two main purposes. The first is to structure data collection by directing the observer's attention towards one specific class of behaviour within a total scene. In the Jenni and Jenni study, the focus is solely on the carrying of books and it follows that carrying other objects, or any other behaviour that involves books, is thereby excluded from the investigation. The second function of the observation system is to define very precisely the categories into which behaviours of interest are divided for the purposes of data collection. In this example the function is performed by the definitions of type A, type B and 'other' forms of book carrying.

Table 4.3   Categories of communicative behaviour in Bales's Interaction Process Analysis

Emotional responses of a positive kind
A   Shows solidarity: raises others' status, gives help, rewards.
B   Shows tension release: jokes, laughs, shows satisfaction.
C   Agrees: shows passive acceptance, understands, concurs, complies.

Task responses
A   Gives suggestion: offers direction, implying autonomy for other.
B   Gives opinion: offers evaluation, analysis expresses feeling or wish.
C   Gives orientation: offers information, repeats, clarifies, confirms.

Task questions
A   Asks for orientation: asks for information repetition, confirmation.
B   Asks for opinion: asks for evaluation, analysis, expression of feeling.
C   Asks for suggestion: asks for possible ways of action.

Emotional responses of a negative kind
A   Disagrees: shows passive rejection, withholds help, shows formality.
B   Shows tension: asks for help, withdraws from field.
C   Shows antagonism: deflates others, defends or asserts self.

Source: Bales, 1950a; reproduced by permission.

While systematic observation is not applicable to every research problem, and may be regarded as involving a rather inflexible approach, it does have a number of advantages. It allows behaviour to be studied in much more detail than would be possible by alternative methods, it allows the collection of quantitative data and consequently the statistical testing of hypotheses, and since the researcher knows exactly what she is waiting to observe, it may also reduce the possibility of distraction. Some further features that make systematic observation a useful way of studying behaviour are listed in box 4.2.

● OBSERVATION DESIGN AND PLANNING ●

This section considers some issues in the planning and design of observational research. All research using observation requires that decisions are made about the environment in which the observations are to be made, the kind of behaviour to be observed, the sampling method to be used, and the form that the observation will take (Banister, 1994). These matters will be considered in turn under the headings of where, what, when, and how to observe. Although much of what will be covered is mainly relevant to systematic observation (and a checklist of key tasks for use in planning is provided later) some is equally applicable to the other forms.

Where to observe?

Observational research does not require any special equipment or particular kind of environment in order to be successful, so in theory at least it can be carried out anywhere that

BOX 4.2 Some strengths of systematic observation

(From Wilkinson, 2000.)

- There is minimal delay between observing and recording. This may mean that more reliable data are obtained than by using indirect methods such as a questionnaire.
- It is highly flexible and can be used to study a wide range of different behaviours on any scale from the micro level (e.g. eyebrow lifts and other elements of non-verbal communication) up to complex social interactions.
- Unlike other methods, observation does not involve any attempt to elicit a specific response from research participants. This makes it appropriate for the study of behaviour in natural situations or when participant reactivity may be an issue.
- It is particularly useful for studying people who may be thought likely to present a managed impression to a researcher in a face-to-face situation, such as an interview. It also offers a way of researching those, such as children, people with learning difficulties, or sufferers of mental disorders, who may be unable to provide introspective data.

the behaviour of interest can be found. However, in practice, the choice of where to observe can depend on factors such as:

- If there is a choice of locations whether one appears more favourable to the observation than the other(s).
- Whether many or few individuals are to be observed. Does one location make the observation of a number of participants easier than the alternatives?
- Whether there are resource limitations to consider. For example, how much time is available to cover different observing sites?
- Whether the target behaviour is specific to, or found with a high degree of frequency in, a particular situation.

The last point can obviously be critical in determining where observations are made. If a form of behaviour can most reliably be observed in one particular environment (e.g. Middlemist, Knowles and Matter, 1976) then the location question is decided. In the research by Jenni and Jenni, mentioned earlier, it was decided that the environment offering the best chance of observing many instances of book carrying is the vicinity of an educational institution, such as a college or university campus. This is not to say that book carrying doesn't occur elsewhere, such as around public libraries, but that it appears in particularly dense and concentrated form in places where education is provided and where it is usually necessary for students to walk some distance between buildings while carrying their belongings.

In thinking about the environment for observation, Foster, Bell-Dolan and Burge (1988) suggest that there is a useful distinction to be made between the '*in vivo*' observation

BOX 4.3   General categories of behaviour

Weick (1968) suggests that the range of observable behaviours can be divided into four general categories:

1   *Non-verbal behaviour* is all forms of body movement including facial expressions.
2   *Spatial behaviour* is any behaviour that alters interpersonal distance.
3   *Extra-linguistic behaviour* is any behaviour that accompanies speech, and including the non-verbal characteristics of speech itself, such as speech rate and volume.
4   *Linguistic behaviour* is the content of speech.

of behaviour in its natural setting, and 'analogue' observation involving some type of intervention by the researcher. (This distinction is sometimes also presented as involving the contrast between 'naturalistic' and 'laboratory' research.) *In vivo* observation is clearly appropriate when a behaviour of interest occurs in its natural setting and there may be reasons why this is to be preferred. In the book-carrying research the possibility of studying a natural behaviour in its normal habitat, allied to the possibility of obtaining a large volume of data were likely to have been the dominant considerations. However, *in vivo* observation is not necessarily always to be preferred over the analogue form. There may be disadvantages attached to *in vivo* observation, that make analogue observation the better option. These might include, for example, the need to obtain permission or co-operation from others, or an inability to control key aspects of the observing environment.

Analogue observation is perhaps more common in psychology than its *in vivo* cousin, and it is typically employed to control the conditions under which data are collected, such as to increase the frequency of a behaviour, or to reduce distractions. The observation suite with facilities for covert observation via two-way mirrors or remote video recording is the most obvious kind of analogue environment, but non-physical versions may also be used, such as when research participants are given specific instructions prior to observation being made to try to ensure that they will behave in a particular way.

What to observe?

As was noted earlier, the aim of conducting observation necessarily implies that some behaviour(s) are selected to be the focus of attention from the total range present in a particular environment. Decisions about what to observe concern, first, *the general type or category* of behaviour (box 4.3), second, the level at which behaviour is to be analysed within that general category and, finally, the *dimensions* of the behaviour.

The second consideration concerns the size of the behavioural units to be observed. This is sometimes referred to as the 'granularity' of observation, and varies depending on the interests of the researcher. One possibility is that observation may take place at the molar (large scale) level of analysis where behaviour consists of complex units that can only be identified through the observer making inferences that rely on the use of contextual knowledge. This is the level at which a 'lay' observer would describe behaviour. In table 4.4 two possible

Table 4.4   Descriptions of behaviour at two levels of granularity

Level of analysis	Description of behaviour
High-level (low granularity)	X approaches a counter, chooses an item, pays for it and leaves.
Lower-level (high granularity)	X walks up to the counter, looks at the goods on display, picks one up and holds it towards the salesperson standing on the opposite side of the counter. The salesperson takes the item from him and puts it in a paper bag. She holds the item in its bag towards X but retains hold of it. X takes out his wallet, extracts some notes, replaces his wallet and holds the notes out to the salesperson who takes hold of them with the hand not holding the item in its bag. As she takes the money she simultaneously relinquishes her hold of the wrapped item just as X grasps it with the hand not holding the money. Now X holds the item and the salesperson holds the money. Next, while X stands by the counter holding the wrapped item, the salesperson operates the till to make the money drawer open and puts the money inside, placing notes of different values into different compartments. She takes some coins out of the other compartments and gives them to X who takes them from her with the hand that is not holding the purchased item. He puts the coins in his pocket and walks away with the item in its bag in one hand.

descriptions of the behaviour 'making a purchase' are shown. The first shows a high-level (molar) approach to observation. Note how, at this level, much contextual knowledge is needed to make sense of the information (for example, that a purchaser and salesperson normally stand on opposite sides of a counter, and that the transaction involves giving money in exchange for the item, neither of which are explicitly stated). Observation that focuses on behaviour at a more micro level might produce the second version, in which the same behaviour is described in much more detail. This is observation where the granularity is considerably smaller (though still not as small as it could be) requiring much less inference (although some is still required – understanding the significance of the terms 'counter' and 'wallet' for example depends on possessing an appropriate cultural background).

Not that the analysis of behaviour need stop at this level, although this may well be detailed enough. But even lower-level actions such as those in the second part of table 4.4 are capable of being reduced to even smaller behavioural units – for example, the moving of limbs in various ways so that fingers can be inserted into a pocket, the wallet located and grasped, money extracted, and so on.

The purpose of this analysis is to make the point that behaviour is constructed, and can be viewed, at several different levels, and that an awareness of this is necessary when planning observation. Behaviour must be observed at the 'right' level for the research. In general, molar behaviours are more meaningful psychologically than those on the micro scale, but they are also more complex and observation of them can involve the observer in a considerable amount of inference (Foster et al., 1988) with the consequent risk of low reliability.

Micro-level behaviours, on the other hand, may carry less psychological meaning. As Sackett, Ruppenthal and Gluck (1978) also point out, most extant behavioural coding systems employ a mixture of levels which suggests that effective observation requires attention to behaviour across different levels from the molar to the micro. Ultimately, the decision about what level to observe depends on the aim of the research: the only criterion is to work at the level(s) of analysis that is most meaningful (valid) in terms of the research goals.

The final consideration in choosing what to observe concerns the ways in which one behavioural instance may differ from another. Box 4.4 below gives examples of some of the key dimensions.

How to observe? Structured observation

All observation must be structured in some way – there must be some ideas guiding the process that tell the observer what to attend to and what to ignore. Other than in casual and participant observation it is usual for the observer's intentions to be organized by means of a structure, or observation system. As was noted earlier, the principal purpose of an observational system is to direct the observer's attention to specific instances of the behaviour of

---

BOX 4.4 Key dimensions of behaviour

Consider the example of a hand coming into contact with the arm of another person. This behaviour may vary from instance to instance on the following dimensions.

Frequency:	How often the contact between hand and arm occurs – either in absolute or relative terms.
Duration:	How long the contact lasts.
Magnitude or intensity:	The amount of force with which the hand is brought into contact with the arm.
Accuracy:	Whether the hand and arm come precisely into contact with each other or just brush against each other.
Social acceptability:	The extent to which the contact is acceptable to the recipient or to other nearby participants.
Antecedent-consequent:	The observed cause of the hand–arm contact and the behaviour that follows, such as the owner of the arm attending more closely than before to the owner of the hand.
Behavioural by-products:	Any physical side-effects of the behaviour, such as finger-marks on the arm, that remain after the contact has occurred.

Source: Based on Foster et al., 1988.

interest in order to minimize observational error. Therefore, once questions about the loca-tion(s) for observation, the general category of behaviour to be studied and the dimension(s) of behaviour that are to be observed have been settled, the next task is to develop an appro-priate observation system for the research (Foster et al., 1988).

An observation system consists of the set of descriptions of lower-level units of behav-iour (at whatever level of analysis judged appropriate) that together define the range of pos-sible forms that may be taken by the behaviour of interest. The observational system developed by Jenni and Jenni (1976) that was discussed earlier illustrates these points.

A more complex example of an observational system that exemplifies the same principles is Bales's Interaction Process Analysis system (Bales, 1950a, 1950b) in table 4.3. This aims to capture communication behaviour that occurs in groups that are engaged in a shared task. In Bales's system, communication is divided into four general types of responses using the concepts of valence (positive or negative) and focus (task or emotion); each valence/focus combination is identified with three types of communication. This gives, at the lowest level of analysis, twelve types of communication in all. Descriptions at this level are supported by detailed definitions and examples of typical, borderline and negative cases that endeavour to make it clear how any particular instance of communication should be categorized.

As the two examples indicate, the construction of an observation system involves describ-ing each one of the various specific forms that the target behaviour may take in such a way that each unit can be easily differentiated from the other(s). The required characteristics of such descriptions are that they should be:

- *Exclusive*: Each of the categories in the observational system is described in such a way that any instance of relevant behaviour can be assigned to one, and only one of the categories.
- *Exhaustive*: The system must be designed to include every form of the behaviour of inter-est that is likely to be observed.
- *Usable*: The descriptions must refer to behaviours that can be differentiated from one another under field conditions.
- *Objective*: The behaviour should be described in a way that requires minimal inference and is free of any specific context in which it might occur.

The construction of the observation system also requires a decision on how many of the lowest level behaviour units to include. This issue is relevant to the question of whether reli-able observations are likely to be possible. Dane (1995) citing Gellert (1955) notes that the number of categories in the observation system is closely related to the number of errors made by observers. With this in mind, how many units should one include? One suggestion, from Foster et al. (1988), is that the optimum number of units is between 8 and 10 with 15 as the maximum, given that observers should be able to memorize the system. The actual number will, however, always depend to some extent on the complexity of the behaviour to be observed and the intended observing situation.

Once an observational system has been constructed, a pilot study is usual in order to check that it possesses the required characteristics, i.e. that it contains all instances of the behav-iour of interest, and that it can be easily implemented in the field. Piloting will also suggest whether there is a need to train observer(s) in the use of the protocol before beginning the main data-collection exercise.

When to observe?

There are two aspects to the question of when observation is to be conducted. The more general issue concerns the possible effect that observing at different times of day may have on the data, and the second concerns the sampling of the behaviour of interest.

The possibility of a 'time of day' effect may be present in some observing environments, giving data that vary when the same situation is observed at different hours of the day. An example might be found in the way the form and content of the talk between workers in an office changes at different times. One would expect there to be some differences in what is said in the first minutes of the working day compared to (say) mid-afternoon or at leaving time.

Clearly, the question of a time of day effect applies only to the collection of certain sorts of data in some observing situations, and it may be irrelevant in others. All observational research, however, requires a plan to collect data by some method of sampling the behaviour of interest. The main types of sampling used in systematic observation are listed below.

Continuous observation

Continuous observation is the non-stop observation of a situation for a given period of time during which all instances of the behaviour of interest are recorded. This approach has the advantage that it is capable of providing a complete record of significant events in terms of their frequency, sequencing and duration/intensity during the period of observation. However, it can also be time-consuming and, if prolonged, makes demands on the stamina and vigilance of the observer, leading to a possible threat to reliability. Nor is it suitable for all situations, such as when a large number of different types of behaviours must be observed, or if behaviour changes rapidly. In these cases a time-sampling method would be better.

The obvious question is, how long should continuous observation last? There appears to be no easy answer to this. The basic requirement is that observation should last long enough to ensure that a representative sample of the target behaviours can be obtained, and this will be longer in some situations than others (see box 4.5). In general, continuous observation is likely to require shorter observing periods when the behaviour of interest is relatively frequent, or consistent or predictable, or when the observation system is relatively simple.

Time-based sampling

The alternative strategies to continuous observation – time interval, time point and random sampling – use the passage of time to trigger data collection. These tend to be used either when behaviour is very variable, or when there are problems with recording behaviour continuously. However, time-based sampling also wastes some quantitative information that could be collected and it is difficult to assess the frequency or duration of the target behaviour using this method. Also, in the case of time-interval and time-point sampling, the time periods must be set to ensure that a representative sample of the behaviours of interest is obtained.

Time-interval sampling

Time-interval sampling divides the whole observation session into periods of a given length, such as 2 minutes. Only the first observed occurrence of the target behaviour is counted in each of these time intervals, regardless of the number of times it actually occurs.

Time-point sampling

In time-point sampling the total observation period is divided into intervals of, say, ten minutes and the observer records any occurrence of the target behaviour only at the very end of each interval. Only if the behaviour is visible at that point in time is it recorded.

Random sampling

Random sampling is time-point sampling conducted on a random basis where the length of interval between one time point of observation and the next is randomly determined. Sampling in this way provides a surer estimate of the overall frequency of behaviour since, if the same behaviour is seen every time a random observation is made, then it can be inferred that it is likely to occur consistently. This contrasts with time-point sampling where it is always possible that the target behaviour is being produced (or not) at intervals that exactly match the observing intervals.

BOX 4.5   Which method of sampling to choose?

The purpose of sampling is to collect data that accurately and reliably reflect behaviour as it occurs in a particular environment. The problem is to choose a sampling strategy from the range of possibilities that serves this purpose. What factors affect the decision? One approach is suggested by Sackett, Ruppenthal and Gluck (1978). They point out that all behaviour varies in terms of both frequency and duration. In principle, therefore, four main behaviour types may possibly be observed – high frequency/short duration; high frequency/long duration; low frequency/long duration and low frequency/short duration. The sampling method selected should be one that maximizes the possibility of capturing all four types of behaviour in any given observing environment.

The same authors also point out that the decision about which sampling method to use depends also on the wider circumstances in which the observation is to be conducted. For example, they suggest that among the considerations that affect the decision are whether observation is of 'live' or filmed behaviour; whether continuous observation is possible in the situation in which behaviour occurs; the number of individuals to be observed, and the complexity of the observation system that must be operated.

● DATA COLLECTION AND ANALYSIS ●

Data collection from observation also requires choosing a method of recording what is observed. A number of different options exist, ranging from paper and pencil up to sophisticated audio and video recording and computer-based systems. The reader is referred to Foster et al. (1988) for a discussion of these methods.

Qualitative data

Qualitative records consist of a verbal description of observed events or behaviour. These may range from a list of brief descriptive points up to a detailed narrative of an entire behaviour sequence and its accompanying events, either as the sole form of data or as an adjunct to qualitative measures. It may therefore include a large interpretive component if it relies on inferences made by the observer. Content analysis or other techniques of qualitative analysis (see chapter 6) can be used on a record of speech.

This is clearly a more demanding form of data to record than that obtained from the quantitative approach and its adoption is likely to depend on a mixture of factors including the complexity of the target behaviour, the use to be made of the results, and the recording skills of the observer.

Quantitative data

The usual form in which raw data are collected from systematic observation is the checklist. This easily generates frequency data for each of the observable categories in the observation system and leads to quantitative analysis and the testing of hypotheses by non-parametric statistics. The first two methods mentioned below are of this type. The third method generates measured data that are treatable by means of parametric statistics such as the t-test or ANOVA.

- *Event recording* offers the most straightforward of all quantitative measures. This method logs the occurrences of the target behaviour to provide measures of relative and absolute frequency. It also provides the possibility of making a record of the order in which events occurred.
- *Interval recording* registers the presence or absence of target behaviours at specified intervals within an observation period, for example, by observing for a 1-minute period every half hour (see time-interval sampling above). By using short observation periods and longer intervals between them it is possible to obtain a record of events over a longer period than can be continuously observed.
- *Duration recording* registers the time taken by a behaviour, for example, how long a panic attack lasts, and, if a MEE (mutually exclusive and exhaustive) observation system is used, it is only necessary to record the onset time of each behaviour.

● VALIDITY AND RELIABILITY IN SYSTEMATIC OBSERVATION ●

Validity

The validity of observational research is concerned with the extent to which the result of a particular observational process can truly be said to provide accurate information about the behaviour of interest. Problems of validity emerge from two sources: the content of an observational system itself, and the sampling procedure through which it is applied to behaviour.

The observational system

The question here is whether the constructs contained in the observational system have been adequately defined in terms both of their relation to relevant theory and of their completeness. If the intention is to test a theory, valid research requires that the descriptions and definitions in the observational system should be constructed in terms of that theory. However, even if no theory is to be tested, the observation system should be designed to include all possible forms of the behaviour to be studied.

Sampling procedure

The other principal source of invalidity comes from inadequate sampling of the situation that is under observation. The more complex the situation the larger the sample that is needed, and the longer that observation should last to secure the full range of instances. Failure to devote adequate time to observation results in a skewed measure of behaviour and thus compromises validity.

Reliability

Reliability in observational research deals with the question of how to obtain a consistent and accurate set of data that are as free of random error as possible. Accuracy in this sense refers to the extent to which the measures of a variable actually reflect the real quantity of that variable which was present. For example, if an observer claimed to see ten examples of a particular behaviour on a single occasion, then accurate observation would require that there were actually ten examples of the behaviour. Consistency is concerned with the extent to which the same standard of accuracy is obtained throughout the observing period.

The usual method of assessing reliability as regards both accuracy and consistency is by means of inter-observer reliability. In this, independent observations of the same events are made by two or more observers, and the extent to which their observations agree provides an index of the overall reliability of their observations. Cohen's *kappa*, which incorporates a

BOX 4.6 Observer drift

The problem of 'observer drift' is the tendency for independent observers to gradually lose their independence if they are able to communicate with each other about the task. Their observations, though initially independent of each other, will show a tendency gradually to converge, in line with the conformity effect. Employing several observers to take an average of their separate observations is therefore unlikely to provide an answer to reliability problems unless it is possible to be sure that each observer (and each separate observation) is truly independent from the others. To complicate matters, it also appears that observers who know that their inter-observer reliability will be computed produce more accurate observations than those who do not (Kent et al., 1977, cited by Foster et al., 1988).

correction for chance agreement, is the statistic most often used for this purpose. Howell (1997) provides a clear explanation of the statistical reasoning and Robson (2002) also has a good discussion of reliability issues in observational research that includes Cohen's *kappa*. Barton and Ascione (1984) cited by Foster et al. (1988) suggest that 85% agreement between independent observers is the normally acceptable minimum.

However, purely numerical estimates of reliability such as *kappa* may be misleading since the extent of agreement between observers is likely to reflect more than their relative accuracy. Among the factors that should also be considered in interpreting such estimates are: the extent to which an observer is required to make inferences, the complexity, or otherwise, of the observation system; and the presence of 'observer drift' (see box 4.6).

Reactivity

Reactivity is the term for the effect on participants' behaviour of knowingly being observed. If participants know (or guess) that they are taking part in research, and their behaviour is being observed it may change from what it would have been if an observer had not been present. For example, some participants may attempt impression management by 'faking good', while others may show social inhibition and suppress the behaviour that would normally have occurred. The problem for a researcher is how such effects may be recognized and allowed for when they occur.

Reactivity effects can be reduced, or at least contained by some combination of the following strategies:

1   Reducing the number of cues that may signal that observation is in progress – by choosing an unobtrusive observation position, for example. The ultimate step in this direction is to use covert observation (with the prior agreement of participants).
2   Increasing the number of planned observation sessions and discarding the data from the early sessions when reactivity is likely to be greatest.

BOX 4.7 Systematic observation: a checklist of design tasks

Preliminaries

- Have described the research problem fully and clearly?
- Have developed an explanation which either links your research to a theory or says why the observations should be made?
- If appropriate, have stated the hypothesis to be tested and identified the test statistic to be used on the data?

The observation system

- Have identified the type(s) of behaviour to be observed?
- Have developed mutually exclusive and exhaustive (MEE) definitions of each category of behaviour?
- Have checked that the categories are complete, distinct and cover all the target behaviours?
- Have checked that each category can be differentiated in the observing situation?

The observation process

- Have identified an appropriate location for making observations?
- Have decided which sampling procedure to use?
- Have decided whether to use overt or covert observation?
- Have decided whether to use one or more observers to collect observations?
- Have reviewed the ethical standards of the investigation and taken any necessary action?
- Have run a pilot study and made any necessary amendments to the observational system, or its implementation?
- If more than one observer has been used, have made a preliminary assessment of inter-observer reliability?

---

3 Allowing time for participants to become familiar with an analogue environment, such as an observing suite, and/or (especially when children are to be observed) providing distracting activities.

4 Debriefing participants after the observations are completed to try to assess the size of any reactivity effects.

The problem in attempting to deal with reactivity is that one can never be sure how much observed behaviour is due to an awareness of being observed and how much it is the genuine result of the situation. Reactivity effects may not be inevitable, as some empirical evidence suggests, but they are difficult to predict and clearly can never be discounted completely.

● OBSERVATION AND RESEARCH ETHICS ●

Planning for observational research almost always includes the decision about whether to observe overtly or covertly. In overt observation, the observer does not hide the fact that observations are being carried out from those being observed, while in covert observation, some degree of concealment is involved, so that those being observed may be (relatively) unaware of the fact. The ethical problems posed by covert observation made without the knowledge or consent of those being observed are obvious. See, for example, Middlemist, Knowles and Matter's (1976) research into the effects of personal space invasion in male urinals and the brief, but intense, debate that followed (Koocher, 1977; Middlemist et al., 1977).

However, even overt observation is problematic in certain situations. In general, it is recognized that there is a distinction to be drawn between wholly public spaces, such as shopping malls, semi-private places such as restaurants, and private environments, such as private homes. The key difference between these three types of situation is the extent to which behaviour in them could normally be expected to come under the scrutiny of others.

Observation of behaviour in a public place, where it can be seen by anyone passing, is generally regarded as unobjectionable whether carried out overtly or not and even if the informed consent of individuals has not been obtained. The justification for this position is that the researcher is doing no more (albeit in a more systematic and concentrated way) than any member of the general public. On the other hand, if the observation of behaviour in private or semi-private situations is planned, then the informed consent of those to be observed would be required because people would normally expect themselves to be shielded from the gaze of the public at large.

EXTENSION ACTIVITIES

Activity 1

Using the 'where, what, when, how' format, plan the observation of a sample of toddlers, that aims to discover whether their play preferences follow gender lines. A collection of toys appropriate to both genders will be available.

Activity 2

Identify a common type of behaviour, such as greetings, and carry out some casual observation in a fully public environment, such as a railway station. Try to construct a typology of greetings that might be used in a systematic study. Among the key variables you could consider for inclusion are extent, duration and frequency of any physical contact, facial expression, and any verbalization.

Activity 3

With consent, observe one individual continuously for a period of about half an hour while s/he engages in a passive activity, such as studying, reading or watching TV. Try to achieve a perfect record of behaviour at the micro level (such as changes to posture) for that period.

Activity 4

Plan a piece of observational research to investigate possible male–female differences in book-carrying on your campus using the definitions from Jenni and Jenni (1976) given in table 4.2. Having done so, what conclusions do you draw about the categories in their observation system?

Chapter Summary

1   Observation is the basic method of data collection across all scientific disciplines. In psychology three main approaches to observation can be distinguished: casual, participant and systematic observation.

2   Casual observation, which comes the closest of the three approaches to 'just looking', involves the unstructured viewing of behaviour. It offers a very flexible method of research that can be applied to almost any situation, and has value as an exploratory method at an early stage of research. However, the lack both of a sampling strategy and protection against observer bias mean that it is impossible to gauge reliability and validity.

3   Participant observation requires the researcher to become involved as part of the social world in which the observation is to be carried out. This approach to observation allows a researcher to see the world through the eyes of the other participants and to obtain access to information that would otherwise remain inaccessible. However, it is a demanding approach to conducting observation, not least because it requires the two contrasting roles, of researcher and participant, to be maintained.

4   Systematic observation allows a researcher to focus more narrowly on a limited range of behaviour by employing an exhaustively defined set of low-level behavioural descriptions to organize the data collection process. In contrast to other forms of observation, the usual result of applying this approach is a quantitative dataset that can be processed statistically in order to test formal hypotheses about behaviour, and this is generally seen as an advantage, since it also facilitates assessment of validity and reliability. On the other hand, its critics cite the supposed narrowness and inflexibility of the method.

5   Planning for observational research requires consideration of where observation is to take place; what is to be observed; how observation is to be conducted and data recorded; and how behaviour is to be sampled. Choices among these issues will be determined by, among others, the purpose of the research, the nature of the environment in which it is to be conducted and the type of behaviour that is to be observed.

6   The concepts of validity and reliability are applicable only to systematic observation. The assessment of these qualities depends on a number of variables, including the nature of any observation system employed, especially its comprehensiveness and usability, and the likelihood of reactivity effects if participants become aware of being observed. Quantitative assessments of the reliability of observations are possible but should be interpreted with care.

7   The most salient ethical issue in observational research concerns the question of whether some form of covert observation may be employed as a way of reducing possible reactivity effects. The ethical acceptability of this strategy depends in general on the situation in which observation is to be carried out, and in particular whether a participant would normally expect to be observed in that situation.

● FURTHER READING ●

Banister, P. (1994). Observation. In P. Banister, E. Burman, I. Parker, M. Taylor and C. Tindall (eds), *Qualitative methods in psychology: A research guide*. Buckingham: Open University Press.

May, T. (2001). *Social research: Issues, methods and process*, 3rd edn. Maidenhead: Open University Press.

Wilkinson, J. (2000). Direct observation. In G. M. Breakwell, S. Hammond and C. Fife-Schaw (eds), *Research methods in psychology*, 2nd edn. London: Sage.

5

EXPERIMENTS

CHAPTER MAP

Introduction

Identifying a causal relation between variables
Testing hypotheses about variables

Essential Features of an Experiment

Independent and dependent variables
Operationalization
Conditions
Control

Types of Experiment

Laboratory and field experiments
True and quasi experiments
Non-experimental correlational research

Experiment Design

The single sample design
The two (or more) groups designs
   Independent groups design
   Repeated measures design
   Before–after design
Other designs
   The N = 1 single participant experiment
   Matched participants design
   Yoked controls design
   Single- and double-blind designs
Simple and factorial experiment designs

Experimental Error

Random and constant error
The main sources of experimental error

Reliability and Validity

Types of validity
Theoretical validity
Internal validity
External validity

Extension Activities

Chapter Summary

Further Reading

THIS CHAPTER

- *Introduces the experiment as a means of testing hypotheses about causal relations between variables.*
- *Identifies the essential features of an experiment.*
- *Explains the different forms of experiment and considers especially the important distinction between 'true' and other kinds of experiments.*
- *Explains and discusses the main experimental designs.*
- *Introduces the concept of experimental error, discusses its main sources, and introduces techniques by which error may be controlled.*
- *Introduces the notions of validity and reliability as the criteria of good experimentation.*
- *Provides a checklist of questions for use when planning a psychology experiment.*

KEY CONCEPTS

Causal relation
independent variable
dependent variable
operational variable
experiment conditions
control condition
field experiment
'true' experiment
'quasi' experiment
between-participants design

within-participants design
experimental error
demand characteristics
experimenter effects
confounding
standardization
randomization
counterbalancing
validity
reliability

● INTRODUCTION ●

In the model of scientific research presented in chapter 1, the development of new knowledge was said to involve the identification of an interesting problem, followed by the formulation of a research hypothesis. This hypothesis is then tested through the careful collection of empirical data and, depending on the outcome of many such tests, a theory may be developed to explain the phenomenon in question. The essential feature of all such explanations is that they are couched in terms of the relationships among *variables* (see box 5.1).

> A variable is anything that, when measured, is capable of taking more than one value. Sex, height, intelligence, attitudes to music, food preferences, reaction time, and personality differences are examples of potentially psychologically interesting variables.

The basic aim of experimental research in all the sciences, including psychology, is thus to identify significant relationships between variables. Of these, causal relations – those where any change to the value of one variable brings about a consequent change to the value of another – are of particular interest because they offer the possibility of a deeper understanding of the phenomenon in question. A causal relationship, once identified, allows more precise predictions to be made about antecedent and consequent conditions and can lead to the construction of a more powerful theory that explains the links between them more fully.

Identifying a causal relation between variables

Identifying a causal relationship between variables is thus highly desirable. But how may causal ties be reliably ascertained, given that they are normally obscured by other influences? Non-experimental methods of research can help by identifying a *regularity*, or co-variation in

---

BOX 5.1 An example of a variable in psychological research

After the appalling murder of Kitty Genovese (see chapter 1 for an account) Latane and Darley began researching to find out more about the 'uninvolved bystander' phenomenon. They believed that one variable, the number of bystanders to an emergency, could have been a contributory factor in the tragedy and they carried out a number of experiments to look at the effect of different levels of this variable on the readiness of bystanders to render assistance. In one, the 'fake fire' experiment (Latane and Darley, 1968) they placed participants in a waiting room and piped white smoke into the room to make it appear that there was a nearby fire. By varying the value of the variable (i.e. the number of participants who were in the waiting room together) the researchers found that readiness to give aid (by raising the alarm, or investigating the source of the smoke) did indeed decline as the number of people in the room increased.

the relation of one variable to another. This, in turn, may *suggest* that a causal link exists between the variables, but there could be any number of alternative reasons. Finding that two variables co-vary falls well short of a *demonstration* of causality. In fact, the only way to exclude alternative explanations and establish that variables are in fact causally related is to conduct an experiment. Experiment alone provides the precise, quantitative data that, on analysis, allows a causal claim to be assessed.

Shaughnessy and Zechmeister (1994) identify three criteria that must be met before a causal relationship can be identified with confidence. They are,

- *The two factors co-vary*: changes to variable A are accompanied by changes to variable B.
- *The co-variation is unidirectional*: there is no change to A when B is varied.
- *All possible alternative influences acting on B have been eliminated*.

The problem in psychology lies in obtaining full implementation of the last requirement. It has been pointed out (e.g. Liebert and Liebert, 1995) that identifying and eliminating every possible alternative influence on a given variable is virtually impossible. Human behaviour is so open to a multiplicity of influences that it is unlikely that they could all be identified. Thus, the most that may reasonably be demanded of an experiment is that it shows that change to variable A is *one*, but not necessarily the *only* cause of change in variable B. Notwithstanding this, the question of how to remove the most obvious of all the undesired influences in an experiment is central to experiment design and will be considered in detail later in the chapter.

Testing hypotheses about variables

The crucial question, of whether one variable has really exerted influence on another, is decided by comparing the results of testing two or more groups of participants, representing different levels of one variable, under controlled conditions, and measuring the other variable in each case. The result of this process will be a number of quantitative datasets that record the changes to the measured variable in those participants. Such data can be tested statistically to determine whether the initial research hypothesis, predicting changes in the value of the measured variable in response to changes in the causal variable, is supported or not. The framework for this decision is provided by precise statistical hypotheses formulated as part of the experiment design process. Chapter 8 provides a detailed explanation of how this testing process operates.

● THE ESSENTIAL FEATURES OF AN EXPERIMENT ●

Independent and dependent variables

How does the experiment set about meeting the criteria of causality listed earlier? Essentially, an experiment is a controlled situation in which one variable (called the independent variable, or IV) is allowed to act on another (called the dependent variable, or DV) when the alternative influences have been removed. If it is then possible to detect changes to the DV as the IV changes, the value of the DV is shown to *depend* on the value of the IV. And if those

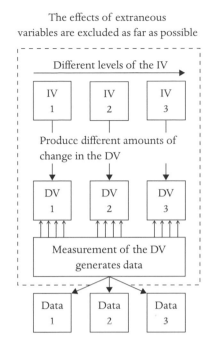

The effects of extraneous
variables are excluded as far as possible

Different levels of the IV

IV 1   IV 2   IV 3

Produce different amounts of
change in the DV

DV 1   DV 2   DV 3

Measurement of the DV
generates data

Data 1   Data 2   Data 3

Figure 5.1 The relationships of IV, DV and data in an experiment

changes are unidirectional the relationship between the IV and DV has been established as a causal one because it meets all the criteria listed above (see figure 5.1).

The independent variable (IV), then, is the variable that is to be investigated as a possible causal influence, so called because it is the *independent* force in the experiment (it is also sometimes called the causal variable). In an experiment, the value (or 'level') of the IV is varied by the experimenter in order to see whether any consequent changes to the dependent variable occur. In the experiment by Latane and Darley (1968) mentioned earlier, the IV is the number of participants in the waiting room.

The dependent variable (DV) is so called because, as noted above, it is considered to be *dependent* on the IV and expected to change when the IV changes. In an experiment this variable is measured (hence its alternative name of the measured variable) to try to detect such changes and it is these measurements that constitute the data of the experiment, as shown in figure 5.1. The DV in Latane and Darley (1968) was the readiness of the participants to act in an 'emergency'.

Operationalization

Frequently, the variables designated as the IV and DV in an experiment are not directly accessible and so can neither be manipulated nor measured directly. Instead, they must be accessed indirectly, by a process known as operationalization. Operationalization involves the selection of another, more accessible, variable that is related as closely as possible to the true variable of interest. In Latane and Darley (1968) the DV was the readiness of the experimental participants to act. However, 'readiness to act' is not directly measurable because it is a mental state. The experimenters therefore operationalized this variable as 'response latency' – the amount of time that elapsed before the participants took any action.

Operationalization is an important consideration in experiment design because it can affect both reliability and validity. As regards validity, the question is how closely a variable that is claimed to operationalize the IV or DV is actually related to the true IV or DV. If this cannot be clearly explained the validity of the results will be in doubt. In using response latency as the operationalization of 'readiness to act' Latane and Darley chose a measure that is strongly related to the 'true' DV on the basis of the largely unassailable argument that those most ready to act can be expected to show the shortest latencies. Response latency, therefore, possesses validity as an experimental measure in this experiment. On reliability, the issue is whether the variable selected for the operationalization of the DV provides measures that are consistent and accurate. The scale of measurement is an important consideration here (see chapter 7). By these criteria, Latane and Darley's choice of operational DV can be argued to allow reliable measures of the DV to be taken.

Conditions

The goal of experiment design is to construct a situation that allows a causal relationship to be identified by varying the value of the IV in order to cause concomitant change to the value of the DV. However, change has to be accomplished in a controlled way so that one can be sure that the DV is responding to deliberate manipulation rather than just varying at random. To do this different values or levels of the IV are provided as separate conditions in an experiment:

1   The control condition is a 'nil intervention' condition. This is created when research participants receive no treatment at all (apart from any procedures intended to disguise that this is the case). The measures of the DV obtained in this condition therefore provide a measure of the untreated, or baseline, performance of the participants. Not all experiments include a control condition (see below).
2   The experimental condition is the 'intervention' condition, representing a change to the level of the IV *away* from the control condition. If the looked-for causal relationship exists, consequent changes to the value of the DV can be expected in the data produced by this condition. One or more experimental conditions may be used.

The research described in box 5.2 shows how data obtained under different conditions allow conclusions to be drawn about the influence of the IV.

Control

The purpose of an experiment is to arrange the situation so that one IV acts on only a single DV in a controlled way and then to measure any changes to the value of the DV that follow. However, there are always more variables in an experiment than just the IV and DV, and many

BOX 5.2   Comparing conditions to identify a causal link between variables

In an investigation widely recognized as a classic, Schachter and Singer (1962) explored the effects of cognitive, social and physiological factors on the experience of emotion. In the experiment, whose ostensible purpose was the testing of the effects of a vitamin, all participants were given an injection followed by different kinds of information about its effects. The participants were then placed in a room with a confederate of the experimenters who simulated an emotional state and their behaviour was observed.

The conditions

The experiment had four conditions with two independent variables (injection type, provision of information) and different levels of each variable (saline/adrenaline and accurate information/no information/misleading information).

- *Group 1*: Received an injection of saline and no information about its effects (the control group).
- *Group 2*: Received an injection of adrenaline and no information about its effects.
- *Group 3*: Received an injection of adrenaline and misleading information about its effects.
- *Group 4*: Received an injection of adrenaline and accurate information about its effects.

The comparisons among conditions

Comparing results from group 1 with those from group 2 showed whether the combination of an adrenaline injection plus exposure to simulated emotion could cause emotional experience (it did). Comparing the results in groups 2, 3 and 4 showed the effect of different types of knowledge about the effects of adrenaline when the physiological effects of adrenaline and the exposure to emotional behaviour were held constant across all three experimental groups. (It was found that groups 2 and 3 responded emotionally, but groups 1 and 4 did not). See e.g. Eysenck (2000) for a fuller discussion of this experiment.

---

of these are also potential influences on the DV. These are called the extraneous variables. The attempt to control or exclude the influence of extraneous variables is an essential aspect of designing an experiment so as to be sure that the observed changes to the DV are attributable only to the effects of the IV. If this is not done, one or more of the extraneous variables may become a source of experimental error.

Experimental error is any change to a DV produced by a factor or variable in an experiment other than the IV.

● TYPES OF EXPERIMENT ●

Experiments are not all alike. There are important differences between experiments carried out in a laboratory and those that are done 'in the field' and, in both situations, between 'true' and 'quasi' experiments.

Laboratory and field experiments

Laboratory experiments arguably represent the most common method of data collection in psychology, though they may not take place in anything that would be recognized as a laboratory by, say, a chemist. The term laboratory simply designates a room or similar situation that contains the equipment needed for the experiment and which allows for the control of key variables, such as the noise and lighting levels, and interactions with and between the participants. The close control of variables and careful measurement procedures afforded by a laboratory setting can be found described in most standard psychology texts. For primary accounts see, e.g. Sperling (1960), Stroop (1932) and Shepherd and Metzler (1971) among many others.

Field experiments are experiments conducted in any non-laboratory environment, where people engage in the normal tasks of everyday life – such as working, studying, playing etc.

In contrast to lab-based research, field research uses locations, such as schools, hospitals, streets, where behaviour can be observed under more natural conditions than is possible in a lab. For this reason, this type of data gathering is sometimes called naturalistic research. (See box 5.3 for an example.)

In a typical field experiment, the researcher creates different situations in the field that represent different levels of an IV and then observes the participants' unconstrained responses in those situations (Doob and Gross, 1968, in box 5.3; or for an extreme example, see Middlemist, Knowles and Matter, 1976). This carries the advantage of allowing the sampling of the range of possible responses in that situation, rather than, as in the lab situation, the measurement of a single specific piece of behaviour. It also reduces the likelihood of reactivity effects because participants need not be aware that the experiment is taking place.

Reactivity effect is the effect (on the data) of knowing that one is participating in an investigation.

On the other hand, arranging a satisfactory field experiment may be difficult. The fact that the researcher has no control over the situation or the events that take place renders the outcome unpredictable and there may be ethical issues around the need to obtain the informed consent of participants and employment of covert observation.

True and quasi experiments

Experiments do not only differ in terms of the location chosen. Differences in the way they are designed create more and less powerful forms and lead to the important distinction

BOX 5.3   An example of a field experiment

Doob and Gross used the field experimental approach to test the hypothesis that aggression would be a more likely response to frustration when the source of the frustration was of low status than when it was of high status. The source of frustration was one car blocking another at traffic signals. The experimenters drove up to traffic lights in Los Angeles in either a high-status car (large, expensive, clean) or a low-status car (smaller, inexpensive, rusty/dirty) arriving as the lights were turning red. When the lights turned green they remained immobile for up to 15 seconds. The dependent measures of frustration were time that elapsed after the lights changed before the driver behind honked, and the number and length of honks produced. These data along with descriptions of the frustrated car and driver were collected by an observer. Throughout, the participant drivers were unaware that they were taking part in an experiment.

The experiment found that status did have an inhibitory effect on horn honking in this situation. Eighty-four percent of drivers in the 'low-status' condition honked at least once and 47% honked twice compared to only 50% and 19% of those in the 'high status' condition. The time taken to produce the first honk was also lower in the 'low-status' condition than in the other and in both conditions men were more likely to honk than women. All these differences were significant at $p < 0.05$.

Source: Doob and Gross, 1968.

between 'true' experiments, 'quasi' (Latin for 'as it were') experiments and other forms of data collection.

The 'true' experiment

A 'true' experiment is one that, because of its basic design features, can allow a causal link between an IV and a DV to be inferred with a high degree of confidence, as long as a high degree of control of extraneous variables is also achieved.

The essential design features required of a 'true' experiment are (see figure 5.2) as follows.

• *Random assignment to conditions*: The research participants must be *randomly* assigned to the different levels of the IV (conditions) in the experiment. Random assignment is a *necessary* condition for making causal inferences about the relation between IV and DV because it ensures that any differences between individual participants are evenly spread across the conditions.
• *Equal treatment of participants*: The treatment of research participants must be equal in every way *except* in relation to the variable being investigated as the IV.

In addition, the presence of a control condition to provide a baseline 'nil treatment' measure of the DV is highly desirable, since it helps confirm the presence of a causal effect in the other conditions. However, it is not an absolutely essential requirement. (The experiment by

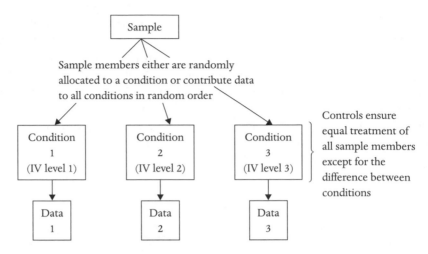

Figure 5.2   Features of a 'true' experiment
Comparison of one dataset with another indicates whether measures of the DV change as the level of the IV changes, and thus whether it may be concluded that the IV caused the change to the DV.

BOX 5.4   Research with no control group

The absence of a control group is sometimes unavoidable. Lewin, Lippett and White (1939) trained graduate students to lead groups in one of three styles – authoritarian, democratic or laissez-faire – in order to assess the relative effectiveness of different styles of leadership. It was impossible to provide a control group in this experiment because a true control would involve nil treatment, that is, no leadership. This could have been achieved only by creating a completely leaderless group which would have introduced a confounding variable (leaderlessness) into the investigation.

Schachter and Singer described in box 5.2 is a 'true' experiment because it meets both essential requirements. The fact that it also possesses a control condition does not affect its ability to reveal causal effects: see also box 5.4.)

'Quasi' experiments

A 'quasi' experiment is one in which either random assignment to conditions is not carried out, or in which participants are not treated equally, or both. Therefore, a 'quasi' experiment does not allow a firm inference to be drawn that the IV *caused* observed changes to the DV. However, it *may* be possible to conclude that a causal relationship is *suggested*, with confirmation awaited from the results of a 'true' experiment.

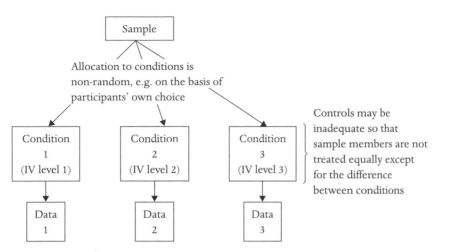

Figure 5.3 Features of a 'quasi' experiment

Comparison of one dataset with another may find differences that *suggest* that different treatments of the IV caused different levels of the DV. However, it cannot be concluded that a causal relationship exists.

BOX 5.5 An example of correlational research

Segall et al. (1963) compared the perception of geometric illusions, including the Muller–Lyer illusion, in different national and ethnic groups that included black Africans, Filipinos, white South Africans, and white Americans, finding that members of the black African and Filipino groups were much less susceptible to the illusions than the others.

This investigation was not an experiment because it involved sampling from different groups formed solely on the basis of their ethnicity and/or nationality and the participants in all groups were treated identically.

A variation on this approach is the 'single group one-shot' design that involves collecting a single set of data from one sample of participants, e.g. Milgram (1963). This type of investigation may have some of the features of a 'true' experiment in that extraneous variables may be controlled, a random sample of participants is employed. However, because there is no manipulation of the value of the IV it is impossible to say whether it is causally linked with the DV. One-shot research is thus essentially a way of establishing the frequency of a particular variable within a given population.

Non-experimental correlational research

A common form of research that resembles an experiment (but isn't) employs the correlational or 'natural groups' design (see box 5.5). This approach compares groups that differ in

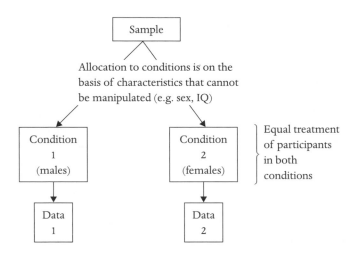

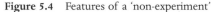

Figure 5.4   Features of a 'non-experiment'
Comparison of one dataset with another indicates whether the conditions differ consistently from each other, but *not* that group characteristics caused such differences.

terms of a particular characteristic, such as sex, intelligence or handedness) with a view to trying to detect a measurable difference between the groups in terms of a variable of interest. Investigations of this type are not experiments because the allocation of participants to a group is not carried out at random by the researcher but is determined by the presence or absence of qualifying characteristics in the participants. These characteristics are imported into the investigation by the participants themselves. The variable acting as the IV cannot therefore be manipulated inside the investigation to see whether the 'DV' changes (see figure 5.4). A further point is that this style of research typically treats the members of all groups identically. For these reasons it is only possible to use this kind of research to see how strongly a 'natural' variable and a measured variable co-vary, as in Segall et al. (1963).

● EXPERIMENT DESIGN ●

Two early decisions in designing an experiment involve determining the number of groups and their relation to each other. The first point depends on the levels of the IV to be used and the second means making a decision on whether the independent samples, repeated measures, or some other design will be used. The choice between these depends largely on whether differences *between* individuals are seen as posing a greater source of experimental error than the likely effect of testing a single group of participants more than once. However, more complex designs are also possible and are discussed later in the chapter, particularly in the section on simple and factorial experiments.

The single sample design

The single sample design is also called the 'one-shot' design because it takes one sample of participants who generate a single set of scores. This design has two uses. It can be employed

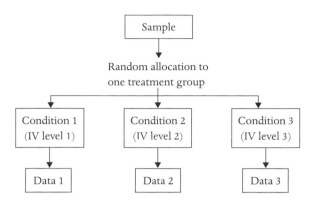

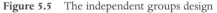

Figure 5.5   The independent groups design
Comparison of one dataset with another indicates whether measures of the DV change as the level of
the IV changes.

when it is not possible to construct a control group, and when only one level of the treatment variable is applied. In such situations a researcher typically wishes to find out whether a particular treatment can cause the sample to differ significantly from the known population. Milgram's (1963) research into obedience is an example of this application.

Two (or more) groups designs

The independent groups design

In this design, a single sample of individuals is divided into two or more groups (conditions) representing different levels of the IV. The groups are each given a different treatment and the participants tested only once, so every item of data can be considered to be independent of every other one. It follows from this that any differences in the data obtained from the various groups is the result of the difference between groups in terms of their participant members plus the difference caused by the different treatments that were applied.

   The aim of the independent samples design is to prevent the possible introduction of error due to the effect of testing the same individuals more than once, so its use is particularly indicated when that possibility is judged to be more serious or more likely than the error introduced by the presence of individual differences (see figure 5.5).

The repeated measures design

The purpose of this design is to control for error due to individual differences between participants and this is achieved by using a single sample whose members contribute data to all conditions in the experiment (figure 5.6). Each participant is tested more than once and acts as her own control. Any difference between groups seen in data is thus attributable to the difference between treatments applied to each group plus the effect of the multiple testing

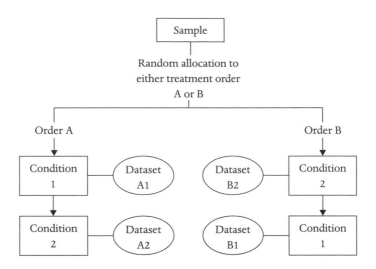

Figure 5.6   A repeated measures design with counterbalanced treatment order
Comparison of datasets A1 and B1 with A2 and B2 controls for both within-group differences and order effects.

of the same individuals. The latter point is the main vulnerability of this design. Without some control, such as placing an adequate interval between repeated occasions of testing, this design can introduce error from sources such as fatigue, practice, or familiarity with the experimental task.

The before–after design

The before–after design combines the features of the two previous designs. In it, participants are first randomly assigned to different treatment conditions, as in the independent groups design, and pre-treatment tasks are administered to establish base-line values of the DV in each group. The experiment is then run, with different experimental tasks for each group and second sets of data collected. Subsequently, comparison is made between the pre- and post-test results in each condition, so that, in each group, participants act as their own controls (figure 5.7). The value of this design is that it not only offers the same degree of control over individual differences between participants as the repeated measures design, but it provides an indication of the extent of difference between the groups by means of the pre-test.

Other designs

In addition to the experiment designs described above, there are a number of other designs about which it is useful to be aware, although they are perhaps less frequently needed by researchers than their more straightforward relatives.

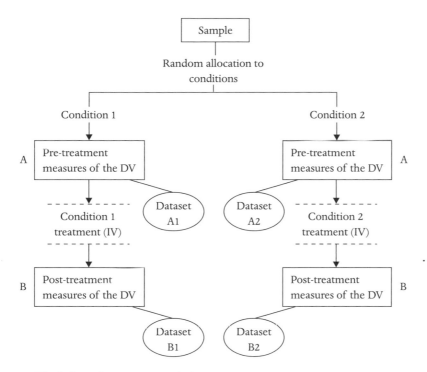

Figure 5.7 The before–after two-groups design
Comparison of datasets A1 with B1 and A2 with B2 allows change due to the IV to be identified since within-group differences are controlled. The comparison of datasets B1 with B2 shows any between-group difference attributable to different levels of IV.

The N = 1 single participant experiment

In an N = 1 experiment the sample consists of a single individual only, and is used mainly in clinical case studies and as a method of conducting exploratory research or testing a novel procedure. However, despite some famous examples of its application, such as Ebbinghaus (1885 / 1913) and Watson and Rayner (1920), its susceptibility to sampling error seriously limits its usefulness. A review of the more famous N = 1 studies and a discussion of the situations in which it may be useful can be found in Dukes (1965).

The matched participants design

The matched participants design is a version of the independent groups design with two groups that aims to improve the comparability of the data obtained from different conditions by controlling for one interpersonal variable (such as IQ) that might otherwise act as a major source of error.

To implement this design, each participant is given a pre-test (perhaps an IQ test) and then each is paired with another member of the sample whose score is closest to their own. One participant in each pair is then assigned at random to one treatment condition with the co-participant placed in the other condition. This arrangement means that, although the participants contribute data independently, the two treatment groups are balanced in respect of the matching variable. The error that could possibly arise from that source is thus partially controlled.

There are, however, difficulties of implementation. Control of the matching variable can only be as good as the reliability and validity of the technique used to provide the pre-test measure and unless the participant pool is large it may be difficult to find a satisfactory match for all participants.

The yoked controls design

The standard independent groups design aims to deal with all treatment groups equally except, crucially, in relation to the IV. The yoked controls design is a two-group variant of the standard design that can be used to ensure that, if necessary, both control and treatment groups receive an absolutely identical experience in at least one respect. In this design, participants are first randomly assigned to either the control or the treatment groups and one member of each is paired, again at random, with a member of the control group. Subsequently the treatment group members are given the required experimental procedure and the response of those individuals to the procedure determines the experience of their control. In effect, the individuals in one group are 'yoked' to those in the other. A literal example of experimental yoking is the 'kitten carousel' experiment of Held and Hein (1963) in which the movements of an active kitten were transmitted to a basket containing a 'passive' kitten as its yoked control. The passive kitten was thus able to receive exactly the same visual input as the active kitten while nevertheless remaining immobile in the basket.

Single- and double-blind designs

As Martin Orne has shown (Orne, 1962) the participants in an experiment frequently attempt to identify the purpose of the experiment, and the nature of their own role within it, from the clues in the experimental task. If this seems likely to affect the outcome of the experiment single- or double-blind procedures can be used. These use one of the standard designs, but in a single-blind design, extra care is taken to prevent the participants from knowing whether they are in a control or treatment condition. This can be achieved if all clues that could possibly identify the conditions are removed.

If the behaviour of the experimenter is also thought to be a source of influence on the participants, the double-blind design can be employed, in which both the participant and the person running the experiment are unaware of whether any given participant is in the treatment or control group.

Simple and factorial experiment designs

In addition to the differences within the range of experiment designs discussed above, there is one further design variation that should be considered. This is the distinction between 'simple' and factorial experiments. Simple experiments are those in which a single IV is mani-

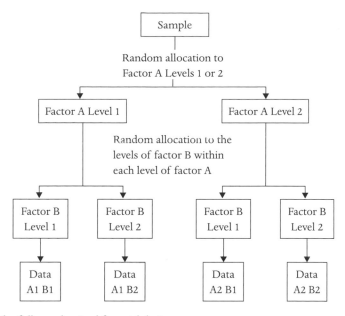

Figure 5.8 The fully randomized factorial design
In the block design version factor A consists of two (or more) levels of the un-manipulated grouping variable.

pulated – in the most clear-cut form this involves only two conditions, but as many conditions as required may be present without affecting the essential simplicity of the design.

If it is suspected that the value of the DV reflects the interaction of two or more IVs then a more complex design is necessary. Such designs are called factorial designs because they involve the simultaneous manipulation of two or more factors each of which may have several levels. The simplest possible factorial design is the 2 × 2 design (two factors each with two levels – see figures 5.8 and 5.9) but experiments involving more factors and levels are possible. The main limiting factor is the need to increase sample size as the number of factors and levels increases. The investigation by Herrman, Crawford and Holdsworthy (1992) into sex differences in the recall of stereotypical 'masculine' and 'feminine' material is an example of this kind of design.

Factorial designs come in three varieties (see Liebert and Liebert, 1995, for fuller information):

- *Fully randomized*: the participants are assigned to a factor or level entirely at random. This approach is mainly used when the sample is homogeneous.
- *Block design*: the participants can be subdivided on one or more grouping variables such as sex or age, and these can be combined with one or more treatment variables. This allows both experimental and correlational data to be generated from the same investigation.
- *Repeated measures*: the participants are assigned at random to one level of a variable and contribute to all levels of a second variable. This allows within- and between-groups effects to be assessed.

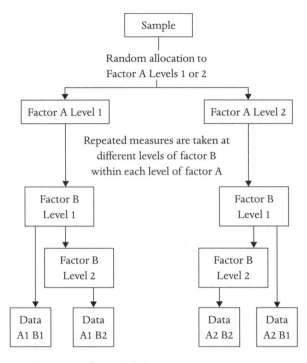

Figure 5.9   The repeated measures factorial design

The advantage of factorial designs over simple designs lies in the fact that in addition to the identification of any 'main effect' on the DV caused by a single variable they also allow the interaction between variables to be examined. The ANOVA statistical tests (chapter 9) provide the means of identifying such interactions.

● EXPERIMENTAL ERROR ●

The concept of experimental error has already been mentioned a number of times in this chapter in the context of the various experiment designs. Experimental error is the difference between the data *actually* obtained and that which *would* have been obtained if it could have been possible to ensure that the IV was the sole influence on the DV, and that any changes to the DV had been measured with complete accuracy.

It will be apparent from this definition that it is impossible to design or carry out a perfectly error-free experiment. The presence of some degree of error is inevitable simply because it may emerge from so many different sources. This means that much of the effort in designing an experiment must be directed at devising methods of controlling those sources of error that seem most likely to interfere with the action of the IV on the DV. If this is not done then one or more of the uncontrolled variables are said to be *confounded* with the effects of the IV.

Confounding has occurred when the influence of the IV on the DV cannot be distinguished from the influence of one or more other variables.

Random and constant error

Anderson (1971) points out the important distinction between two general types of experimental error: random error and constant error.

- Random error is error that sometimes affects one condition in an experiment and sometimes another causing the measures of the DV to be sometimes greater and sometimes less than their true value in an entirely random fashion.
- Constant error is error which has a consistent character throughout an experiment, producing the same degree of overestimate or underestimate of the true value of the DV. Constant error may affect only one, or more, of the conditions in an experiment.

Random error thus affects the sensitivity of the experiment, obscuring the true picture and making it harder to see the effect of the IV on the DV. Like dirt on a windowpane it reduces visibility, but the view itself is essentially undistorted. Constant error, on the other hand, actually distorts the information obtained in the experiment. Like a pattern worked into the glass, it makes it impossible to obtain a true view, no matter how clean the windowpane itself may be.

The main sources of experimental error

Each of the sources of error mentioned below are capable of contributing both random and constant error to an experiment. Clearly, constant error, because it makes it impossible to see whether the IV caused the DV to change at all, poses the greater problem and should be the first concern in experiment design. However, the aim is always to try to reduce *both* types of error to as close to zero as possible. The extract from Stroop (1932) in box 5.6 illustrates the close attention to detail required in designing an experimental task in order to identify and remove sources of error.

Error due to sampling

This form of error is caused by a failure of the sampling procedure to generate a sample that is adequately representative of the population of interest (see chapter 3 for more information about sampling). If the planned sample is small a highly representative sample is unlikely to be achieved, so the only effective remedy is to take a random sample to ensure that any constant error present in the sample is converted to random error. Random error from this source can be reduced in turn by maximizing the size of the sample and/or by increasing the sensitivity of the measurement procedure to reduce the possibility of tied scores.

Participant-related error

The participant variables are those, such as intelligence, motivation, expectations, manual dexterity, handedness that, in a repeated measures design, account for the variance *within*

BOX 5.6   Controlling error in the Stroop colour naming task

When this experiment was contemplated, the first task was to arrange suitable tests. The colors used on the Woodworth–Wells color-sheet were considered but two changes were deemed advisable. As the word test to be used in comparison with the color test was to be printed in black it seemed well to substitute another color for black as an interfering stimulus. Also because of the difficulty of printing words in yellow that would approximate to the stimulus intensity of the other colors used, yellow was discarded. After consulting with Dr Peterson, black and yellow were replaced by brown and purple. Hence the colors used were red, blue, green, brown and purple. The colors were arranged so as to avoid any regularity of occurrence and so that each color would appear twice in each column and in each row, and that no color would immediately succeed itself in either column or row. The words were also arranged so that the name of each color would appear twice in each line. No word was printed in the color it named but an equal number of times in each of the other four colors; i.e. the word 'red' was printed in blue green brown and purple inks; the word 'blue' was printed in red green brown and purple inks; etc. No word immediately succeeded itself in either column or row. The test was printed from fourteen point Franklin lower case type. The word arrangement was duplicated in black print from same type. Each test was also printed in the reverse order which provided a second form. The tests will be known as 'Reading color names where the color of the print and the word are different' (RCNd) and 'Reading color names printed in black' (RCNb).

Source: Stroop, 1932.

conditions and, in an independent groups design, for variance occurring both *within* and *between* conditions.

Participant-related error also arises from treatment variables – the way participants are allocated to different treatments, or the order in which tasks are taken – which may constitute a source of error if they are able to confound the IV. The appropriate countermeasure here is to assign participants to different conditions at random in order to randomize both the within-conditions and the between-conditions sources of variance. If a participant variable is known to correlate highly with the DV a matched participants design also be considered.

Task-related error

Task variables are those concerned with the procedures that participants are required to perform in an experiment. They include such things as: the degree of difficulty of the task; the time allowed for its completion; the nature of the instructions given to the participants and, in repeated measures designs, any effects on performance attributable to fatigue or practice.

BOX 5.7 Countermeasures against experimental error

Randomization

Randomization distributes the effects of a potential source of error at random throughout the experiment, or through one particular condition, thus converting constant error into the (somewhat) less serious random error. Allocating participants to conditions at random controls for individual differences by ensuring that such differences are randomly distributed.

Standardization

Standardization involves ensuring that some aspect of the experiment is the same for all participants within a condition, and perhaps across conditions as well. For example, the environment in which an experiment takes place should normally be the same for all participants in all conditions and the instructions and experimental procedures should be identical within each condition.

Counterbalancing

Counterbalancing attempts to ensure that error from one possible source is neutralized by being balanced (as far as possible) by an equal amount of error from another, similar source. For example, in a repeated measures design the order in which two tasks are performed is a possible source of error. Counterbalancing the order in which they are performed so that half the participants complete task 1 before task 2, while the other half take the tasks in the reverse order, removes or reduces error from this source.

The essential countermeasure is to standardize all experimental procedures (such as instructions, number of trials, the inter-trial interval, any feedback) so that the experience of all participants is as far as possible identical. Counterbalancing or randomizing task order across the groups also ensures that error from this source is reduced (see box 5.7).

Error due to measurement

This error arises when an experiment produces an inaccurate estimate of the true value of the variable being measured. This may be divided into (1) error inherent in the measuring technology (such as is present in most psychometric tests) and (2) human error such as using a manual stopwatch, rather than one triggered electronically, to record response times. The appropriate countermeasure is to seek to reduce both constant and random error by standardizing the measurement procedure for the DV across all conditions and to average each participant's performance across several trials so as to reduce the contribution of human error.

Error due to the environment of the experiment

Many environment variables can also act as a source of experimental error. These include not only the physical characteristics of the space, such as its temperature or noise level, but also features such as the demeanour of the experimenter, or the presence of other people. The purely physical variables can be dealt with by standardization or counterbalancing as appropriate but those involving the other human participants in the experiment are less easy to reduce since they arise from the social psychology of the situation. Among the most important of this latter group are the following.

Error due to 'demand characteristics'

Orne (1962) suggests that, motivated mainly by the desire to be helpful, the participants in an experiment try to read the available 'demand characteristics' for clues to its 'real' purpose. On the basis of their deductions they may attempt to produce data that confirm what they believe to be the real aim. This acts as a potential source of error in an experiment because in trying to infer the purpose of the experiment participants may arrive at a wrong conclusion and thus shape their behaviour entirely inappropriately. Even if not, their normal behaviour may still be exaggerated or changed in some way.

Clearly the problem of demand characteristics is a particular issue for designers of laboratory-based experiments. This is particularly true since the wide publicity given to Milgram's research on obedience (Milgram 1963) may lead participants to overestimate the possibility that deception has been employed as part of the design of the experiment. To make matters more complicated, a negative version of the demand effect called the 'screw-you effect' has been discussed by Argyris (1968). In this participants deliberately try to generate data that would disconfirm (screw up) the research hypothesis.

It seems that the only effective countermeasure to both the positive and negative consequences of demand characteristics is to provide as full information as possible about the aims and goals of the research and to try to ensure that one is believed. The problem posed by disaffected or unmotivated participants can be partially alleviated by pre-experiment screening to try to remove them from the sample. Post-experiment debriefing can also be used in order to check participants' perceptions of the experiment.

Error due to 'experimenter effects'

This is the error introduced (unconsciously) into the research by the researcher herself through interaction with participants that has been investigated in a long series of experiments by Rosenthal and others. Rosenthal (2002) identifies four general types of experimenter effect.

- Biosocial effects are produced by the personal characteristics of experimenter and participants, such as sex, age and ethnicity. Male participants have been found to be less smiled at than female participants and smiling at participants was also found to predict the results of the experiment (Rosenthal, 1967).
- Psycho-social effects are produced by the personality and perceived competence and authority of the experimenter. Researchers with a warm demeanour were found to elicit higher intelligence test scores than those with a cooler demeanour (Rosenthal, 1969).
- Situational effects, such as the level of experience of the researcher and the trend visible in incoming results (i.e. whether they appear to conform to the research hypothesis) are also good predictors of the eventual result (Rosenthal, 1976).
- Expectancy effects, also called the 'Pygmalion effect', refer to the self-fulfilling effects of an experimenter's expectations about the results of an investigation. The classic demonstration (Rosenthal and Jacobson, 1968) involved 18 American elementary school classes whose children were given an IQ test at the beginning of the school year. The teachers were told, on the basis of the results, that 20% of the children possessed high intellectual potential although in fact they had been chosen at random. At the end of the academic year the children were re-tested and those randomly selected to have 'high potential' were found to have gained significantly more in IQ than those not selected.

Social psychological effects such as these represent a major challenge to experimenters. Because they are so subtle and operate largely unconsciously they are extremely difficult to predict or to control. Clearly, an attempt to reduce the effects of (say) a 'cold' demeanour by adopting a jolly persona merely introduces a different source of potential error into the situation in place of the one removed. The usual strategy to deal with effects from this source is to try to reduce the interaction between participants and experimenter to a standardized minimum, so as to limit the opportunities to 'read' any cues that may be provided by the experimenter. Another possible strategy is to use the double-blind technique, in which someone who is uninformed about the aim of the experiment is coached to act as the experimenter in place of the 'real' researcher.

● RELIABILITY AND VALIDITY ●

In seeking to demonstrate that a causal relationship exists between variables, the researcher's goal is to design an experiment that both delivers a true view of that relationship and also gives an identical picture whenever the experiment is performed. That is, the aim is to design an experiment that possesses the essential qualities of validity and reliability.

Types of validity

Questions of validity deal with the extent to which an experiment can be relied upon to present a true picture of the relationship

The issue of validity is concerned with the extent to which any conclusions drawn from an experiment are justified, i.e. it deals with the value of the inferences made on the basis of experimental results.

Reliability refers to the extent to which a given experimental phenomenon can be replicated and thus shown to be independent of a specific situation.

between two variables. Data from an experiment are assessed as valid if they meet the following criteria (Liebert and Liebert, 1995).

Theoretical validity

This form of validity, also called construct validity, looks at whether the concepts (constructs) that are implemented in a piece of research are derived from a theory for which empirical support exists, and can therefore be linked to other well-researched phenomena. This quality is important as psychological knowledge slowly moves beyond the accumulation of unconnected empirical findings to become more systematic. For example, the experiment by Doob and Gross (1968) summarized earlier is based on the empirically well-established connection between frustration and aggression (Dollard et al., 1939).

Internal validity

This deals with the internal features of an experiment. The main threats to internal validity come from the repeated testing of participants (affecting within-participant validity) or the presence in the experiment of systematic differences between one treatment group and the other(s) (between-groups validity). If left uncontrolled either of these factors can seriously weaken the validity of any conclusions that are drawn from the results.

External validity

This is concerned with the extent to which results can be generalized beyond the experiment from which they were obtained to other times, places and populations. One important aspect, known as population validity, expresses the extent to which the experimental sample accurately captures the characteristics of the required population. Clearly, if there is a wide divergence between population and sample in terms of age, social class or other factors, the validity of any conclusions is likely to be undermined.

A second form of external validity is ecological validity. This is present when the conclusions of the experiment are shown to be generalizable across to other situations. The partial replication of an experiment, in which some aspect of the original design is changed, is the main method of demonstrating external validity. If successful, such partial replication shows that the results do generalize, thereby increasing confidence that the effect is a real one rather than an artefact.

This completes the review of the essential information needed to design and implement experiments in psychology. Box 5.8 provides a checklist of the matters to be considered during the design and planning of investigations that employ this method. Further advice on conducting research by experiment can be found in sources such as Underwood and Shaughnessy (1975), Liebert and Liebert (1995) or Coolican (2004).

BOX 5.8   Experiment planning checklist

The following checklist covers the main design issues to be considered in planning an experiment.

The research question

- Can the problem be expressed in terms of the causal relations between variables?
- How will the IV and DV be operationalized?
- How will the DV be measured? Are the measures likely to be reliable?

Design issues

- How many levels of the IV should be tested? (See the section preceding box 8.5 in chapter 8.)
- Can the difference between levels be explained in terms of predictions made from a theory or from previous research? Is the difference between levels sufficiently great to allow the effect of the experimental manipulation to be seen?
- Is a control condition required? Is one possible?
- Consider which extraneous variables will need to be controlled by randomization, standardization or counterbalancing – such as instructions to participants or environmental factors.

Sampling

- Can the population of interest be clearly defined?
- How will the population be sampled?
- Is the sampling method one that minimizes the possibility of sampling error?
- What sample size will be aimed for?
- What strategy will be used to ensure that the sample is not smaller than planned (e.g. due to 'no shows')?

Test statistics

- Which is the appropriate test statistic(s)?
- Is there a good fit between the requirements of the statistical model of the intended test and the design features of the experiment?
- Is the test likely to be powerful enough to identify correctly when the null hypothesis may be rejected, given the intended sample size?

Ethics

- Does the experiment entail any potential ill-effects of any kind?
- Has informed consent been given?
- Has there been no deception about the purpose or procedure?
- Have the right to withdraw and eventual use of data been explained?
- Has the post-experiment debriefing been planned?

EXTENSION ACTIVITIES

Activity 1

Look up an account of the experiment by Held and Hein (1963). What do you consider to be the true and operationalized versions of the independent and dependent variables in this case?

Activity 2

The researches of Sherif (1935), Asch (1955) and Crutchfield (1955) were all directed at the same basic effect. Evaluate their results in terms of the different types of experimental validity discussed in this chapter.

Activity 3

The famous Stanford prison study (Zimbardo et al., 1982) is sometimes called a field experiment and sometimes a simulation. Which description do you think is the more accurate, and why? (see www.Stanfordprisonexperiment.edu for an account of this research).

Activity 4

Read again the extract from Stroop (1932) in box 5.6. Identify each possible source of error mentioned in the extract, state whether it is likely to be random or constant error and name the counter-measure that Stroop applied.

Chapter Summary

1 The purpose of this chapter has been to introduce the essential features of the psychology experiment. The importance of this method of research in psychology lies in its potential to identify causal relations by means of the manipulation and measurement of variables across different experimental treatments and under controlled conditions.

2 However, only 'true' experiments – those possessing the key characteristics of random assignment, and equal treatment of participants – have this capacity. Other forms of investigation such as 'quasi' experiments or correlational studies may indicate interesting relations between variables but fall short of demonstrating causality.

3 The question of how an experiment should be designed is initially concerned with the way in which the participants are grouped and tested in the experiment, This is an important issue since it defines how one critical source of error – inter-participant differences – will be managed. The main distinction here is between the 'within-groups' and 'between-groups' designs, but there are variations on this basic theme, such as the matched participants, yoked controls and before–after designs.

4 The many possible sources of experimental error can be grouped under a number of general headings, including sampling error; task-related error, and measurement error.

Perhaps the most interesting (and least tractable) of these is the error arising from the social nature of the experiment itself. Social psychological effects such as 'faking good'; the response of participants to the 'demand characteristics' of the situation and effects generated by the researcher herself all contribute to the general difficulty of obtaining reliable measures and, it appears, can never be entirely eradicated from an experiment.

5 Productive experiments are those that are designed in such a way that the data generated are as reliable and valid as possible. This can only be achieved if attention is paid to the control of both random and constant error from the design stage onwards. The successful control of error from different sources involves combinations of standardization, randomization and counterbalancing, depending on the expected source of error, as well as appropriate design, sampling and statistical decisions.

● FURTHER READING ●

Coolican, H. (2004). *Research methods and statistics in psychology*, 4th edn. London: Hodder Arnold.

Shaughnessy, J. J., Zechmeister, E. and Zechmeister, J. (2005). *Research methods in psychology*. New York: McGraw Hill.

Part II

DATA ANALYSIS

6

INTRODUCTION TO QUALITATIVE DATA ANALYSIS

CHAPTER MAP

Introduction: Paradigms Old and New

Philosophical Underpinnings of Qualitative Research

Constructivism
Interpretivism
Realism

What Is Qualitative Research?

Qualitative research as interpretation
Acts and actions
Feminism and qualitative research

Analysing Qualitative Data

'Giving voice'
Grounded theory
Thematic analysis
Discourse analysis

Evaluating Qualitative Research

Extension Activities

Chapter Summary

Further Reading

THIS CHAPTER

- *Places the rise to prominence of qualitative research in the context of the emergence of a 'new paradigm' in psychology.*
- *Defines qualitative research as the collection and analysis of linguistic materials (texts) in order to understand the meanings that participants ascribe to their experiences.*
- *Points to the connections between feminism and qualitative research.*
- *Outlines four methods of conducting qualitative analysis: 'giving voice', grounded theory, thematic analysis and discourse analysis.*
- *Provides general guidance on how to carry out a qualitative analysis.*
- *Presents some approaches to the evaluation of qualitative research.*

KEY CONCEPTS

Constructivism	'giving voice'
interpretivism	themes
realism	grounded theory
indexicality	discourse analysis
inconcludability	interpretative repertoire
reflexivity	extreme case formulation

● INTRODUCTION: PARADIGMS OLD AND NEW ●

The discussion of 'science and psychology' in chapter 1 introduced 'new paradigm' research as a concept that emerged within psychology from the late 1970s onwards. The precipitating cause of this development was dissatisfaction with an 'old paradigm' that had come to be dominated by quantitative, largely experimental, investigations. Among the particular weaknesses that came to be perceived in the research conducted within the old paradigm were the following.

The impoverished nature of quantitative data

- 'Old paradigm' research was strongly centred on collecting quantitative measures of behaviour. However, as the focus shifted towards a greater interest in human experience this approach was increasingly seen to offer only a very restricted view of what might actually be taking place within an investigation. It was argued that much of what was ignored by experimenters was to be found encoded in language, which was consequently viewed as offering a rich alternative source of information about human behaviour and experience.

The social psychology of experiment

- Work by Orne (1962) showed that research participants will try to make their own sense of an experiment by trying to 'read' its 'demand characteristics', in other words by trying to figure out what hypothesis is being tested. This interpretation of the 'real' purpose of the experiment influences participants' behaviour as they try either to provide the data that they believe the experimenter is looking for or attempt to withhold it. Efforts to prevent these tactics succeeding (for example, by resorting to deception) are essentially self-defeating since a range of further problems of validity and ethics are likely to emerge as a result.

Vulnerability to strong experimenter effects

- Experimenters are usually very hopeful that they will obtain results that confirm their alternate hypothesis. This can introduce a strong, though usually unconscious, bias to an investigation, for example, when a researcher gives a participant 'the benefit of the doubt' in scoring an experimental task.

Poor ecological validity

- Laboratory-based experimental research was seen as lacking in ecological validity because its results were difficult to replicate in other, less controlled, situations.

The problem of ethics

- The demand for 'good data' tended to place the rights of research participants behind the demands of the research. This was not a new problem, as the case of 'Little Albert' (Watson and Rayner, 1920) demonstrated, but the issue came to particular prominence after the publication of studies such as Milgram's investigation into experimentally induced obedience (Milgram, 1963) and Zimbardo's controversial prison simulation (Zimbardo, Haney, Banks and Jaffe, 1982).

Participant characteristics

- The use of volunteers, and/or students as the principal types of participants in psychological research was regarded as introducing further possibilities of bias to the results. A number of studies demonstrated that such groups possess characteristics that render them significantly unlike members of the wider population. The practice of generalizing to the wider population on the basis of data obtained from such restricted samples increasingly came to be regarded as questionable.

In the course of the 'paradigm crisis' of the late 20th century it was argued that these issues fatally undermined the claim by psychologists to be practitioners of a discipline that operated on the same lines as the natural sciences. The obvious weaknesses of the narrow quantitative and experimentalist model of psychological inquiry motivated some (but not all) psychologists to search for better ways of capturing the richness and variety of human experience. There was the desire to open up to scientific study questions that were inaccessible under the old approach and this required both new definitions of what counted as data, and different approaches to data collection and analysis.

By the 1990s it was clear that a 'new paradigm' had indeed begun to emerge. A British Psychological Society report (Nicolson 1991) acknowledged that future developments within psychology would be assisted by the increased use of qualitative approaches in both teaching and research. This report and a conference that followed did much to establish the respectability of qualitative methods among psychologists and there was wider acceptance of the view that much of potential value is ignored when the quantitative approach alone is used. Researchers thus increasingly started to look for different ways of exploring and understanding their phenomena, and began to borrow methods, such as ethnography and discourse analysis, from nearby disciplines such as sociology and anthropology. Essentially, what eventually emerged from the 'new paradigm' debate was the advocacy of a more comprehensive approach to methodology rather than the complete rejection of the quantitative approach. Rather, there was a desire to develop a range of qualitative methods of inquiry in psychology that could complement and extend the work being done within the existing quantitative tradition.

● PHILOSOPHICAL UNDERPINNINGS OF QUALITATIVE RESEARCH ●

The movement towards qualitative research in psychology also received considerable impetus and direction from parallel work in philosophy and in particular in the philosophy of the social sciences. At its base lay Ludwig Wittgenstein's re-appraisal of the nature of mental activity (Wittgenstein, 1953). According to Gillett (1995) Wittgenstein argued that mental activity is not an 'inner set of processes' (such as would, in principle, be accessible to a traditional scientific approach) but rather 'a range of moves or techniques defined against a background of human activity and governed by informal rules' (Gillett, 1995, p. 112). In this view, it is impossible to understand human behaviour without taking into account both the effect of context and the self-positioning of the individual in relation to the complex of rules and practices to which they are subject. Researching human experience thus becomes an interpretive task leading to the goal of 'verstehen' – the imaginative identification with the subjective world of the research participant.

Constructivism

Against this background, the 1960s onwards saw interesting developments in the philosophical domains of ontology and epistemology. In ontology, the position known as constructionism/constructivism became influential. This takes the view that the phenomena of the social world (including all our knowledge of it) are not objective entities but are constructs of the mind arrived at (constructed) through social interaction (e.g. Berger and Luckman, 1967).

For example, constructivism would deny that there is any objective human quality called 'royal' that possesses general properties that can be isolated and examined. Instead, it asserts that 'royalty' is a human construct referring to a particular quality of difference, that is ascribed to some parts of the social world but not to others. 'Royalty' is thus one of many constructed meanings, specific to a particular time and place that people may use to organize and make sense of their world.

Ontology is concerned with providing an account of the nature of being as applied to social entities. So an example of an ontological question would be to ask, 'of what does this social phenomenon fundamentally consist?' Different ontological conceptions require equally different epistemologies – theories about the nature of knowledge and how it may be attained.

Epistemology, or theory of knowledge, is that part of philosophy that concerns itself with questions about what knowledge is and how it may be validly achieved.

Interpretivism

An ontology requires an appropriate theory of knowledge (or epistemology) that specifies how the world may be validly and reliably known. In the case of constructivism this role is fulfilled by the methodology called interpretivism. The interpretivist view is that humans, though part of the natural world, are fundamentally different from other natural phenomena and therefore research aimed at understanding them requires an entirely different approach. In particular, humans appear to be unique in possessing both self-consciousness and language and this has important implications for their study. Self-consciousness leads humans to be aware of themselves as social actors and to modify their behaviour to take into account both their internal mental states and external conditions. Language, too, is important because it permits the formulation and communication of complex meanings. Consequently, people are able to represent, comment on, and ascribe meanings to their experiences in various ways. Interpretivism is the attempt to *understand* this process, specifically to understand how language is used to construct a set of meanings in relation to some specific feature of social existence.

Realism

An alternative epistemological position that has also exerted considerable influence within the new paradigm is that of realism (Harre, 1986). Realism is sympathetic to the objectivist ontological position in the sense that it believes that social reality is distinct from its human actors and can be studied as a separate phenomenon. However, it also takes the view that each natural phenomenon must be studied by appropriate methods. In the case of a social phenomenon such as human behaviour this means that the methods applied must take into account the nature of the human subject – and especially the key characteristics of self-consciousness and possession of language.

● WHAT IS QUALITATIVE RESEARCH? ●

Qualitative research adopts a broadly constructivist/interpretivist approach to the social world, although as Potter (1996) points out, it does not embody a single unified method of approach. On the contrary, it is more of a broad set of research methods and different ways of analysing data. Thus, within qualitative research, one can move between observation, interview, ethnography, diary method, protocol construction, the 'grounded theory' approach of Glaser and Strauss (1967), discourse analysis, and several other methods. What is common to all is that they involve the collection or interpretation of linguistic materials (texts) that can be subjected to analysis and interpreted for information about how social experience is constructed in particular situations. The goal is to understand the meanings that are attached to experiences by human actors, i.e. understanding the forms of interpretation that are applied by them to raw experience in different situations.

Qualitative research as interpretation

Interpretation therefore plays a central role in qualitative research because it is the only way to address the problem of how to move across the gaps that exist between the researcher, the object of research, and the way it has been represented. For example, imagine being given a text that contains an account of a schizophrenic episode. Clearly the *account* of the episode cannot be treated as if it were the episode itself. Rather, it is one (more or less accurate) representation of the episode. That means that the original experience underwent interpretation when the writer decided what to put in the account and what to leave out. A second process of interpretation follows when the text is read, and again decisions are made about what to notice and what to ignore. Thus an experience leads to an account of the experience which leads in turn to a reading of the account, with interpretative gaps occurring between each stage. These gaps cannot be removed but they can be bridged, to some extent, by acts of interpretation.

Therefore, *it is always impossible to access experience directly through a text*. The best that can be said is that an original experience may be *mediated* more or less accurately through a text, but that in the process it undergoes at least two interpretative processes, one when it was written and one when that written account is read.

The existence of interpretive gaps between experiences as objects of study and the formation and reading of those accounts leads to the three defining characteristics of qualitative research: indexicality, inconcludability and reflexivity – that clearly distinguish it from its quantitative cousin.

- *Indexicality* is the idea that an interpretation is always tied to a particular temporal, physical or social situation, and thus will change with these. There are no universal explanations because everyone will 'read' a text in a slightly different way and will extract different things from it.
- *Inconcludability* recognizes the fact that we can always add more to whatever explanation we have given, and this in turn expands (and changes) it. We never arrive at an end to interpretation because there is always more that could be said.

- *Reflexivity* acknowledges that researcher and researched can influence each other in ways that also influence the outcomes of the research. Thus talking to someone who suffers from schizophrenia will change our previous perception of the disorder, change the way we think about it and influence the way we carry out research into it.

Acts and actions

Harre and Seccord (1972) distinguished between these concepts in a way that is helpful for understanding the particular perspective offered by qualitative research.

- Acts are essentially movements that have been given a small amount of interpretation, such as when observing a particular facial expression (an act) leads to the interpretation that a particular mental state, such as fear, was experienced. This is the level at which non-qualitative approaches to research tend to operate.
- The deeper level of analysis that turns acts into actions is obtained by adding more interpretation so that the full meaning of an expression of fear *in that context* can be understood. Typically, uncovering the meaning of actions in a specific situation involves trying to clarify and make explicit the social roles and rules that determine what life is like in that social context. Only then can the full significance of what has been observed be understood.

In general, new paradigm research is interested in placing actions in their wider social context in order to understand the complex social meanings that they carry. Because meanings are encoded in the form of language qualitative research is directed towards the analysis of language in use, for example, to the ways in which texts may constructed by different people under different circumstances and for different purposes.

Feminism and qualitative research

Some of the most enthusiastic practitioners of qualitative methods have been found among the feminist critics of psychology, so it is appropriate at this point to consider briefly the connections between feminism and qualitative research.

At the general level, the feminist critique of the social sciences provides an analysis of the effects of the prevailing (sexist) ideology on the production of knowledge. As Burman (1994b) points out (p. 124) the feminist view sets out to challenge existing ('masculinist') power-relations within the discipline by giving alternative answers to questions such as, 'How should new psychological knowledge be created?' and 'What is the nature of the responsibilities of the researcher to her research participants?'

Two versions of the feminist critique identified by Burman (1994b) have particular implications for research methodology (box 6.1). The 'essentialist' version of the feminist position asserts that, because of the unequal power relations between the sexes, women necessarily construct a different version of the social world than men. Their social and psychological experiences and personal perspectives

> Feminism is a gendered ideology that insists on the separateness and distinctiveness of women's experience.
>
> Sexism is an ideology that insists on the superiority of one sex over the other.

BOX 6.1   Feminist reflexivity

Reflexivity is the idea that research data are shaped by the researcher as well as by the participants. The researcher is not a neutral agent of data collection, but brings her own experiences, perspectives, assumptions to the task and these contribute as much to the shape of the research and its results as the contributions of the participants. The feminist understanding of reflexivity, however, takes a more collaborative view of the nature of research. In this view, researchers should not just aim to conduct studies in ways that minimize any possible negative consequences. They should also be concerned for the possible effects of participation on those being studied and should attempt to promote positive outcomes in the shape of personal and institutional change.

Source: Burman, 1994b.

are consequently quite different from any male versions and must be approached on their own terms, rather than in terms of categories and concepts constructed by men. This leads to a view that is highly critical of the ability of 'masculinist' quantitative research to capture female experience. In particular the impersonality, power imbalance and manipulation inherent in the quantitative approach are seen as inimical to the feminist understanding and are therefore to be avoided. By contrast, qualitative research methods, and in particular the interview, are seen to offer a more satisfactory approach by allowing the experiences of research participants to be explored in a way that tends to equalize the statuses of researcher and researched (see, for example, Oakley, 1981).

The second position pushes beyond the view that the inadequacies of masculinist social science simply require rebalancing by the application of a more sympathetic methodology. This version of the critique challenges all power relations in the social sciences by arguing that scientific activity is fundamentally androcentric in its orientation, operates in various ways to defend the sexist *status quo* and endorse the subordination and invisibility of women. This bias can be seen, for example, in the power differentials existing between researchers and participants and female researchers and their male colleagues as well as in the widespread use in psychology of non-reflexive quantitative methods. The radical feminist response to this is to argue that the social sciences should do more than simply move towards the more equal treatment of the sexes. They should also become more accountable to society in general and to its research participants in particular, with the ultimate goal of transforming research practice, the academy and ultimately society itself.

● ANALYSING QUALITATIVE DATA ●

When research in psychology generates qualitative data, in the form of an interview transcript, or diary, the data take the form of a text, a body of language that has become available for analysis. Work on such texts can be pursued in different ways – to different degrees of depth and detail – that depend ultimately on the purposes of the research. At the simplest level, qualitative analysis involves asking questions about the manifest meaning of a text and

BOX 6.2 Managing qualitative analysis

- Make a copy of all documents and keep one set as an untouched 'master' copy. The second 'working copy' can be re-organized, cut up, scribbled over, and coded in various ways during the analysis. The close engagement with the text in this way facilitates creative thinking and the generation of understanding and insight.
- Transcribe audio recordings, or other data, into a double-spaced format with numbered lines and paragraphs or sections for ease of reference.
- Begin by cross-referencing sections of text to each other at the word, sentence, and paragraph levels. There are a number of commercially produced software packages, such as N6 (formerly NUD*IST) (Richards, 2003) that can help with this process.
- Use file cards to store notes made during the analysis. If one main idea is recorded per card they can easily be shuffled into different orders during the construction of an analytic argument.

about the connections between its structure and content. On the other hand, much deeper and more intensive analyses are also possible, such as the exploration of the multiple relationships between manifest and latent content, the speaker's or writer's intentions, and the intentions and actions of the researcher, as co-producer of a text. A fundamental point is that, as Foster and Parker (1995) point out, qualitative data are never 'gathered fresh from the world' (p. 165). Rather, they are always the result of collaborative effort by researcher and participants. An awareness of this should therefore form the starting point for every analysis.

If a qualitative analysis is to be successful it is necessary for the process of dealing with the data to be well organized. Data volumes can be large and it is important to find an effective way of managing the purely administrative aspects of the process. To that end, the suggestions in box 6.2 may be helpful.

Foster and Parker (1995) identify four main approaches to analysing textual data – 'giving voice', grounded theory, thematic analysis, and discourse analysis. The following discussion will be restricted to these four, although there are at least two further forms not covered here, namely, conversational analysis (see Heath and Luff, 1993) and protocol analysis (e.g. Gilhooly and Green, 1996).

'Giving voice'

This approach to analysis goes beyond simply importing an interviewee's words into the researcher's account by means of quotation or paraphrase. The aim in 'giving voice' is to try to achieve an empathic understanding of the meaning that the experiences described in the text might hold for the person concerned. To see, as it were, the world represented in the text through the respondents' eyes and then to voice those experiences as the respondents would wish them to be told. Analysis in this form is a 'political' activity in the sense that one of its intentions is the empowerment of those whose lives provide the source of data.

Working in this fashion with a text such as an interview transcript is, as Foster and Parker say, primarily a task of re-presentation or 'reflecting back', of 'witnessing to a story'. The relation between the words of a text, their meaning, and the intentions of its producer are thus regarded as essentially unproblematic. The text is seen primarily as a vehicle for expressing manifest meanings that may be extracted directly from its surface features without the need for much exploration beneath the surface. For example, the question of what motivated the production of a text is generally not regarded as an issue, nor is there likely to be any analysis of how the producer's world view has been constructed or articulated within the text.

Grounded theory

'Grounded theory' is an approach to analysing any textual material developed within sociology (Glaser and Strauss 1967) that involves systematically reading and re-reading a text in order to identify the categories and concepts that are expressed in it. The aim is to render the implicit content of the text fully explicit so as to produce 'a conceptually rich, dense and contextually grounded account' (Pidgeon, 1996, p. 78). 'Grounding' therefore refers to the processing of data in great detail so that any theory that finally emerges can be seen to be based firmly in the data. The nine stages of a grounded theory analysis proposed by Glaser and Strauss (1967) are as follows.

- *Develop categories.* From multiple readings of the text proceed to identify and group together all instances of like (or related) categories – these are concepts that serve to organize the constructs identified at the next stage.
- *'Saturate' the categories.* Accumulate as many instances of the categories as can be found in the data, stopping only when it is apparent that any future instances of the category can be predicted.
- *Create abstract definitions.* Create a 'master definition' of the categories that abstracts the key features found in the category instances at the previous stage.
- *Use the definitions.* Apply the definitions already constructed to guide further fieldwork and to stimulate theoretical reflection.
- *Fully exploit the categories.* Use the categories already found to identify any further categories of interest. These may be more specific, more general or otherwise different from those already found.
- *Develop links between categories.* Construct hypotheses about the possible links between categories.
- *Review the links.* Look for evidence of when the links hold true and specify the conditions that hold when this is the case.
- *Connect to existing theory.* Make clear the connections between existing theory and any emerging hypotheses.
- *Test emerging relationships.* Use extreme comparisons to test emerging relationships. Identify key variables and dimensions and see whether relationships hold true even at the extremes.

Two features of grounded theory analysis are particularly noteworthy. One is the use of constant multiple comparison among elements identified in the text in order to expose the full richness in the data and to foster theory development (as, for example, in the last two of the steps listed above). The other is 'theoretical sampling', i.e. the addition of new cases (data) to the analysis as the theory develops. This and negative (or extreme) case analysis, in which cases that do not fit the candidate theory are actively sought, is an important feature of the grounded theory method because it is seen as a way of checking, and possibly correcting, the initial assumptions (Pidgeon, 1996).

Further accounts of the grounded theory method can be found in Henwood and Pidgeon (1996), Turner (1981), Strauss and Corbin (1990), as well as the Glaser and Strauss source referred to earlier.

Thematic analysis

Thematic analysis involves the development of a coherent reading of a text, such as an interview transcript, where the researcher's interventions are also part of the text to be analysed (Burman, 1994a). Reading a text in this way is a multi-stage process that begins with the tentative identification of large-scale themes or systems of meaning. The second stage of analysis then aims to look closely at the specific form taken by the instances of each theme, both in relation to each other, and also in relation to the interviewer's own contributions. Initial assumptions about the thematic coherence of the text may thus be modified by allowing conflicting agendas and perspectives to be identified.

Discourse analysis

In using language to create or convey a particular reality we always convey more than we intend. This 'additional content' is produced by linguistic and rhetorical structures that are inseparable from language, but that also operate independently of any overt meaning. These 'additional' meanings are the discourses that exist within a given piece of spoken or written language. They are, as Coyle (2000) puts it, 'sets of linguistic material that have a degree of coherence in their content and organization and which perform constructive functions in broadly defined social contexts' (p. 245).

The basic theoretical position taken by discourse analysis is constructivism. As mentioned earlier, this is essentially the idea that there is no social reality 'out there' that waits to be discovered. Instead, what we call 'reality' is what we have put together from the range of linguistic resources available to us, so that our language simultaneously contains and creates experience. To some extent we are conscious of this in our everyday interactions.

For example, calling an example of verbal interaction between two people an 'argument' rather than a 'discussion' may be an intentional choice to create a particular version of reality around that interaction. Among the features that are imported with the verbal label 'argument' may be the implication that someone 'started' the argument (with further implications of blame), that there were particular motives at work, that information was distorted or suppressed, that someone 'won' and someone 'lost', and so on. 'Argument' is more than just a label to be applied to some forms of interaction and not others. Rather, it is a label that can be used to create a new version of reality by bringing an entirely new range of social meanings to bear upon the situation. Language therefore provides us with the building blocks of reality, by both reflecting *and* constructing our inner experience. And, by analysing the discourses present in a text, we can begin to see how this occurs in particular instances.

If the concept of discourse seems rather vague, the notion of rhetorical purpose may help to clarify the sense in which it is used here. All texts (including this one) possess rhetorical purposes by virtue of the fact that they can produce effects on the reader or hearer – they may explain, intimidate, persuade, justify a course of action and so on. Such purposes are constructed by the patterns of language (forms of words) that make up a text. For example, a self-justifying rhetorical purpose (to get oneself out of trouble) might be constructed from such linguistic resources as 'I only . . .'; 'I thought . . .', 'I didn't know . . .', 'I didn't mean to . . .', etc. These and other purposes exist in the text *whether or not* they were those intended by the producer of the text and also whether or not the reader/hearer responds to them. They are there by virtue of the fact that the text has been constructed from language that offers a range of possibilities. Purposes in text are expressed through the construction of discourses, and it is such discourses that are the focus of this form of analysis.

The primary focus in discourse analysis is, thus, the text itself, and the rhetorical purposes that are visible there. The analysis says, in effect, 'the text at this point is constructing this kind of discourse by using this kind of linguistic construction' Discourse analysis, therefore, involves a shift away from analysing a text in terms of its manifest meaning to looking at the way it has been constructed (whether consciously or unconsciously) in order to achieve one or more rhetorical purposes.

If a single text is constructed to fulfil more than one function then multiple readings may be found within it. As Potter (1996) suggests, social life is characterized by conflicting points of view – in effect a clash between different versions of reality – and we can expect that similar conflicts will emerge in a text. The analysis of such texts can thus be expected to reveal different discourses that serve entirely different rhetorical intentions.

Doing discourse analysis

Discourse analysis, then, seeks to expose the ways in which language is used to construct a version of reality in a particular situation, as it might in an interview, or a political speech, a lecture, or a trial. How is this achieved?

The first point to make is that discourse analysis is not an easy form of analysis to implement. On the contrary, it is widely recognized to be a difficult, time-consuming and frustrating process (Gill, 1996, p. 146) not least because, unlike quantitative analysis, there is very little in the way of rules or formal procedures to be followed in conducting the analysis, and relatively little guidance has been published. The following section presents one way that doing discourse analysis can be approached that is based on Potter and Wetherall (1987). Other suggestions can also be found in Coyle (2000), Gill (1996), Parker (1994), Foster and Parker (1995) and Wooffitt (1993).

Suspend belief

The first step is to suspend belief in the taken-for-granted aspects of language use . This is simply another example of 'rendering strange what we take as given' (Toren, 1996) involving the abandonment of the usual assumption that a text simply means what it says. Coyle (2000) refers to this as the adoption of an 'analytic mentality' – essentially taking a new perspective on a text by asking how it represents a constructed version of reality. One should look at the way a text is constructed and assess its intended functions instead of what is conveyed on the surface.

Immerse oneself in the text

A text should be read and reread until one is completely familiar with every word, phrase and nuance. The linguistic patterns and other features that are present in the text can only begin to be recognized through the experience of total immersion.

Code the text

Next a text is coded for recurring elements (words, phrases, sentences) using appropriate categories. This is done until no more instances of the categories can be found. Not all instances of the categories will necessarily be apparent at the first pass through the text, so several passes may be necessary before exhaustive coding is achieved. At this stage, hypotheses may be formed about what discourse(s) are present. Potter and Wetherall (1987) suggest two stages of approach here, beginning with the identification and coding of any 'interpretative repertoires' that are apparent, followed by coding of individual utterances at the micro level, to see how each unit of the text contributes to (or undermines) the discourse.

> Interpretative repertoires are related sets of terms that may be threaded throughout the text, especially when the discourse is framed around one (or more) metaphors or images. The concept of interpretative repertoire captures the 'off-the-peg', clichéd, character of some forms of expression.

Analyse the discourse(s)

The final step is to identify the possible functions of the discourse(s) found in the text. Potter and Wetherall (1987) suggest that segments of text may be analysed to identify nuances, contradictions, qualifications, vagueness and similar constructs. Recurring patterns and 'interpretative repertoires' may be evidence of a particular rhetorical purpose, so all the possible functions of particular features of the text should be considered. For example, one can ask what problem a piece of text may be attempting to solve and what solution it provides. The presence of rhetorical techniques such as 'extreme case formulations' should also be looked for and their effects and functions assessed. Wooffitt (1990) cited by Gill (1996) suggests that specific questions can be asked at this stage, such as, 'What business is being attended to during the discourse?', 'How do speakers display their orientation to (or away from) this business?', 'What strategies do they adopt to accomplish this?'

> Extreme case formulations employ words like 'never', 'no one', 'everyone', 'absolutely', 'always' (as in 'I have never stolen anything', 'I always wear a tie', 'I am absolutely certain that . . .') to help present a particular version of reality within a text and thus to serve a particular rhetorical function in the overall discourse.

● EVALUATING QUALITATIVE RESEARCH ●

The evaluation of the results of qualitative research, and especially discourse analysis, appears problematic at first. The absence of agreed systems for conducting the analysis renders the whole approach vulnerable to the charge of producing idiosyncratic interpretations that are difficult to challenge effectively. To make matters worse, the same piece of text can almost always be subjected to several analyses that produce different, but apparently equally valid, results. And, while it is always possible to repeat a piece of qualitative research, it is not possible to attempt replication, because the result on the second occasion will be a different piece of work. Clearly the standard concepts of reliability and validity are very difficult to apply to qualitative research, since they assume that replication of good research is always possible. How then is it possible to arrive at a reliable judgement of the value of such research?

The first point that should be made is that qualitative analysis, especially if it involves discourse analysis, aims to produce 'a reading' of a text and its context that represents a *version* rather than a definitive interpretation. The constructivist perspective does not recognize the possibility of a definitive single interpretation. Instead, every interpretation of a text represents a constructed reality just as much as did the original, unanalysed text. (This leads, of course, to the possibility of an infinite regress of texts, as Coyle (2000) points out. Any analysis of a text generates a further text that can be analysed in the same way, and so on, and so on.

Stiles (1993) suggests that reliability is a matter of the trustworthiness of the interpretation, and not of whether the same method can be applied again and again with similar results. He identifies internal consistency, usefulness, robustness, and fruitfulness – meaning that the research has stimulated further inquiry – as key criteria of trustworthiness rather than the degree to which a study can be replicated. Robson (2002) also notes that trustworthiness is more useful as a criterion than attempts to pursue validity, reliability and generalizability in the qualitative context. For him trustworthiness means that the results should be credible, dependable and its insights capable of being transferred across contexts.

Potter (1996) argues also that qualitative accounts can be tested against the participants' own understandings and against the evaluations of readers. If the 'reading' contained in the analysis has succeeded in making explicit and reflecting back the participants' meanings and understandings of the world, then it can be said to have value. Readers, on the other hand, must evaluate the results of qualitative research for themselves.

The problem is that none of the criteria mentioned above offers a particularly objective way of assessing 'good' qualitative research. However, Henwood and Pidgeon (1992) have compiled a set of criteria that are more satisfactory in that respect, and it is appropriate to end this chapter with their list (box. 6.3). Those contemplating the execution of qualitative research should also note that these points also offer very helpful reminders and guidance on how the analysis of textual material should be conducted.

BOX 6.3   Evaluation criteria for qualitative research

- *Is the analysis close to the data?* Good qualitative research is explicit about the chain of reasoning leading up to every conclusion. For example, if one stage of qualitative research involves labelling the phenomena being studied then the researcher should also explain why such labels have been applied.
- *Is the research reflexive?* Good qualitative research acknowledges the way in which the research activity itself shapes the outcome of the inquiry. The researcher should not only be aware of this but should attempt to account for and record all such influences on the research.
- *Is the documentation comprehensive?* Good documentation is essential. The reader should be provided with a complete account of what has been done, and why, at all stages of the research process. The aim should be to build up a comprehensive paper trail for the project.
- *Is sampling theory-driven?* Within qualitative research there is no need to examine many cases simply in order to achieve a large enough sample if this does contribute to the theory that is being developed. Sampling should proceed only as long as required to ensure that the theory is sufficiently comprehensive.
- *Is negative case analysis applied?* Negative case analysis involves fully exploring cases that do not fit the emerging conceptual system as well as those that do. This gives a way of making explicit and challenging the initial assumptions of the research in order to generate a better theory.
- *Is there negotiation between researcher and participants?* Qualitative research recognizes that not all participants' accounts can be taken at face value, not because they necessarily seek to mislead, but because they may not be fully aware of the reasons for their actions. If researcher and participant engage in negotiation in these areas it facilitates the exploration of reasons why their interpretations of a particular account may differ.
- *Are the conclusions transferable?* Qualitative research does not aim for generalizability so much as transferability. The test is not whether the findings can be generalized to explain situations beyond that in which the data were gathered, but whether the insights can be transferred to aid the understanding of similar contexts.

Source: Henwood and Pidgeon, 1992.

EXTENSION ACITIVITIES

Activity 1

Find an article in a newspaper or magazine and practise adopting an 'analytic mentality' to the text by reading it as you imagine a Martian would. Ask yourself what implicit (taken for granted) knowledge is required to understand the text. List the examples you find. What is the reality that the text seeks to construct for the reader? (Magazine articles on show-business topics are particularly good for this.)

Activity 2

Consider any piece of writing (such as a journal article, or a passage from this book) as an item of constructed text and again assess it from the perspective of the 'analytic mentality'. Can you identify its rhetorical purpose(s)? What is the evidence for the purpose(s) you found? How are the discourse(s) constructed to achieve those purposes?

Activity 3

Find a piece of text in which someone describes an experience of a particular situation. Consider whether the respondent's world has been presented as they would wish. What aspects of the account would you concentrate on in order to represent that world empathically and in a way that empowers the respondent? Which aspects would you de-emphasize because they do not represent empathy and empowerment? Is anything left after these two types of text have been removed?

Chapter Summary

1   This chapter begins with an outline of the 'paradigm crisis' that occurred in psychology during the last quarter of the 20th century, and the consequent influence of 'new paradigm' thinking about research methodologies. As a result of that debate, research using a qualitative methodology increasingly began to appear alongside the traditional quantitative methods and is now widely accepted as offering an alternative and complementary approach to psychological inquiry.

2   The approach to qualitative data is grounded in the related philosophical doctrines of constructivism and interpretivism. Taken together, these assert, first, that the social world is constructed only from inter-subjective meanings encoded in language and shared by the actors in a specific situation. Second, such meanings can only be uncovered through the interpretation of a corpus of language, such as might be obtained from a research interview.

3   In addition to its focus on language use, the methods of qualitative data analysis possess three features that distinguish them from quantitative methods. These are: indexicality – the fact that interpretations are always tied to specific situations; inconcludability – the idea that analysis is never complete; and reflexivity – the recognition that a researcher is just as much a contributor to research as the other participants.

4   The feminist wing within psychology has regarded qualitative methods as offering a chal-
    lenge to the sexism that they believe can be found in 'old paradigm' research practice. In
    particular the qualitative approach to data collection has been argued to offer a better
    alternative to the 'masculinist' qualities of impersonality, power and manipulation that
    they found within the positivist paradigm. These 'improvements' take the form of
    research based on more equal and open relationships between researcher and researched.

5   The analysis of qualitative data section takes as its starting point the reminder by Foster
    and Parker (1995) that qualitative data are invariably the outcome of a complex process
    of collaborative construction involving both researcher and participants. Four specific
    methods of treating qualitative data are reviewed and some suggestions made about how
    the more demanding forms (grounded theory analysis and discourse analysis) may be
    approached.

6   The evaluation of qualitative research presents particular problems since reliability, valid-
    ity and generalizability are seen to be inappropriate concepts. Some writers such as
    Robson (2002) argue that concepts such as 'trustworthiness' and 'credibility' can be
    applied successfully to the results of analysing qualitative data. An alternative view (e.g.
    Henwood and Pidgeon, 1992) avoids the problem of how such criteria should be imple-
    mented by suggesting a set of more specific features that not only could be used to iden-
    tify 'good' qualitative research, but could also help to guide the activities of researchers
    as they plan research using qualitative methods.

● FURTHER READING ●

Banister, P., Burman, E., Parker, I., Taylor, M. and Tindall, C. (1994). *Qualitative methods in psychology:
    A research guide*. Buckingham: Open University Press.
Richardson, J. T. E. (1996). *Handbook of qualitative research methods for psychology and the social sciences*.
    Oxford: B. P. S./Blackwell.
Robson, C. (2002). *Real-world research*, 2nd edn. Oxford: Blackwell.

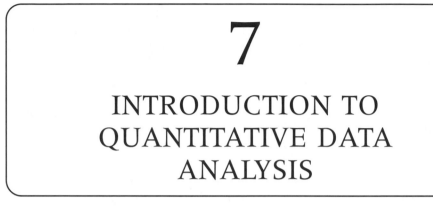

7

INTRODUCTION TO QUANTITATIVE DATA ANALYSIS

CHAPTER MAP

Variables, Data and Measurement

Introduction
Scales of measurement
Reliability, validity and measurement error

Data Presentation

Distributions
Stem and leaf diagrams
Box and whisker plots
Centiles and quartiles
Simple, cumulative and relative frequency
Histograms
Bar graphs
Line graphs

Descriptive Statistics

Central tendency
Dispersion
Skewness and kurtosis
Co-variation: graphical and statistical approaches

Extension Activities

Chapter Summary

Further Reading

THIS CHAPTER

- *Introduces important concepts in quantitative research, such as operational definition, variables and the types of quantitative data.*
- *Describes S. S. Stevens's classic account of scales of measurement and introduces the concept of measurement error.*
- *Introduces the concept of a distribution and describes some different approaches to representing distributions including EDA techniques, centiles and frequency tables.*
- *Describes the most frequently encountered measures of central tendency and dispersion and their strengths and weaknesses.*
- *Introduces skewness and kurtosis as descriptions of the shape of a distribution.*
- *Introduces the concept of co-variation and explains graphical and statistical approaches to describing the relationship of two sets of scores.*

KEY CONCEPTS

Conceptual and operational definitions
discrete and continuous variables
categorical and measurement data
nominal, ordinal, interval and ratio scales
   of measurement
measurement error

simple relative and cumulative frequencies
measures of central tendency and
   dispersion
skewness and kurtosis
co-variation

● VARIABLES, DATA AND MEASUREMENT ●

Introduction

The theme of this chapter is the representation and exploration of quantitative data – the collections of numbers that are deemed to be of interest to psychological inquiry. How do such data come about?

All research in psychology can be said to begin with an idea (a concept or construct), formed from observation or some other source, that is usually expressed in a conceptual definition. 'Schema', 'self-esteem' and 'intelligence' are all examples of psychologically interesting concepts that each have their own conceptual definition. However, conceptual definitions in psychology refer to mental processes that can only be explored by indirect means, and for this an operational definition is always required.

The purpose of an operational definition is to make measurement possible. It does this by identifying a variable that can readily be measured, and thus can yield quantitative data. For example, the concept of intelligence might be operationalized as a person's

An operational definition is a description of observable events that are likely (or predicted by theory) to follow from a concept (see box 7.1).

BOX 7.1   Conceptual and operational definitions: the example of locus of control

The conceptual definition of locus of control (Rotter, 1954) refers to general beliefs about what determines whether people are successful in their endeavours to obtain the things they desire. Those whose locus of control is strongly *internal* believe that success or failure is due to their own efforts, while those whose locus of control is strongly *external* tend to believe that success and failure are determined by factors outside their control such as chance or fate. Expressed in this form, the concept is difficult to quantify or measure directly. In order to research the concept, Rotter defines locus of control operationally as *the subjective probability that a given behaviour will lead to reinforcement*. This definition readily leads to quantified observations by means of self-report scales such as the Locus of Control Test (Rotter, 1966) in which people are asked to express numerically the subjective probability of a range of events. Data can thus be collected that can be compared across individuals and situations.

A variable is any thing that is capable of taking different values on different occasions.

---

ability to solve complex puzzles – the more intelligent the person, the more puzzles that can be solved in a standard time. Thus, defining intelligence operationally as the variable 'number of puzzles solved' leads directly to quantification because a person will always solve some number of puzzles correctly.

Two types of variable are generally distinguished. Discrete variables are those having several different possible instances, each of which is distinct from the others. The variable 'handedness', for example, can be instantiated in any particular case as left-handedness, right-handedness, or as neither. Continuous variables are those where any instance of the variable represents a position on a continuum. Reaction time, degree of autonomic arousal, or the strength of a friendship are all examples of continuous variables.

Quantitative data are obtained when a variable is subjected to a measurement process. The measurement of a variable involves assigning a numerical value to each observed instance of the variable and this leads, in turn, to two types of data. Categorical data (also called frequency data) use numbers to measure discrete variables in the simplest way possible, by counting observations within several categories of interest. These data therefore consist of integers (whole numbers) that represent the different instances observed. Typically, they are obtained from measurement of a discrete variable. Measurement data, on the other hand, are typically obtained from instances of continuous variables. Each data item (which may consist either of integers or decimal values) in this case represents a position on a measurement scale that is assumed to correspond to a magnitude of the variable.

Scales of measurement

Measurement was earlier defined as the process that assigns numerical values to different instances of a variable. This is essentially the definition proposed by S. S. Stevens in his classic

---

BOX 7.2   Scales of measurement and the ruler analogy

A helpful way of thinking of the differences between the scales is to consider how each scale would be realized as a ruler (see figure 7.1).

- The nominal scale ruler is of finite length and has no markings. One can therefore only determine whether an object is the same length as the ruler, or not.
- The ordinal scale ruler has index marks that are unevenly spaced along its (potentially infinite) length and is labelled with an ordered set of numbers. One can therefore only say whether an object is longer or shorter than another, and indicate this by the relative magnitudes of the numbers assigned.
- The interval scale ruler is infinitely long and has index marks that are placed at equal intervals from each other and labelled consecutively. As the ends of the scale are inaccessible it is impossible to see whether the ruler has a zero point, so no absolute measurement is possible. However, one can nevertheless accurately measure the difference between two lengths.
- The ratio scale ruler has equally spaced index marks labelled with consecutive numbers that begin at zero at one end. This ruler allows the absolute lengths of objects to be compared, and for measures made using one set of units to be translated into any other with no loss of information.

---

treatment of measurement issues in psychology. As he also makes clear, there is more than one way of conducting measurement and each way carries different consequences for the kind of information that can be produced:

> measurement is the assignment of numerals to objects or events according to rules. And the fact that numerals can be assigned under different rules leads to different kinds of scales and different kinds of measurement. (Stevens, 1951, p. 1)

The important ideas here are, first, that measurement involves the application of one from a number of possible rules; second, that when applied, different rules create different scales of measurement; and, third (though not mentioned explicitly in this quotation), that each scale allows different operations to be performed on the data. Stevens is led by this reasoning to identify a hierarchy of four scales of measurement for psychology – the nominal, ordinal, interval and ratio scales – in which each scale represents a different way of using numbers to capture the content of observations (box 7.2).

The nominal scale

The nominal scale uses numbers to sort a set of observations into categories by arbitrarily assigning different numbers to indicate observations that are equal in some respect. Nominal

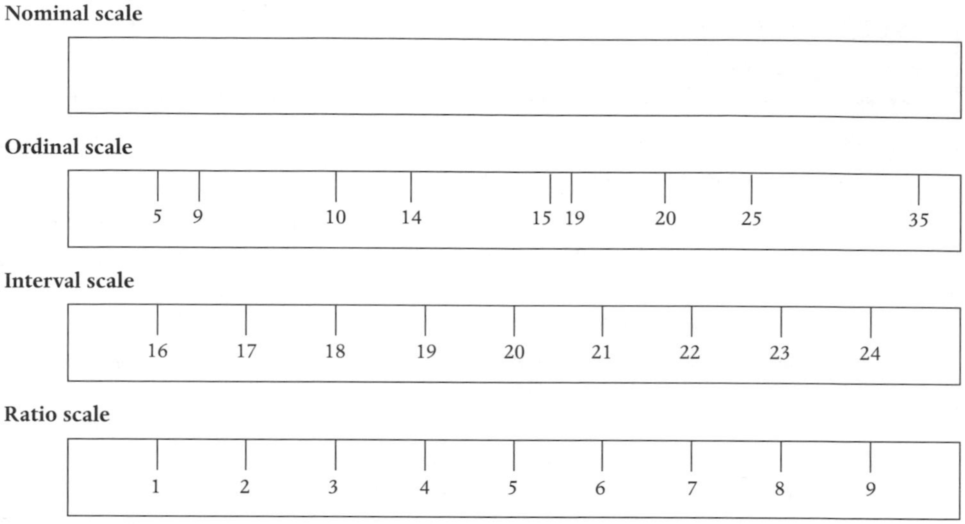

Nominal scale

Ordinal scale

| 5 9 | 10 | 14 | 15 19 | 20 | 25 | 35 |

Interval scale

| 16 | 17 | 18 | 19 | 20 | 21 | 22 | 23 | 24 |

Ratio scale

| 1 | 2 | 3 | 4 | 5 | 6 | 7 | 8 | 9 |

Figure 7.1   Scales of measurement: the ruler analogy

scale measures are achieved when, for example, the members of a group are sorted by sex by assigning (say) a 1 to indicate a male and 2 a female. The assignment of numbers is arbitrary, so the numeral 1 could be replaced with 9, or 900 or any other number with no loss of information.

The ordinal scale

Measurement on the ordinal scale is achieved when numbers are assigned in a way that preserves the relationships of magnitude among the observations. For example, respondents who rate, on a 10-point scale, the subjective intensity of a pain stimulus (such as a pinch) are generating measures on an ordinal scale. A rating of 10 would indicate a greater intensity of pain than a rating of (say) 5, which in turn would indicate greater intensity than a rating of 1. Making the assumption that the participants' ratings are reliable, the ordinal relationship of the scores therefore preserves the relationship of the pain experiences because larger numbers indicate more pain. Measures on the ordinal scale are therefore monotonic and can be subjected to any order-preserving transformation, such as squaring, without loss of information.

The term monotonic refers to any series of numbers that increases or decreases consistently throughout its range.

The interval scale

To achieve measures on an interval scale numbers must be assigned to observations in a way that not only preserves the ordinal relationships, but also allows equal distances on the scale to indicate equal differences between observations. For example, a Celsius thermometer measures temperature on the interval scale. Not only does 5 degrees C indicate a cooler temperature than 15 degrees C, but the difference between them indicates the same amount of temperature change as would occur between 5 and 15 degrees, 20 and 30 degrees, or 40 and 50 degrees. The differences between numbers exactly reflect differences of temperature. In psychology, interval scale measures exist, but are less common than ordinal measures. This is because, as Stevens (1951) points out, of the difficulty of devising ways of measuring psychological quantities that provide equal units on the scale. Some instruments, such as intelligence tests, are often assumed to provide measures on the interval scale but probably do not, because of the difficulty of establishing precisely what a difference between two test scores actually means in terms of difference in intellectual capacity.

The ratio scale

The ratio scale possesses all the qualities of the preceding three scales, but additionally has a true zero point that indicates the complete absence of the variable being measured. On this scale, therefore, the numbers that are assigned to observations preserve their absolute magnitudes and the ratio of any two scale values is invariant. Because it is possible to conceive of the zero quantity the variable of age could be argued to provide a rare example of measurement made on the ratio scale that is also of interest to psychologists. A 20-year-old is twice as old as a 10-year-old (a ratio of $2:1$) whether the units are years, months, weeks or fractions of a century. However, ratio scale measurement of other variables in psychology is very rare, and it is safe to assume that the limit of what can be achieved in measurement in psychology is represented by the interval scale.

With exceptions (e.g. Howell, 1997), Stevens's typology of measurement scales provides the usual starting point for approaching measurement issues in psychology. Certainly, in order to interpret data accurately, it is essential to understand his fundamental point that, depending on how they are used, numbers carry differing amounts of information. However, among some other problems raised by the typology is the fact that the scales of measurement are often erroneously used to determine the selection of a significance test. For those interested, both MacRae (1995) and Fife-Schaw (2000b) provide concise discussions of the issues surrounding the application of Stevens's scales of measurement in psychology.

Reliability, validity and measurement error

The quality of the measurement of psychological variables is generally assessed against the criteria of validity, reliability and measurement error.

Validity

Questions of validity are concerned with the integrity of the relationships between a concept and the variable(s) identified in its operational definition. If a variable used to define a concept operationally cannot be accounted for in terms of theory (if, for example, the use of the variable 'number of puzzles solved' to measure intelligence cannot be explained in terms of some theory of intelligence), then the validity of the operational definition, and any measurements derived from it, is open to question.

Reliability

Reliability is concerned with the stability of measurements – the extent to which it is possible to repeat a measurement using the same instrument under the same conditions and obtain the same result. This has two aspects: the variability of the behaviour of human research participants and measurement error.

Variability

It is part of the nature of human beings that their behaviour is highly variable in the sense that it lacks predictability and consistency. Any person generating data on two or more occasions will always produce somewhat different results each time even if tested by identical methods, and different individuals will also generate results that are different one from another. This means that the results of measurement always vary within and between persons from one occasion to another, whatever the variable that is being measured.

Measurement error

Measurement error, E, is expressed in classic measurement theory by the relation $T = O + E$ where O is the observed score and T is the unknown 'true' score. The problem, for researchers (happily dealt with through the application of statistics), is that of the three variables only the value of O is ever known for certain.

The concept of measurement error expresses the fact that all measurement is inaccurate to some degree so that while it may approach a 'true' value it will, nevertheless, always differ from it. Among the several sources of this difference are the design of the investigation, the researcher and her behaviour and, most crucially, the measurement process used to generate the data.

The existence of variability and error raise important problems for the reliability of measurement since, clearly, it is impossible to guarantee that any psychological measurement will be perfectly reliable. This is why psychology is sometimes described as an 'inexact science'. It is simply not possible to conduct research into human behaviour or mental processes with the same precision that is achieved (say) in physics or chemistry. However, the techniques developed by statistics provide ways of dealing with this problem. For example, sampling theory allows the effect of many individual human variabilities to be smoothed so that a generally reliable picture can be seen (Kruskal, 1968). And, as discussed in the next chapter, it is also possible to quantify the probable contribution that error makes to a set of scores.

We now move from the realm of measurement theory to the practicalities of dealing with data. When faced with the task of understanding the information contained in a set of raw data where does one begin?

Table 7.1 Number of faces recognized from 75 photographs (N = 40)

38	48	18	22	27	36	47	29	31	55
36	29	38	13	39	67	41	58	55	43
43	59	46	29	46	49	15	49	63	52
54	42	36	57	41	59	44	46	40	64

Table 7.2 Scores from table 7.1 placed in order

13	15	18	22	27	29	29	29	31	36
36	36	38	38	39	40	41	41	42	43
43	44	46	46	46	47	48	49	49	52
54	55	55	57	58	59	59	63	64	67

● DATA PRESENTATION ●

One way of beginning is simply to re-present the dataset in a way that gives a clearer picture. This form of analysis tries to see the overall 'shape', the *distribution*, of data, and includes both tabular and graphical techniques.

Distributions

Placing scores in order turns a random assembly of numbers into a simple distribution. When scores are treated in this way some information, such as the range of values, becomes much clearer. For example, consider the randomly ordered set of scores in table 7.1. It is difficult to conclude much from this arrangement (or rather lack of arrangement) of the data, other than that some scores seem to be repeated.

Now consider table 7.2. You can see that this simple rearrangement has made it easier to see both the range of values in the dataset, and exactly how many times some scores are repeated.

However, because the data are presented in tabular form, understanding the information still requires some effort. An even clearer representation can be achieved by using the stem and leaf display from John Tukey's collection of techniques of exploratory data analysis (EDA) (Tukey, 1970).

Stem and leaf diagrams

This form of representation allows the presentation of all the individual data values together and reveals very clearly the shape of the distribution, as well as easily permitting recall of the original dataset from the display (see box 7.3). The example stem and leaf display in table 7.3 has been generated from the dataset in table 7.2. The digits on the left (the stem) are the first

BOX 7.3   Stem and leaf displays with very large numbers of leaves

When there are very large numbers of trailing digits, constructing a clear stem and leaf by hand may be difficult as they may not all fit across the page. If so, the size of the interval of each point on the stem can be reduced. The single interval of 40–49 in table 7.3 could be divided into the 5 intervals 40–41, 42–43, 44–45, 46–47, 48–49. If this is done a code is needed to identify each of the 5 intervals, because they all share the same leading digit (4).

The code is based on the second digit of the lower value in each stem pair. The first pair, 40–41, receives the symbol 4* (where * stands for 0), the second pair, 42–43, receives the symbol 4t, (where t stands for 'two'), and so on. The result (for part of the data), is shown in table 7.4.

Table 7.3   Stem and leaf display of the data in table 7.2

Stem	Leaves
0	
1	3 5 8
2	2 7 9 9 9
3	1 6 6 6 8 8 9
4	0 1 1 2 3 3 4 6 6 6 7 8 9 9
5	2 4 5 5 7 8 9 9
6	3 4 7
7	
8	
9	
etc.	

Table 7.4   Subdividing the stem intervals of large datasets: part of the data in table 7.3 showing the coding system

Stem	Leaves
4*	0 1 1
4t	2 3 3
4f	4
4s	6 6 6 7
4e	8 9 9

digits of each data value and are called leading digits. The digits on the right (the leaves) are the second digits in each score and are called trailing digits. We can see now clearly that the distribution is narrow, but quite symmetrical, can easily estimate the range and the central value and also see where repeated scores occur.

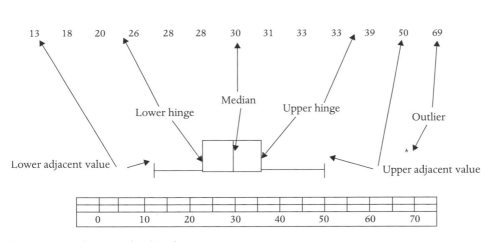

Figure 7.2 A dataset and its boxplot

The values of the leading digits can, if needed, continue to 10 and beyond, but they don't have to go right to the very ends of the range. Outliers (any extreme values at either end of the distribution) can be grouped together at the ends of the display, and given a simple verbal label such as 'very low values' or 'very high values'. This allows concentration on the scores that are most closely grouped together.

Box and whisker plots

This technique (Tukey, 1977) provides a simple and effective way of representing distribution as the dispersion of a set of scores around a central point (usually the median) that can either be sketched by hand quite quickly and accurately or drawn using SPSS. The components of the example boxplot in figure 7.2 are as follows

- The *upper hinge* is the median of the scores in the upper half of the data (i.e. the half above the median of the whole dataset).
- The *lower hinge* is the median of the scores in the lower half of the data. The hinges enclose the middle 50% of the scores called by Tukey the *H-spread* – essentially the interquartile range.
- The *inner fence* encloses 1.5 or 2 times the H-spread (there is no fixed rule) above the upper hinge and below the lower one.
- The *adjacent values* are the scores that lie immediately inside the *inner fence*.
- The inner fence also marks the boundary beyond which values may be considered as *outliers*. Beyond them lie the most extreme values of the dataset and these are shown on a boxplot by asterisks (*).

Four features make the boxplot a particularly useful technique of data representation.

- It is easy to spot the presence of outliers in the dataset. These extreme values may indicate the presence of error in the process of data collection and should be re-examined with this possibility in mind.

BOX 7.4   The basic data entry procedure in SPSS

In the **Data View** screen click on the **Variable View** tab in the bottom left corner of the screen.
In **Variable View**
Enter name for the variable (e.g. 'data') in the column under **Name**
   Click on the **Data View** tab
In **Data View**
   Enter the scores in the named column.

(See appendix 2 for more information on data entry into SPSS.)

BOX 7.5   Navigation in SPSS

Throughout this book, the instructions for obtaining output from SPSS employ the following conventions:

*   The names of the main menus in SPSS are in bold upper-case: e.g. **ANALYZE**
*   Dialogue box items or menu items are shown in bold title case: e.g. **Compare Means**
*   The successive selection of menu or dialogue box items is indicated by the right facing arrowhead: e.g. **ANALYZE > Descriptive Statistics > Frequencies**.

---

*   Skewed distributions are revealed by the presence of whiskers of different lengths.
*   Two (or more) distributions can easily be compared by drawing their boxplots against a common scale.
*   The ends of the box correspond closely to the limits of the interquartile range.

Exploratory data analysis in SPSS

SPSS can produce a stem and leaf display and a boxplot, either together or separately on the same output screen, or a boxplot alone. These can be cut and pasted into a word-processor document by clicking on the required element and continuing in the usual way. The boxplot can be resized using the grab boxes around the frame, and its appearance (thickness of lines, fill colours) can also be edited by double clicking on the feature you wish to change (see boxes 7.4 and 7.5).

To obtain a stem and leaf display and boxplot

ANALYZE > Descriptive Statistics > Explore
Then in the **Explore** dialogue box:

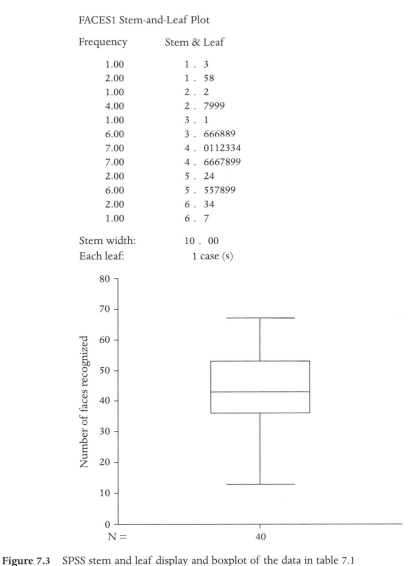

FACES1 Stem-and-Leaf Plot

Frequency   Stem & Leaf

1.00   1 . 3
2.00   1 . 58
1.00   2 . 2
4.00   2 . 7999
1.00   3 . 1
6.00   3 . 666889
7.00   4 . 0112334
7.00   4 . 6667899
2.00   5 . 24
6.00   5 . 557899
2.00   6 . 34
1.00   6 . 7

Stem width: 10 . 00
Each leaf: 1 case (s)

Figure 7.3   SPSS stem and leaf display and boxplot of the data in table 7.1

Highlight the name of the variable

Click on the top arrow button to move it into the **Dependent List** box

Click on the **Display Plots** radio button on the left of the box

[In SPSS versions 12 and 13, click on the **Plots** radio button in the **Display** control box at bottom left of the **Explore** dialogue box]

Click on the **Plots** button on the right of the box

Click on **Stem and leaf** and/or the radio button **Boxplots Dependents together** [**Dependents together** in v. 13].

Click on **Continue**

Click on **OK** to see the result in the **Output View** screen. (See both plotting options in figure 7.3.)

To compare boxplots of more than one set of scores

Data entry

In the **Data View** screen click on the **Variable View** tab in the bottom left corner of the screen.

In **Variable View**

Enter a data label (e.g. 'number') in the column under **Name**

> Enter a category name (e.g. 'Conditions') below it in the same column

Click on the **Data View** tab

In **Data View**

Enter the data from all samples one after the other in the first column. In the second column indicate the sample (category) of each score by placing an identifying digit in the second column next to each data item.

GRAPHS > Boxplot

Then in the **Boxplot** dialogue box:

> Click on the **Simple** option
>
> Click on the **Summaries of Groups of Cases** radio button
>
> Click on **Define**

In the **Define Simple Boxplot: Summaries for Groups of Cases** dialogue box

> Highlight the name(s) of the variable(s) to be plotted
>
> Click on the arrow button to move the names into the **Boxes Represent** field
>
> Click on **OK** (see figure 7.4).

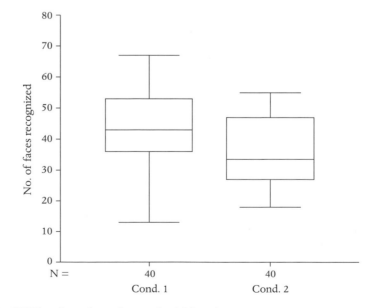

Figure 7.4   SPSS boxplots of two datasets (each N = 40)

[In SPSS Versions 12 and 13, starting from the **Define Simple Boxplot: Summaries for Groups of Cases** dialogue box,

>Highlight the data label and click on the arrow to move it to the **Variable** box.

>Click to highlight the category label and click on the arrow to move it to the **Category Axis** box

Click on **OK**.]

Note how this facilitates comparison of the two datasets in figure 7.4, as one can see clearly how they differ in their central tendency, interquartile range and skewness.

Centiles and quartiles

Once scores have been placed in order individual scores can be located in relation to the entire dataset. A centile (also called a percentile) is defined as the point on a distribution below which lie 1% of all the scores (note 1% of all scores not 1% of the range). So a dataset of 100 different scores consists of 99 centiles, with the second lowest score occupying the first centile. The 10th centile (also known as the first decile), is that score below which lie 10% of all the scores.

However, centiles and deciles are not very useful if the dataset is small or contains many scores with the same value. Then it is more meaningful to use just three: the 50th (the median), which is the point on the distribution below which exactly 50% of all the scores occur; and the 25th and 75th, called the first and third quartiles (symbols Q1 and Q3). The difference between the first and third quartiles, embracing the middle 50% of all scores, is called the interquartile range (IQR).

Quartiles are useful for giving a quick fix on where a single value stands in relation to a mass of data. It is immediately informative to know that, for example, a particular score is located below Q1 in the first (bottom) quartile of a sample, or lies within the interquartile range Q1 to Q3 (see figure 7.5).

The interquartile range has another useful application: that of helping to identify outliers (extremely low or high values) in a dataset. Tukey (1977), for example, has suggested that the upper and lower points of a distribution beyond which scores should be regarded as outliers can be identified by the simple formulae Q1 – 1.5 × IQR and Q3 + 1.5 × IQR (i.e. the value of the score at the first quartile plus and minus one and a half times the interquartile range).

Centiles in SPSS

The analysis of a dataset in terms of any desired set of percentiles is available in SPSS as part of frequency analysis. The program not only identifies values at the percentile and quartile points, but also allows a dataset to be divided into *any* desired number of groups.

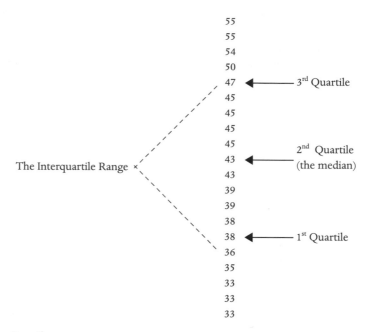

Figure 7.5   Quartiles

Data entry

Follow the basic procedure described in box 7.5, then in **Data View**

ANALYZE > Descriptive Statistics > Frequencies
Then in the **Frequencies** dialogue box:
> Click to tick the box **Display frequency tables**
> Highlight the name of the variable in the left-hand area
> Click on the arrow button to move it into the **Variable(s)** area
> Click on the **Statistics** button at the bottom of the box.

Then in the **Frequencies: Statistics** dialogue box:
> Click on any or all of
> **Quartiles** to obtain quartile values
> **Cut points for** and enter the number (e.g. 7) in the adjacent box to obtain values for any desired number of equal percentile points
> **Percentile(s)** and enter any value from 1 to 99 in the adjacent box. **Output View** will give the score at the selected percentile
> Click on **Add**, if active
> (In v. 13 the **Add** button only becomes active when a value is entered in the **Percentile(s)** box)

Click on **Continue**
Click on **OK** to see the **result in Output View** (table 7.5 shows the result of taking the **Quartiles** option).

Table 7.5   SPSS output showing quartile point values for the data in table 7.1

Statistics

N	Valid	40
	Missing	0
Percentiles	25	36.00
	50	43.00
	75	53.50

Simple, cumulative and relative frequency

Even more can be achieved by counting the data items to create frequency tables. Counting scores in slightly different ways provides a basic, but revealing, profile of the whole dataset in the form of a *frequency distribution*. Among other advantages, this allows one set of scores to be easily compared with another and forms a worthwhile preliminary to statistical calculations.

Simple frequency

Starting with a table of raw data, a simple frequency table is created by putting the scores in order and then noting the number of times each value occurs (see column 2 of table 7.6). It is now possible to see easily which scores have the highest and lowest frequencies, and exactly where they are located in the range of scores. Note also that the original unorganized dataset can still be easily retrieved.

Relative frequency

Relative frequency is more informative because it expresses individual frequencies as a proportion of the whole dataset. Relative frequency is computed by dividing each simple frequency by the total number of observations. This is often expressed as a percentage, as in column 3 of table 7.6.

Cumulative frequency

Cumulative frequencies are useful for identifying where a particular value stands in relation to the sample as a whole. Ascending cumulations are calculated by adding simple frequencies together to create a running total upward from the lowest score and indicate how many scores lie *below* a given point. The opposite, descending, cumulations start with the highest value and proceed to the lowest, indicating how many lie *above* any point. SPSS provides this statistic as a cumulative relative frequency expressed as a percentage (column 5 of table 7.6).

Table 7.6   SPSS table of frequencies from the data in table 7.1
FACES1

		Frequency	Percent	Valid %	Cumulative %
Valid	13.00	1	2.5	2.5	2.5
	15.00	1	2.5	2.5	5.0
	18.00	1	2.5	2.5	7.5
	22.00	1	2.5	2.5	10.0
	27.00	1	2.5	2.5	12.5
	29.00	3	7.5	7.5	20.0
	31.00	1	2.5	2.5	22.5
	36.00	3	7.5	7.5	30.0
	38.00	2	5.0	5.0	35.0
	39.00	1	2.5	2.5	37.5
	40.00	1	2.5	2.5	40.0
	41.00	2	5.0	5.0	45.0
	42.00	1	2.5	2.5	47.5
	43.00	2	5.0	5.0	52.5
	44.00	1	2.5	2.5	55.0
	46.00	3	7.5	7.5	62.5
	47.00	1	2.5	2.5	65.0
	48.00	1	2.5	2.5	67.5
	49.00	2	5.0	5.0	72.5
	52.00	1	2.5	2.5	75.0
	54.00	1	2.5	2.5	77.5
	55.00	2	5.0	5.0	82.5
	57.00	1	2.5	2.5	85.0
	58.00	1	2.5	2.5	87.5
	59.00	2	5.0	5.0	92.5
	63.00	1	2.5	2.5	95.0
	64.00	1	2.5	2.5	97.5
	67.00	1	2.5	2.5	100.0
	Total	40	100.0	100.0	

If the scores in a large dataset have been grouped into classes (see box 7.5 for an explanation of how this is done), an ascending cumulation always takes the upper limit of the class interval as its reference point for identifying the highest score of any proportion of the sample. Similarly, for a descending cumulation, the reference point is always the lower limit of an interval.

Frequencies in SPSS

SPSS generates a table containing a listing of the raw data, and simple, relative and cumulative percentage frequencies. There are processing options to allow the information to be displayed in either ascending or descending order.

Data entry

Follow the basic procedure described in box 7.5. Then in **Data View**,

ANALYZE > Descriptive Statistics > Frequencies
Then in the **Frequencies** dialogue box:
 Click to tick the box **Display frequency tables**
 Highlight the name of the variable in the left-hand area
 Click on the arrow button to move it into the **Variable(s)** area
 Click on **OK** to see the output screen.

Further options

- If you wish to have data from two or more variables displayed make sure all the names are in the **Variable(s)** area of the **Frequencies** dialogue box.
- Click on the **Format** button on the right of the **Frequencies** screen to bring up the **Frequencies:Format** dialogue box that allows you further options.
  - **Compare variables** produces the frequency tables one after the other with a common summary table
  - **Organize output by variables** produces separate summary tables followed by each frequency table
  - The **Suppress tables with more than n categories** option in the Format box removes any frequency table with more than the required number of categories from **Output View**. Click **Continue** to confirm your selection
  - Click on the **Statistics** button to see a dialogue box that allows you to select from possibilities that include Central Tendency and Dispersion. These will be discussed later in the chapter.

Class intervals and grouped data

Often, the range of a dataset (the difference between the lowest and highest score) is larger than ten or twelve units. This can create difficulties, especially when the intention is to create a graph. In such cases, the difficulty of accommodating all the scores individually on the X axis means that it is usually necessary to divide the range into *class intervals* rather than attempting to deal with each score individually. The instructions for creating class intervals are in box 7.6 and the results (again for the data in table 7.1) are in table 7.7.

Graphing frequencies: histograms

Frequency tables are helpful when one wants to see something of the profile of a distribution. However, a clearer impression can be gained by drawing a histogram – a graph that represents frequency.

In the histogram the vertical (Y) axis indicates the frequency with which the various score values occur in the dataset. The area of each 'bar' is therefore proportional to the number of

BOX 7.6   Procedure for grouping scores into class intervals

- Determine the range of the scores. In table 7.1 this is 54 (the difference between 67 (highest) and 13 (lowest). Decide the number of class intervals. It is generally suggested that there are not less than 10 and not more than 20 of these, with a preferred class size of 1, 2, 3, 5, or 10 units. A simple rule is to divide the range by the preferred size of classes, and 'add one'. Thus, the range of 54 divided by a preferred interval size of 5 gives 10 intervals, and adding one gives a total of 11 intervals. So the range must be divided into 11 equal-sized groups, each containing five units of score. The first interval contains scores of 13, 14, 15, 16 and 17; the next holds scores of 18, 19, 20, 21 and 22, and so on up to the 11th interval which has score limits (the boundary scores of the interval) of 63 to 67.
- Whole number (integer) score limits are adequate as long as the scores themselves are integers but not when the scores include non-integers. Then it is necessary to use what are called the exact limits of each interval to sort each score accurately into one, and only one, of the classes. It is good practice to use exact limits even when working with integer values. Usually the exact limits are 0.5 units below the lower integer value, and 0.49 units above the higher. You can see how this works in table 7.7. (Note the convention that places the lowest score value at the bottom of the table and the highest at the top.)

Table 7.7   Score limits, exact class limits and simple frequencies of data in table 7.1

Score limits	Exact Limits	Frequency
63–67	62.5–67.49	3
58–62	57.5–62.49	3
53–57	52.5–57.49	4
48–52	47.5–52.49	4
43–47	42.5–47.49	7
38–42	37.5–42.49	7
33–37	32.5–37.49	3
28–32	27.5–32.49	4
23–27	22.5–27.49	1
18–22	17.5–22.49	2
13–17	12.5–17.49	2

scores it represents. The two key features of the histogram that distinguish it from the similar bar graph are:

- the horizontal (X) axis must have a continuous scale
- the bars must touch each other.

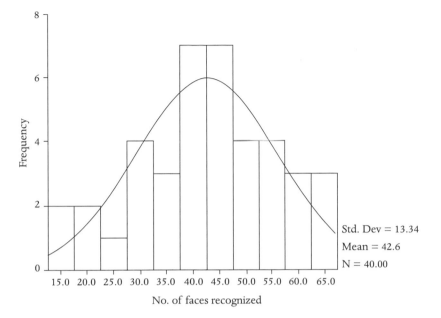

Figure 7.6 SPSS histogram of the data in table 7.1 with normal curve added

Table 7.8 Frequencies of unequally grouped data representing the time taken to complete a standard task (N = 60)

Time-band (seconds)	Class width	Simple frequency	Exact limits	Frequency density simple frequency / class width
0–5	5	10	0–4.99	2
5–10	5	13	4.5–9.49	2.6
10–20	10	19	9.5–19.49	1.9
20–30	10	8	19.5–29.49	0.8
30–60	30	10	29.5–59.49	0.33

When working with (integer) score limits, the scale values on the X axis may be placed under the centres of the bars, though it is better practice to place them under the points at which the vertical lines of the graph meet the X axis. If exact limits are used (the scores having been grouped), a label indicating the class limit must be placed under the lines and for the sake of clarity it is usual for only the lower limit to be provided. SPSS Version 11 can't do this. It automatically selects the appropriate exact limits for non-integer data but displays only the median value of each (see figure 7.6). In SPSS versions 12 and 13 integers representing selected lower score limits are automatically displayed.

Sometimes it is necessary to draw a histogram when the class limits are unequal so that the area of each bar represents frequency by varying both widths and heights. The heights of the bars in these circumstances are known as frequency densities and the formula to determine the bar height appropriate for each class interval is, bar height = simple frequency / class width. Hand-drawing will be necessary to produce this type of graph since SPSS does not support this feature (table 7.8 and figure 7.7).

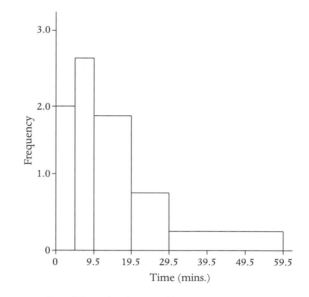

Figure 7.7   Histogram plotted from the data in table 7.8

Histograms in SPSS

Data entry

Follow the basic procedure described in box 7.5. Then in **Data View**,
ANALYZE > Descriptive Statistics > Frequencies
In the **Frequencies** dialogue box,
>   Click to untick the box **Display frequency tables** if you just want a chart on its own,
>   otherwise a frequency table will also be displayed
>   Highlight the name of the variable in the left-hand area
>   Click on the arrow button to move it into the **Variable(s)** area
>   Click on the **Charts** button.
In the **Charts** dialogue box
>   Click on the **Histograms** radio button
>>   Click to tick **With normal curve** if you want a plot of the shape
>>   of a normal curve with your data (as in figure 7.6)

Adding the normal curve
to the plot of your data
allows a visual check of
skewness and kurtosis.

>>   Click **Continue**
>>   Click on **OK** to display the histogram in **Output View**.

>>   Alternatively, using the Graphs menu,
>>   **GRAPHS > Histogram**
>>>   Highlight the name of the variable in the left-hand area
>>>   Click on the arrow button to move it into the **Variable** area

Click to tick **Display normal curve** to plot the shape of a normal curve with the data,
(as in figure 7.6).
Click on **OK** to display the histogram in **Output View**.

The **Chart Editor** provides a number of customizing features for histograms
Double-click anywhere on the field of the histogram to bring up the **Editor**
Double click on the feature you wish to change or use the icons at the top of the **Editor**
screen.

For example, to set the interval width or number of intervals on the X axis manually,
In the **Chart Editor** double click on the X axis scale
In the **Interval Axis dialogue box**
Click on the **Custom** radio button
Click on **Define**
In the **Interval Axis: Define Custom** dialogue box
Manually set the **desired no of intervals**; **interval width** or **range of scale**
Click on **Continue**
Click on **OK**

[In SPSS versions 12 and 13 you can use the drop-down menus in **Chart Editor** to edit the
output.]

For example, **Chart Editor > Edit > Select X axis**
In the **Properties** dialogue box
Set the range and interval type details to either **Auto** or **Custom**
Click on **Close**.

In v. 13,
In the **Properties** dialogue box
Click on **Scale** and set the details
Click on **Apply**
Click on **Close**

To close the Chart Editor use **File > Close** in the main menu.

Bar graphs

A bar graph allows you to represent and compare data from different sources or situations.
They are straightforward to produce but should always be drawn with a clear space between
each bar. One typical use in psychology is to show the average scores achieved in different
conditions in an experiment when the vertical (Y) axis always represents the changes observed
to occur to the Dependent Variable and the horizontal (X) axis represents the different conditions (treatments) of the Independent Variable. The rise and fall of the data values are indicated by the upper edge of the bars and the separation of the bars indicates the discontinuous
nature of the variables that are being represented.

Bar graphs in SPSS

Bar graphs are straightforward to produce in SPSS, and there is a large number of editing options that allow the chart to be tailored to precise requirements. The instructions below provide guidance on producing only the simplest kind of chart in which the values represent the means of separate samples. You should consult a specialist text such as Brace, Kemp and Snelgar (2003) for more detailed information.

Data entry

In the **Data View** screen click on the **Variable View** tab in the bottom left corner of the screen.
In **Variable View**
Enter a label for each category of data in the column under **Name**
Click on the **Data View** tab to return
Enter the raw data under the appropriate heading. The column labels assigned in Variable View will initially appear as labels of the bars in the chart, but these can be edited later if desired.

GRAPHS > Bar
Then in the **Bar Charts** dialogue box:
    Click on **Simple** to select the simple bar chart
    Click on the radio button **Summaries of separate variables**
    Click on **Define**.
Then in the **Define Simple Bar** dialogue box [**SPSS** versions 12 and 13 call this dialogue box **Define Simple Bar: Summaries of Separate Variables**]
    Highlight the variable names in the left-hand area
    Click on the right arrow button to move them into the **Bars Represent** area
    Click on **Change Summary** [**v. 13: Change Statistic**].
Then in the **Summary Function** [**v. 13: Statistic**] dialogue box,
    Click on the radio button **Mean of values**
    Click on **Continue**
    Click on **Titles** to add titles, then **Continue**
    Click on **Options**
    Click on **Exclude cases listwise**
    Click on **Continue**
    Click on **OK**.
A bar chart appears in the **Output View** window (see figure 7.8).

To make the X (horizontal) axis begin at zero (in version 11 only)

Double click on the body of the chart to bring up the **Chart Editor**
Then,
CHART ≥ Axis

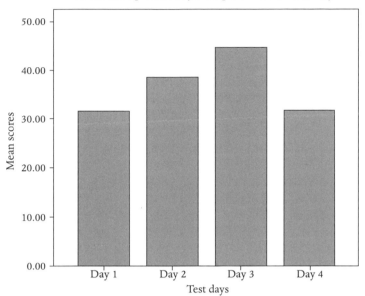

Figure 7.8   SPSS (v. 12) chart showing four score means

Then in the **Axis** dialogue box:
    Click on the **Scale** radio button
    Click on OK.
In the **Scale Axis** dialogue box
    Click on the down arrow by the **Scale Minimum** box until it shows zero
    Click on **OK** and close the **Chart Editor** by clicking in the top right corner.

[In SPSS versions 12 and 13 the X axis automatically begins at zero.]

Line graphs

Line graphs are used to represent the relationship between two (usually continuous) variables, showing by direction of the line any changes to the value of one variable in terms of the other. Either a straight line or a smooth curve may be fitted to the pattern of points. Figure 7.9 shows a line graph (drawn from imaginary data) in which the line represents the mean recall score of one group of 10 participants who were asked to read through a list of words and attempt to recall them at 15-minute intervals.

Line graphs are, unfortunately, easy to draw in a way that provokes misinterpretation and the general guidance of the APA on the drawing of effective graphs is given in box 7.7. Three further points should also be noted. First, the scales on either axis should have equal intervals. Second, information about *rate of change* indicated by the line can only be obtained if three or more points have been plotted, and, third, the slope (angle) of a line depends on the scales chosen for the axes.

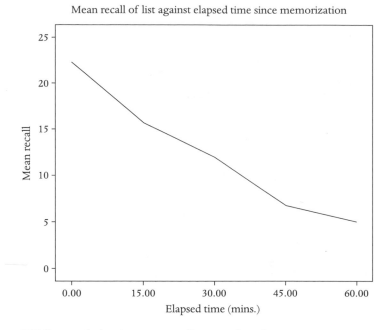

Figure 7.9   SPSS line graph showing mean recall against elapsed time

Line graphs in SPSS

Data entry

In the **Data View** screen click on the **Variable View** tab in the bottom left corner of the
    screen.

In **Variable View**

In the column under **Name** enter a label for each variable (e.g. 'time' and 'recall')

Click on the **Data View** tab to return

Enter the values for each variable in the appropriate column.

For example, to produce the graph in figure 7.9

In the 'time' column the elapsed time intervals (0, 15, 30, 45, 60 minutes) are each entered
10 times because they apply to all 10 of the participants, giving 50 cells filled in total. The
individual recall scores from each test are then entered alongside in column 2.

GRAPHS > Line

In the subsequent **Line Charts** dialogue box:

    Click on **Simple** to select the simple line chart

    Click on the radio button **Summaries for groups of cases**

    Click on **Define**.

Then in the **Define Simple Line** dialogue box,

    Click on **Other Summary Function**

[In v. 13: when **Define Simple Line: Summaries for Groups of Cases** appears

    Click on **Other Statistic** and continue as below.]

Highlight the measured variable name ('recall' in this example) in the left-hand area
Click on the right arrow button to move it into the **Variable** area
Highlight the other variable name ('time' in this example) in the left-hand area
Click on the right arrow button to move it into the **Category Axis** area
Click on **OK**

The line graph appears in **Output View**.

To make the Y (vertical) axis begin at zero,
Double click on the body of the chart to bring up the **Chart Editor**
Double click on the Y axis
Change the value in the **Range Minimum** box to zero
Click on **OK**.

Alternatively, in the **Chart Editor**
CHART ≥ **Axis**
Then in the **Axis** dialogue box,
Click on the **Scale** radio button
Click on OK.
In the **Scale Axis** dialogue box
Click on the down arrow by the **Range Minimum** box until it shows zero
Click on **OK** and close the **Chart Editor** by clicking in the top right corner.

[In SPSS versions 12 and 13, double clicking on the Y axis or the icon at the top of **Chart Editor** brings up the **Properties** dialogue box.
Click on the **Scale** button at the top. If the **Auto** button is ticked against **Minimum**, click to untick and enter a 0 in the **Custom** box alongside.
Click on **Apply**.] (See also box 7.7.)

BOX 7.7 The APA advice on drawing graphs

The American Psychological Association provides definitive guidance on every aspect of scientific writing. The following summarizes its guidance on producing graphs and charts (APA, 1994).

- Plot the independent (causal) variable on the horizontal (X) axis and the dependent variable, or equivalent, on the vertical (Y) axis
- A vertical axis that is 3/4 to 2/3 the length of the horizontal axis gives a well-proportioned chart
- When planning a chart look at the range of the data to be plotted on each axis before deciding the scales
- The scales should maintain the ratio of the units of variable X to variable Y in the data
- Both axes should begin at zero. If this is impossible because of the resulting length of the scale, start at zero but interrupt the axis with a double slash
- The lettering should be parallel to each axis and the numbers on the scales should be horizontal on both axes
- Short labels are always better than long ones.

● DESCRIPTIVE STATISTICS ●

Descriptive statistics are the summarizing statistics that reduce any set of data, no matter how large and apparently unwieldy, to a single, easily comprehended, value that represents a particular property of the entire set. The four types of descriptive statistics are as follows:

- *Measures of central tendency* describe data in terms of a typical or central value.
- *Measures of dispersion* describe the data in terms of the distribution of individual data items around the mean or median The most widely used measure of dispersion is the standard deviation, although the range (simple, interquartile and semi-interquartile) and variance are also important.
- *Measures of skewness and kurtosis* describe a dataset in terms of the shape of the distribution.
- *Measures of correlation* describe the relationship between two sets of data in the form of the correlation coefficient. The two most commonly encountered correlation coefficients are Spearman's rank order correlation and Pearson's product moment correlation.

Measures of central tendency

The mean

The mean is the arithmetic average of a set of data, found by dividing the sum of all the scores by the total number of scores ($\Sigma x / n$) and indicating the point in a distribution at which the sum of the deviations (the difference between the mean and every individual score) is zero. However, although the statistic offers a representative value, in that each individual score contributes to the computation, it is sensitive to the presence of extreme scores, and is therefore best used when score values are reasonably close together – this can be determined by inspection. Should extreme values be present the mean must be regarded as unreliable as a representative value, and the median offers a better alternative.

The statistical symbol for the mean is $\bar{X}$ (pronounced ex-bar)

Example:

105, 110, 128, 130, 154, 164, 171, 173, 176, 179

The mean in this case is 149 (1490 ÷ 10), and it gives a reliable picture of the typical score because the scores are evenly distributed across the range of the dataset.

The median

The median value is the central value (the positional average) of an ordered set of data. To find the median, it is helpful to use the concept of the **median position**, defined as the place in an ordered set of scores that is occupied by the median score. In an odd number of scores, the median position lies exactly in the middle of the set of scores and in the example below the score at this position is 154. If there are an even number of scores, the median position lies midway between the two central scores and the median value is calculated as the mean of these two scores. In the example below the two central scores are 74 and 88 and when added together and divided by 2 give the median value of 81. Because it is insensitive to the actual data values, the median is to be preferred to the mean when there are extreme values in the data, and when the data represent measures on the ordinal scale.

Example:
The median of an odd number of scores
105, 110, 128, 130, 154, 164, 171, 173, 176

The median in this case is 154

Example:
The median of an even number of scores
34, 38, 46, 67, 68, 74, 88, 89, 90, 93, 96, 100,

The median in this case is 81

The mode

The modal value is the most frequently occurring score in a dataset and is found by inspection of the data. Some datasets may have no mode while others may have one or more modal values. These distributions are called bimodal (if there are two modes), or multi-modal (if there are three or more). The mode is useful measure of central tendency when neither the median nor the mean are appropriate, such as when data represent measures on the nominal scale.

Example:
34, 38, 46, 67, 74, 74, 88, 89, 93, 93, 93, 100,

The mode here is is 93

Measures of dispersion

As well as having a central or most representative value datasets also differ in the extent to which scores are bunched together or dispersed. The dispersion of a dataset is the extent to which individual scores differ from one another. If one set of scores all have the same value they have zero variability, and the various measures of dispersion – the range, semi-interquartile range, variance and standard deviation all have the value zero. If, on the other hand, the set of scores differ widely from one another, the greater will be the variability and the measures of dispersion will, in their different ways, reflect this fact.

The range

The range is the least informative and least stable (in the sense that it can vary unpredictably from one sample to another as sample size increases) of all the measures of dispersion, being just the difference between the highest and lowest values of a dataset. Its main advantage is that it is probably the simplest of all statistics to compute but it is very limited in what it can convey. It tells us the size of the space between the top and bottom scores, but says nothing about how all the other scores are arranged inside that space.

The interquartile and semi-interquartile ranges

The interquartile range improves on the crudeness of the range as a measure of dispersion by using the difference between the scores at the 25th and 75th percentiles as a measure of dispersion. This is particularly useful when there are extreme values present that would otherwise distort the value of the simple range. The semi-interquartile range goes yet further in pursuit of a stable range statistic by dividing the interquartile range in half. When combined with the median, this statistic is commonly applied to ordinal data, or other data that are extremely skewed.

The variance/standard deviation

Both the previous measures define dispersion in terms of the size of the difference between two scores in a dataset, and the greater the difference the greater the dispersion. However, this approach says nothing about the way that scores might be distributed between the extremes of the range. It would, clearly, be highly desirable to know whether the scores are mostly closely bunched together or evenly distributed across the range. This information becomes available when the dispersion of a set of scores is characterized in terms of their distribution around a central value, as it is in the variance/standard deviation statistic. An average of the squared differences (deviations) from the mean gives the variance of a dataset and taking the square root of the variance gives the standard deviation. All scores thus contribute equally to the value of the variance/standard deviation. However, as noted above, if strong skew is present or if there are outliers in the dataset, other statistics may be preferred (see table 7.9 for computation instructions).

Why the need for both the variance and standard deviation statistics?

Given the closeness of the relationship between the variance and standard deviation one might wonder why there is a need for both statistics. When computing variance, the problem

Table 7.9   Calculation of variance/standard deviation by hand

	Data X (N = 10)	3, 17, 11, 6, 9, 12, 11, 16, 10, 12
1	Sum the scores;	$\Sigma X = 107$
	Divide the result by N, the number of scores, to find the mean	$\bar{X} = 107 \div 10 = 10.7$
2	Subtract each raw score from the mean to find the difference scores	Difference scores (d) 7.7, −6.3, −0.3, 4.7, 1.7, −1.3, −0.3, −5.3, 0.7, −1.3
3	Square each difference score	Difference scores squared (d^2) 59.29, 39.69, 0.09, 22.09, 2.89, 1.69, 0.09, 28.09, 0.49, 1.69
4	Sum the squared difference scores	$\Sigma d^2 = 156.1$
5	Divide the result of (4) by N − 1 to find the variance	$\Sigma d^2/N - 1 = 156.1 \div 9 = 17.34$
6	The square root of the variance is the standard deviation	$s = \sqrt{17.34} = 4.16$

is that the squaring operation not only changes the numerical values but the units of measurement also. For example, squaring deviations measured in seconds produces a variance value measured in new units of 'squared seconds'. Not only are such units difficult to understand, they also make it difficult to relate the measure of dispersion back to the original set of scores. The solution is, of course, to return to the original units by taking the square root of the variance – the standard deviation – thereby allowing the dispersion statistic to be easily related to its parent dataset.

The formula for the standard deviation is

$$s = \sqrt{\frac{\Sigma d^2}{N-1}}$$

s   is the symbol for the standard deviation
d   is the difference between each score and the mean
N   is the number of scores
Σ is the instruction to sum all the (squared) differences.

The sample standard deviation can estimate the standard deviation of the population

The computation in table 7.9 using N − 1 to divide the sum of the squared differences at step 5 is the formula for finding the variance/standard deviation of a sample (symbol s.). This is the version usually employed. When the sample is smaller than the population of interest and has been obtained from a structured sampling process (typically a random sample), this statistic gives a reliable estimate of the variance/standard deviation of the population from which the sample was taken. See Howell (1997) for the criteria of whether a statistic is a good estimator of its corresponding parameter.

The formula that divides by N alone at step 5 gives the variance/standard deviation of a whole population (symbol σ). It is therefore only useful when there is no need to estimate the population variance/standard deviation because every member of a population is included in the sample.

Descriptive statistics in SPSS

Data entry

Follow the basic procedure described in box 7.5. Then in **Data View**,
ANALYZE > Descriptive Statistics > Descriptives
Then in the **Descriptives** dialogue box:
> Highlight the name of the variable
> Click on the arrow button to move it into the **Variable(s)** box
> Click on the **Options** button.

In the **Descriptives: Options** dialogue box select whichever descriptive statistics you wish to use.
> Click on **Continue**
> Click on **OK** to see **Output View**.

Alternatively,
ANALYZE > Descriptive Statistics > Frequencies
Then in the **Frequencies** dialogue box:
> Click to untick the box **Display frequency tables**

[SPSS v. 13 displays a warning message after this action: Click **OK** on the warning and continue as below (unless you wish to see frequencies displayed).]
> Highlight the name of the variable in the left-hand area
> Click on the arrow button to move it into the **Variable(s)** area
> Click on the **Statistics** button at the bottom of the box to get to the same dialogue box as before and make your selection. [In SPSS versions 12 and 13 the **Frequencies: Statistics** dialogue box appears that contains a range of similar options.]
> Click on **Continue**
> Click on **OK** to see **Output View**.

Or, to produce all the descriptives in table 7.10 at once,
ANALYZE > Descriptive Statistics > Explore
Then in the **Explore** dialogue box,
> Highlight the name of the variable
> Click on the top arrow button to move it into the **Dependent List** box
> Click on the **Display Statistics** radio button on the left of the dialogue box
> *(Click on the **Both** button and the stem and leaf display and boxplot will be shown as well)*
> Click on the **Statistics** button on the right of the dialogue box
In the **Explore: Statistics** dialogue box
> Click on the box to put a tick against **Descriptives**
> Click on **Continue**
> Click on **OK** to see them in **Output View**.

Most of the information in table 7.10 will already be familiar. Of the remainder, skewness and kurtosis are dealt with immediately below and the 95% confidence interval is discussed in chapter 8. The 5% trimmed mean is simply the mean recalculated after the top and bottom 2.5% of scores have been removed to eliminate any very extreme values.

Table 7.10   SPSS descriptive statistics for the data in table 7.1

Descriptives

FACES1	Mean		Statistic	Std error
	Mean		42.6000	2.10975
	95% confidence interval for mean	Lower bound	38.3326	
		Upper bound	46.8674	
	5% trimmed mean		42.9167	
	Median		43.0000	
	Variance		178.041	
	Std deviation		13.34320	
	Minimum		13.00	
	Maximum		67.00	
	Range		54.00	
	Interquartile range		17.5000	
	Skewness		−.333	.374
	Kurtosis		−.283	.733

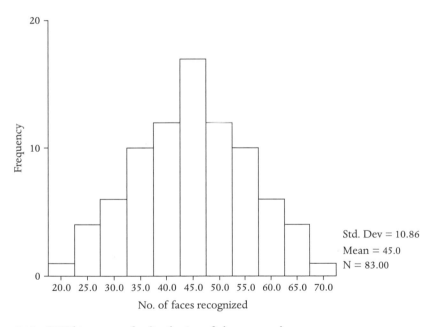

Std. Dev = 10.86
Mean = 45.0
N = 83.00

Figure 7.10   SPSS histogram of a distribution of almost zero skew

Measures of skewness and kurtosis

Table 7.10 contains the two statistics that are quite different from those already discussed. The skewness and kurtosis statistics characterize the *shape* of a distribution. The qualities that they capture can be seen most clearly in the histograms of differently shaped continuous distributions (figures 7.10 to 7.13)

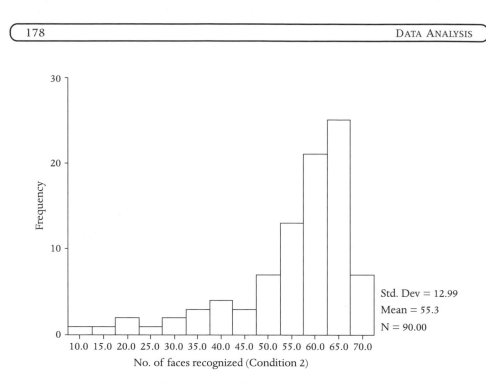

Figure 7.11   SPSS histogram of a distribution of negative skew

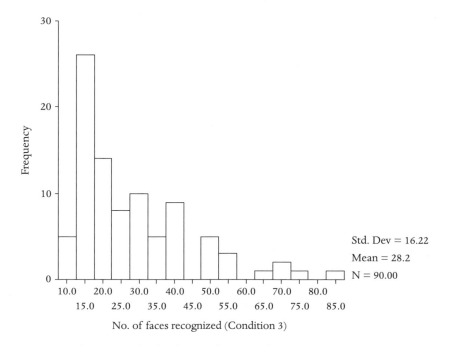

Figure 7.12   SPSS histogram of a distribution of positive skew

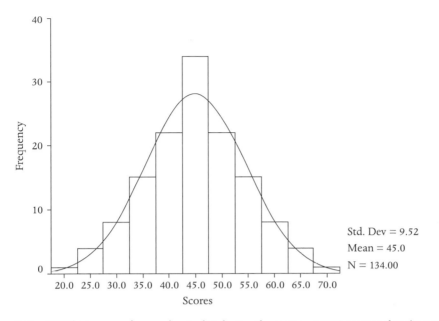

Figure 7.13 SPSS histogram of a mesokurtic distribution (kurtosis – −0.008) compared to the normal distribution

Skewness

This refers to the extent to which a distribution is asymmetrical about its mean and median (i.e. the left half is not a mirror-image of the right half). In a perfectly symmetrical distribution such as the theoretical distribution known as the normal distribution (see next chapter), these measures of central tendency have the same value and the skewness statistic has a value of zero. Empirically obtained distributions, on the other hand, are always likely to contain some degree of skew, either positive or negative, as indicated by a non-zero value of the skewness statistic. The greater its value diverges from zero the greater the skewness of the data. (However, while symmetry in a distribution means that the mean and median always have the same value, it must also be pointed out that the opposite is not always true. Identical values of the mean and median do not necessarily mean that the distribution is symmetrical.)

Negative skew is present when the distribution has greater frequencies (including the mode) located towards the high end of the variable, with the mean of the dataset being less than the median, as in figure 7.11.

Positive skew is present when the majority of scores are located towards the low end of the variable, and the median of the dataset is greater than the mean, as in figure 7.12.

It is important to be aware of the possible significance of the skewedness of a distribution. Skew may indicate that problems of measurement have produced floor or ceiling effects in the data. It can also suggest that the population distribution from which the data were taken was not normal in form – an important issue that must be assessed when the use of parametric statistics such as the t-test are contemplated.

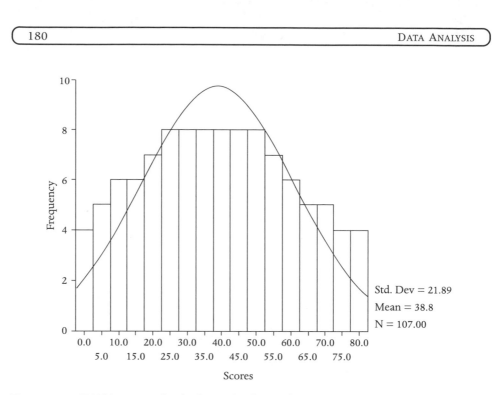

Figure 7.14   SPSS histogram of a platykurtic distribution (kurtosis = −0.895) compared to the normal distribution

Data can be assessed for skew by comparing the mean and median. The greater the difference between these statistics the more asymmetric the distribution, with the direction of skew indicated by their relative values. A visual assessment of the presence of skew (and also of kurtosis) can be made in SPSS, which provides for the histogram of a dataset to be superimposed on a normal distribution curve (see figures 7.13–7.15).

Kurtosis

This is simply a measure of the 'flatness' of a distribution compared to the shape of the standard normal distribution (see next chapter for an introduction to this important distribution). The closer a distribution follows the shape of the normal distribution (a mesokurtic distribution), the closer the value of the kurtosis statistic tends towards zero (as in figure 7.13). When the distribution is more vertically compressed, such as figure 7.14 (a platykurtic distribution), the statistic has a negative value tending towards −1 as it becomes 'flatter' (negative kurtosis). On the other hand, leptokurtic distributions, such as figure 7.15, are narrow and high in the centre compared to the normal distribution and the statistic has a positive value (positive kurtosis). The greater the value (positive or negative) of the kurtosis statistic, therefore, the more the distribution of the sample data diverges from the mesokurtic form. This can give an indication of how close, or not, the population distribution may be to the normal distribution. It should, however, be approached cautiously. Howell (1997), for example, points out that large samples are generally needed to obtain an idea of the true shape of a population distribution. He therefore suggests that, given the small sample sizes

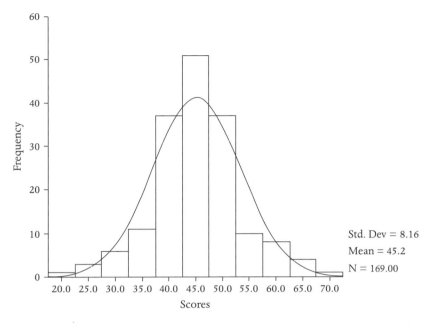

Figure 7.15 SPSS histogram of a leptokurtic distribution (kurtosis = 0.990) compared to the normal distribution

that are common in psychology, the kurtosis statistic is unlikely to offer a very reliable guide to the shape of a population distribution.

Skewness and kurtosis in SPSS

Data entry

Follow the basic procedure described in box 7.5. Then in **DataView**,
ANALYZE > Descriptive Statistics > Frequencies
Then in the **Frequencies** dialogue box,
    Click to untick the box **Display frequency tables** (if desired)
    Highlight the name of the variable in the left-hand area
    Click on the arrow button to move it into the **Variable(s)** area
    Click on the **Statistics** button at the bottom of the box.
In the **Frequencies: Statistics** dialogue box
    Click to tick **Skewness** and/or **Kurtosis**
    Click on **Continue**
    Click on **OK**.

Co-variation: graphical and statistical approaches

In psychology, it is often necessary to be able to relate one set of scores to another in order to establish whether two variables can be said to co-vary. For example, given the two sets of

Table 7.11   Self-estimates of hours of sleep per night and scores on
a test of problem-solving of 12 students

	Estimated average hours of sleep per night	Problem-solving test score/20
1	7	13
2	5	9
3	8	16
4	9	17
5	4	5
6	6	11
7	7	10
8	8	12
9	5	15
10	8	14
11	6	12
12	9	18

data in table 7.11, the obvious questions to try to answer would concern the direction and strength of any relationship between the number of hours of sleep and scores on the problem-solving test. Does sleeping longer seem to be positively related to problem-solving performance in this sample? One can begin to obtain answers to questions of this type by drawing a scatterplot of the two sets of data in question.

There are two techniques for assessing the relationship between two sets of scores – graphical methods using the scatterplot, and statistical methods that employ the correlation coefficient. As the former offers a natural route of approach and is an essential tool for assessing the co-variation of two collections of scores, even before a correlation coefficient is calculated, we begin there.

Scatterplots

A scatterplot consists of a set of points, in which each point represents one pair of scores (figure 7.16). From it one can check the overall shape of the relationship and, if appropriate, estimate the direction and magnitude of any co-variation.

Scatterplots are quite intuitive and are easily sketched by hand, so detailed instructions for drawing them are not likely to be required. In addition to the general guidance applicable to all graphs given in box 7.6, an essential point to bear in mind is that the link between each member of a pair of scores is maintained through any subsequent processing.

What does figure 7.16 tell us about the data? It suggests that the relationship between these variables is a linear one and quite strongly positive (although this conclusion must be qualified by the small size of the sample and the presence of one or two values that diverge from the overall trend). In general, the scatterplot seems to indicate that the more hours of sleep one estimates oneself to have had, the higher one scores on the problem-solving task. However, it would be necessary to collect much more data using more refined measures of sleep duration and problem solving before one could be clear about the relationship.

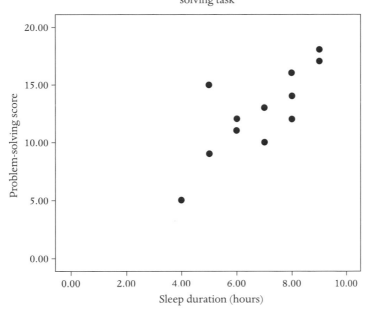

Figure 7.16   Scatterplot of the data in table 7.11 (SPSS v. 12)

Scatterplots in SPSS

Follow the basic procedure described in box 7.5 above to create two columns of data. Then, in **Data View**,

GRAPHS > Scatter [in version 13: **GRAPHS > Scatter/Dot**]

Brings up a dialogue screen offering a choice among different types of scatterplot. To produce a simple scatterplot

Click on **Simple**

Click on **Define**.

In the **Simple Scatterplot** dialogue box

Highlight the name of the criterion variable in the left-hand area and click on the arrow button to move it to the Y Axis box. Repeat the process to move the predictor variable to the X Axis box.

Click on the **Titles** button to insert titles

Click on **OK** to see the Output View screen

To edit the scatterplot double click anywhere on the body of the chart

In the **Chart Editor**

Click on **Format** to bring down the menu or [In SPSS versions 12 and 13 Click on the **Edit** menu]

Click on one of the icons at the top of the editor screen. (Pop-up labels appear when you rest the cursor on an icon.)

In paired datasets if one variable appears logically to precede the other it is called the predictor variable, and the other is called the criterion (see also below).

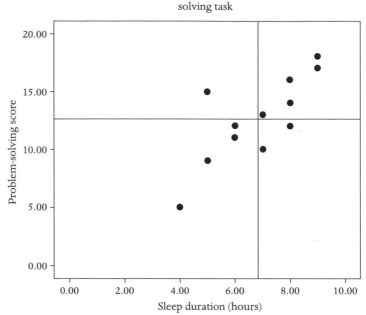

Figure 7.17   Scatterplot of the data in table 7.11 with reference lines added at the data means (SPSS v. 12)

[In v. 13: Click on the item you wish to edit and select **Edit > Properties** to see an appropri-ate dialogue box.]

Further scatterplot techniques

When a scatterplot contains many data points, or when the trends in the data are unclear, the following techniques can help the information in the data to be seen more clearly.

Reference lines

A clearer view of the information in a scatterplot can be obtained simply by dividing the field of the graph into four quadrants by means of reference lines. These are probably most helpful if placed at the means of the X data and Y data, but they can be located to intersect anywhere on the field of the graph. The number of data points in each quadrant gives more informa-tion that may help interpretation. For example, consider the scatterplot in figure 7.16 of data from N = 12 participants showing the co-variation of the two variables of sleep hours and scores on a problem-solving task. Applying the technique to figure 7.16 produces figure 7.17. The number of data points in each quadrant is shown in table 7.12.

This simple procedure confirms that the trend of the data is strongly from top left to bottom right of the graph, indicating a strong positive relationship between sleep duration and problem-solving score. Most of the intersection points occur in the top-right and bottom-

Table 7.12 Number of data points above and below the means of the data in table 7.10

Sleep estimate	Problem-solving score	
	Cases below the mean	Cases above the mean
Cases above the mean	2	5
Cases below the mean	4	1

left quadrants, the points are quite evenly spaced and form a rough line within these quadrants. A chi-squared test could be carried out on the frequencies to determine whether the association is statistically significant (see chapter 9).

To insert reference lines in SPSS

Double click anywhere on the field of the graph to enter **Chart Editor**

For vertical line(s)
Select **CHARTS > Add Chart Element > X Axis Reference Line**.
[In v. 13 use **OPTIONS > X (or Y) Axis Reference Line** to call the **Properties** dialogue box.]
In the **Properties** dialogue box
    Click to select the **Reference** tab if not already the active one
    In the **X Axis Position** box enter the X axis value (e.g. the mean of the X data) at the
        desired insertion point for the reference line
    Click on **Apply**
    Click on **Close**

For horizontal line(s)
Follow the instructions above but select **Y Axis Reference Line** from the **Add Chart Element** menu.

Select **FILE > Close** to exit **Chart Editor** and return to **Output View**. The reference lines will be added to the scattergraph in **Output View**.

The line of best fit

The line of best fit (or 'regression line') is a line drawn on a scatterplot that passes through, or close to, as many of the points on the plot as possible to provide an indication of the trend of the data. The more points that are touched by or are close to the line, the higher the correlation coefficient that would be computed from the data. In the example in figure 7.18, the line touches or runs close to most of the data points, indicating that the two variables covary strongly in a positive direction.

    The usual way of establishing a precise line of best fit is the method of 'least squares', as found in advanced texts such as Howell (1997). SPSS also uses the 'least squares' method to add a line of best fit to a scatterplot, the procedure for which is given below. If neither of these options is available, a hand-drawn approximation can be made by joining the first and last datapoints, plus as many of the others as possible and this may be sufficient for many purposes.

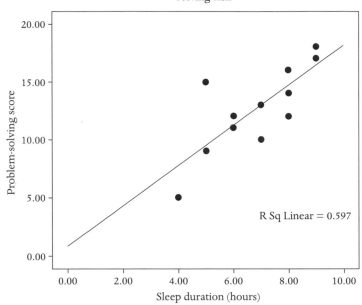

Average hours of sleep per night and scores on a problem-solving task

Figure 7.18   Scatterplot of data in table 7.11 with regression line added (SPSS v. 12)

To add the line of best fit in SPSS

With the scatterplot visible in **Output View**
Double click on the scatterplot to open the **Chart Editor** window.
Click **CHART > Options**
In the **Scatterplot Options** dialogue box
> Click to tick **Fit Line Total**
> Click on **Fit Options**
> Click to highlight **Linear Regression** (ignore all other boxes)
> Click on **Continue**
> Click **OK**.

To edit, click on the appropriate icon at the top of the **Chart Editor** screen. First, double click on any data point in the scatterplot to make the icons 'live'.

[To place a regression line on the graph in v. 12,
Double click on the field of the graph to activate **Chart Editor**
> In **Chart Editor** double-click on any data marker to activate them all (a **Properties** dialogue box appears which you can use to edit the data field if desired).
> Next click on the **Chart** tab and select **Add Chart Element > Fit Line at Total** from the drop-down menus.]

(A line of best fit is inserted on the graph in **Chart Editor** and a new **Properties** dialogue box appears that provides various editing options. Check that the **Linear** radio button is active.)

Click **Close** to remove the **Properties** dialogue box
Click on the shaded graph to exit **Chart Editor**

In v. 13: select **ELEMENTS > Fit Line at Total**
In the subsequent **Properties** box click the **Linear** radio button
Click **Close**
Exit **Chart Editor**.

[SPSS automatically places the value of the linear regression statistic on the field of the graph. This may be easily removed in **Chart Editor**, if desired.]

Linear regression

Linear regression is the prediction of one variable from another in order to specify values that lie outside the range of the sample. That is, given a sample of scores, it allows one to find the value of Y that is predicted by any desired value of X. This possibility may be useful when one wishes to look beyond a given set of data towards establishing some general principle, but should be used cautiously. Howell (1997) has the formulae for the hand computation of the regression statistic, together with a detailed discussion of the issues involved and SPSS also provides the statistic in the **ANALYZE** menu (see Brace, Kemp and Snelgar, 2003).

The statistical approach to co-variation

The co-variation of two sets of scores has two dimensions. The *direction* of co-variation concerns whether the scores vary directly or inversely. *Magnitude* indicates the strength of the relationship. Both are captured in a single statistic, the *correlation coefficient* (box 7.8), in which,

- *Direction* is indicated by the sign of the coefficient. A positive coefficient indicates that any two sets of scores co-vary directly with each other (any change in the values of one is accompanied by a change of the other in the same direction). A negative coefficient indicates the opposite relationship, where each increase in the value of one is accompanied by a change to the other in the opposite direction.
- *Magnitude* is indicated by a value in the range from 0 to 1, with the zero indicating a nil (random) relationship between the two sets of scores and 1 indicating a perfect (consistently proportional) relationship. The values between 0 and 1 indicate the degree to which the relationship is less than perfect (see table 7.13 and figures 7.19 to 7.21).
- Figure 7.19 shows a strongly positive correlation in which the points on the scatterplot clearly run from the lower left-hand towards the top right-hand corner indicating a strong positive relationship. The Spearman coefficient computed by SPSS from these data is $r = 0.979$.
- Figure 7.20 shows almost perfect negative correlation in which the points on the graph run from the top left-hand to the bottom right-hand corner. The Spearman coefficient computed in SPSS from these data is $r = -1.0$.
- Figure 7.21 shows a zero or random correlation. There is no consistent pattern visible in the scatterplot and the two sets of scores hardly co-vary at all. The Spearman coefficient computed in SPSS from these data is $r = -0.011$.

Table 7.13 Coefficient values and the relationship between two variables

Coefficient (+ or −)	Relation between variables
1.0	Perfect correlation: Any change to the value of the X variable is accompanied by a proportional change (either direct or inverse) to the value of the other. Indicates a straight-line relationship.
0.9	A less than perfect but still a very high correlation indicating an almost straight-line relationship.
0.7 or 0.8	A high correlation indicating a reasonably strong, close straight-line relationship.
0.5 or 0.6	Some degree of correlation, but not a close relationship.
0.3 or 0.4	A low correlation indicating a weak relationship. Considerable departure from a straight-line relationship.
0.1 or 0.2	A very low correlation with virtually no relation between variables.
0	A random relationship.

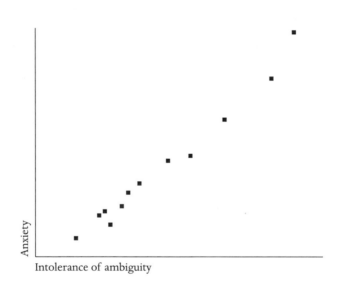

Figure 7.19 A strong positive correlation (Spearman's r = 0.989)

Predictor and criterion variables

Sometimes, though not always, it is possible to differentiate between pairs of variables, where one of them, called the predictor variable *in some sense* precedes, the other. If one variable is clearly the predictor variable it should be assigned to the X (horizontal) axis of a scatterplot. The other variable is called the outcome (or criterion) variable, and this is the variable that represents the particular point of the research – the variable about which one wishes to make a statement. In table 7.11, and the three scatterplots drawn from it (figures 7.16, 7.17 and 7.18), sleep duration is a better candidate for the predictor variable. The most plausible relationship between the two variables is for sleep duration to allow the prediction of problem-solving performance rather than the other way round.

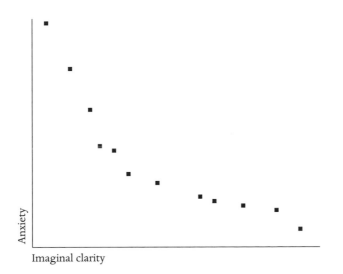

Figure 7.20   A strong negative correlation (Spearman's r = −1.0)

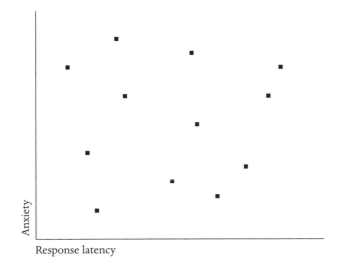

Figure 7.21   An almost zero correlation (Spearman's r = −0.11)

Instructions for computing the two most frequently required coefficients – Spearman's Rank Order Coefficient and the Pearson Product Moment Coefficient – can be found in chapter 9.

This completes the introduction to the most commonly required descriptive statistics and graphing techniques. For more information on any aspect consult the sources listed at the end of this chapter.

BOX 7.8   Three essential points about correlation coefficients

- Measures of correlation only produce a meaningful result if the pairs of scores are related in some way (for example because they have both been obtained from the same group of individuals).
- Even though two sets of scores are related in some way the correlation coefficient itself says nothing about the possibility of a causal relationship between them. 'Correlation does not imply causality' (anon.). It may be possible to *infer* the existence of a causal relationship through the correlational research design, but this is not the same as establishing a causal relationship by experiment.
- The relationship between the variables must be a linear one. This means that the scores must be related in the same direction (either positive, or negative) across the whole range of the data. If the relation between the sets of scores, as revealed by the scatterplot, appears curvilinear, then a correlation coefficient will produce a misleading result. Even if a scatterplot appears to be linear, caution is needed because it may be that only part of the range of a curvilinear relationship has been sampled. In such case, both the shape of the scatterplot and the value of the coefficient depend on the shape of the curve and the location of the sample on the curve.

EXTENSION ACTIVITIES

Activity 1

Match the following everyday examples of data to their scales of measurement. Your bank account PIN; the number of cheques in your chequebook; the amount written on a cheque; your car registration number; your rating (five-point scale) of the last film you saw; a telephone number; the winners of the Oscar awards.

Activity 2

Construct a stem and leaf display by hand from the dataset in table 7.14. Use the same technique on the dataset in table 7.15. How would you characterize the differences between the two displays? Now use the SPSS stem and leaf command on the same data (see p. 156 above for instructions). Are there any differences in the results?

Activity 3

Practising grouping data using exact limits is worth doing so you know what is involved. Construct a frequency table containing score limits, exact limits and simple frequencies from the data in table 7.14.

Table 7.14 Scores from a logical reasoning test

35	49	46	55	54	74	81	118	32	39
67	38	41	32	37	65	37	46	69	57
38	58	67	35	48	58	35	91	45	28
31	77	58	77	38	43	37	76	69	76
66	42	39	87	45	30	47	55	49	33
47	38	63	90	43	68	78	38	47	75

Table 7.15 Time taken (in seconds) to find the target letter in a complex array

4.44	4.69	3.01	4.66	3.42	3.02	4.15	3.51	3.45	4.88
2.82	4.41	4.75	3.21	4.88	2.80	4.14	3.45	5.33	2.92
5.3	3.99	3.37	3.79	4.16	3.45	4.01	3.13	3.73	3.17
3.8	3.29	4.09	2.77	4.65	4.00	4.37	4.55	3.17	4.01
3.03	4.44	3.41	3.08	3.99	3.45	3.51	7.54	3.12	5.50

Activity 4

How could you check the claim that the distribution of scores in table 7.14 indicates that the test was too difficult for most of the participants? Is the claim correct?

Activity 5

Construct two separate boxplots by hand using the datasets in table 7.14 and 7.15. Compare the results with the stem and leaf displays constructed in Activity 2. Does the boxplot gives you more information about the datasets? Now use the SPSS boxplot command on the same data (see p. 156 above for instructions). Are there any differences between your boxplot and the one produced by the program? How do you account for them?

Activity 6

Enter the data from tables 7.16 and 7.17 into SPSS and generate two boxplots on the same scale. How would you describe any differences between them?

Activity 7

Enter the data in table 7.17 into SPSS and generate a table of frequencies. What information about this distribution is now available to you? If SPSS is not available carry out the exercise by hand.

Continued

Table 7.16   Fifty estimates (in minutes) of the duration of a standard interval (silence condition)

6.4	8.7	5.8	5.6	4.7	4.8	4.9	8.3	8.4	5.6
7.0	7.6	6.2	7.5	6.6	5.5	7.2	9.0	6.1	4.6
6.2	8.3	5.4	6.9	7.8	7.5	6.7	6.6	7.2	5.5
5.7	6.4	4.9	6.0	5.4	5.5	5.3	7.9	7.9	6.7
6.8	7.7	6.9	4.6	8.4	5.7	6.6	8.1	6.9	6.5

Table 7.17   Fifty estimates (in minutes) of the duration of a standard interval (white noise condition)

7.0	7.4	6.1	6.0	6.6	6.7	4.0	7.8	8.3	8.7
7.9	8.8	6.8	7.6	4.6	8.1	7.2	7.6	4.2	8.6
8.4	7.6	7.0	6.6	7.7	7.5	4.8	8.1	8.2	7.7
8.1	7.8	7.0	6.0	5.4	7.9	5.3	6.2	7.0	3.5
6.3	5.7	5.1	4.5	7.2	5.9	6.6	4.9	6.8	7.0

Table 7.18   Error scores of 10 participants on (a) a time-estimation task and (b) eye–hand co-ordination task

	1	2	3	4	5	6	7	8	9	10
Time-estimation	5	7	4	6	8	8	9	7	8	6
Eye–hand	12	0	9	7	8	6	8	10	7	8

Activity 8

Draw a histogram from the data in table 7.17 using SPSS. Add the Normal Curve to the display and use the Chart Editor to enter a title, axis labels and change the fill colour and line thickness of the histogram.

Activity 9

The best way to understand what a formula is doing is to compute the statistic by hand. For practice, use the formula given on p. 175 to compute the Standard Deviation for each of the two sets of scores in table 7.18. What does the result suggest about the dispersion of one compared to the other? Check your computations by entering the scores into SPSS.

Activity 10

Draw a sketched scatterplot of the data in table 7.18, add a hand-drawn line of best fit and estimate the direction and extent of the co-variation. Then enter the same data into SPSS to obtain a scatterplot with line of best fit and compare your version with that obtained from SPSS. Are there differences?

Table 7.19 Scores on a measure of marital attitudes taken at different intervals after marriage

	1	2	3	4	5	6	7	8	9	10
After 2 weeks	12	14	15	10	13	10	15	9	14	10
After 3 months	14	19	12	12	17	18	18	9	16	10
After 6 months	15	10	13	10	16	10	17	11	16	14
After 1 year	10	6	13	10	12	8	13	13	15	9

Activity 11

Using SPSS, choose to draw either a bar graph or a line graph of the means of the four sets of scores in table 7.19 in order to highlight the differences between them. Would the same type of graph indicate change over time equally clearly? Check your conclusion by comparing this graph with the alternative.

Activity 12

Enter SPSS, and in **Variable View** label a column Group 1 (or similar). Change to **Data View** and enter one of the datasets from tables 7.14 to 7.19 in the first column. Go to the **ANALYZE** menu and select **Descriptive Statistics > Descriptives**. The result will be shown in **Output View**. Click on the right-hand corner to remove it. Now explore the menus and dialogue boxes to see whether you can obtain a table showing all the descriptives at once. How many of them do you recognize? When you have the table, see if you can paste it into a document in your word processor.

Chapter Summary

1   The theme of this chapter has been the descriptive treatment of quantitative data. Such data are generated when a psychologically interesting variable such as intelligence is defined operationally and can thus be subjected to a measurement process of some kind.

2   Measurement involves assigning numbers to instances of a variable. The various ways in which such assignments can be made creates different scales of measurement. Stevens (1946, 1951) proposes a well-known typology of such scales for psychology – the nominal, ordinal, interval and ratio scales – providing a starting point for consideration of measurement issues.

3   Measurement is assessed against the criteria of reliability and validity. Validity is concerned with the extent to which a measurement technique is capable of capturing the concept in question. Reliability is concerned with the extent to which repeated measurements of the same event are able to produce identical data. Two factors threaten the reliability of measurement in psychology: the intrinsic variability of human behaviour and the fact that all measurement contains an unknown proportion of error.

4 The concept of the distribution provides the essential basis for organizing a set of scores and there are a range of approaches for investigating the shape and other characteristics of a distribution. These include different types of frequency distribution, and graphical methods such as the histogram and the techniques of exploratory data analysis.

5 Descriptive statistics extend the range of information that can be extracted from a dataset. The measures of central tendency summarize the data in terms of a single central value, while the measures of dispersion describe the way that scores are spread, or scattered around a central point. The mean and standard deviation are probably the most widely used of all these statistics.

6 Skewness and kurtosis are concepts used to describe the shape of a distribution and can be examined graphically when the histogram of a dataset is plotted. Skewness concerns the extent to which the shape of the histogram departs from left–right symmetry about its central point while kurtosis describes the relationship between the height and width of a histogram, especially departures from the symmetrical bell-shape of the normal curve. Both skewness and kurtosis can also be described statistically.

7 The description of the relationship (co-variation) of two sets of scores can also be achieved by either graphical or statistical methods. The scatterplot provides a succinct graphical representation of such a relationship and this may be supplemented by other techniques such as by drawing a line of best fit to clarify the trend of the data. Co-variation can also be described by means of the correlation coefficient – a statistic that captures both the direction and magnitude of the relationship between sets of scores.

● FURTHER READING ●

Frank, H. and Althoen, S. C. (1994). *Statistics: Concepts and applications.* Cambridge: Cambridge University Press.

Howell, D. C. (1997). *Statistical methods for psychology,* 4th edn. Belmont, CA: Duxbury Press.

Howell, D. C. (1995). *Fundamental statistics for the behavioural sciences,* 3rd edn. Belmont, CA: Duxbury Press.

For more information about SPSS contact SPSS UK Ltd, St Andrew's House, Woking, Surrey, UK, GU21 1EB.

8

INTRODUCTION TO
INFERENTIAL STATISTICS

CHAPTER MAP

The Foundations of Statistical Inference

Simple probability
The normal distribution
The standard normal distribution
Using the SND to compare different populations
Using the table of areas to establish probabilities
   Some examples of the SND in use

Parameter Estimation

Point estimates and their limitations
   Sampling error
Interval estimation
   Key concepts in interval estimation
      Sampling distributions
      Standard error
      A central limit theorem
   Estimating μ when σ is known.
      Confidence level and significance level
   Estimating μ when σ is unknown
   Beyond the sampling distribution of the mean
Parameter estimation in SPSS

Hypothesis Testing

Statistical hypotheses – null and alternate
The sampling distribution of the test
Significance level
Region of rejection
Critical value

Decision errors in hypothesis testing
    Type 1 error
    Type 2 error
    Test power

Extension Activities

Chapter Summary

Further Reading

THIS CHAPTER

1. Describes the important features of the normal distribution and standard normal distribution and shows how these may be used.
2. Introduces parameter estimation as the technique for obtaining knowledge about populations from the evidence of samples.
3. Explains how the provisions of a central limit theorem allow the normal distribution to be used to estimate the mean of a population.
4. Shows how to estimate a population mean from sample data.
5. Explains how test statistics are used to make inferences from samples of quantitative data to their parent populations.
6. Shows how key concepts such as significance level and region of rejection form a framework for making decisions about statistical hypotheses.

KEY CONCEPTS

Population
sample
statistics
parameter
simple probability
outcome
sampling distribution
normal distribution
standard normal distribution
z-score
statistic parameter
parameter estimate
point estimate
sampling error
interval estimate
confidence interval
confidence level
upper and lower confidence limits

confidence coefficient
sampling distribution
standard error
standard variate
unbiased estimate
hypothesis
statistical hypothesis
research hypothesis
null and alternate hypothesis
directional and non-directional
    hypothesis
sampling distribution
significance level
region of rejection alpha level α
critical value
one-tailed test
two-tailed test type-1 error
type-2 error

● THE FOUNDATIONS OF STATISTICAL INFERENCE ●

Research in psychology almost always finds it necessary to explore data in greater depth than descriptive statistics alone are able to do, and this requires the application of inferential statistics. There are two aspects to this. In the first place, the techniques of inferential statistics allow researchers to use the information in a single sample to say something about the population from which it was taken. (See chapter 5 for more information about samples and populations.) Commonly, this involves estimating population parameters, such as the mean or standard deviation, from the corresponding statistic, a process known, for the obvious reasons, as 'parameter estimation'.

Inferential statistics is the branch of statistics concerned with drawing reasoned conclusions from samples of data.
Statistic: A value computed from a sample.
Parameter: A value computed from a population.

Second, researchers often wish to analyse data in two (or more) samples to assess whether the differences between them indicate that they could have been taken from the same or from different populations. Usually, such questions are posed to test an explicit hypothesis within a formally structured investigation, such as an experiment. Finding answers to these questions relies on the key concepts of probability and the normal distribution.

Simple probability

Probability theory is concerned with quantifying the likelihood that specific things will happen under different kinds of conditions. The terminology of probability theory speaks of probability as associated with the *outcome* of some *event*. It enters statistics because in the absence of certain knowledge, we wish to assess the likelihood of such outcomes as obtaining data within a given range of values, or whether a given dataset could have been drawn from a particular population.

To establish some key principles, consider the simplest situation involving the outcome of a single independent event such as throwing a die or drawing a card at random from a pack.

The probability of observing a particular outcome of an event when all possible outcomes are equally likely is found from the formula,

$$\text{Probability of a particular outcome} = \frac{\text{No. of outcomes of interest}}{\text{Total no. of possible outcomes}}$$

To find the probability of drawing a specified card from a standard pack we need to know how many cards *of that type* there are in the pack, and how many possible outcomes of all types there are. In the standard pack there are 52 possible outcomes of drawing a single card, thus,

- The probability that a single card drawn from the pack is a red card is 26/52
- The probability that the first card is a Heart is 13/52
- The probability that it is the Ace of Hearts is 1/52.

Fractions such as these are cumbersome to compute, so it is usual to convert them to decimal form. This always yields a value in the range from zero and 1 because the number of outcomes of interest cannot exceed the number of possible outcomes. So, if there are zero *possible* outcomes the value of p must also be zero because, logically, there must also be zero outcomes of interest. Similarly, if there are the same number of outcomes of interest as there are possible outcomes, then the former are certain to occur, and p = 1. The probabilities associated with all other situations, such as drawing the Ace of Hearts from a shuffled pack on the first attempt, have values between zero and 1.

These are examples of simple probability – the outcomes of single independent events when all possible outcomes are equally likely. Of course, it is also possible to calculate the probability of an outcome in much more complex situations, such as joint probability (where one wishes to determine the probability of two (or more) independent outcomes), or conditional probability (where the likelihood of one outcome depends on whether another has already occurred). The procedures for calculating these and other complex probabilities are beyond the scope of this book, but instructions can be found in many advanced statistics texts.

> In behavioural research the equal likelihood of all possible outcomes is achieved by random sampling from the population of interest.

The normal distribution

The normal distribution is central to the application of statistics in psychology for two reasons. First, it can be shown that many empirical distributions are modelled accurately by the normal distribution. When plotted from sufficiently large samples, the distribution of human variables such as height, grip strength or cranial circumference in the general population all turn out to be approximately normal in form. Furthermore, it has long been argued that many of the variables of interest to psychologists are also likely to be distributed normally.

> The insight concerning the normal distribution of psychological variables is generally attributed to Francis Galton in the course of his pioneering investigations into the heritability of intelligence (Galton, 1869).

The second reason is that when the appropriate conditions (such as minimum sample size) are met, many random sampling distributions (i.e. the distributions of statistics such as the mean and standard deviation obtained from repeated random sampling from a population) are also found to be normal, or nearly so. This fact provides the rationale for statistical tests of significance, since it allows users of statistical tests to make inferences about the relation of samples to their parent population(s), even though the parameter values of the latter may be unknown. The normal distribution is a class of theoretical population distributions that is specified by two parameters – the population mean and population standard deviation. The exploration of the properties of these distributions is generally attributed to Carl Friedrich Gauss (1777–1855) and for that reason they are sometimes also known as Gaussian distributions.

In formal statistical terms, the normal distribution is a graph of the density function of a variable, X. (Density is related to, but not exactly the same as, frequency: density = the height of the curve for any given value of X, whereas a frequency is the number of times a given value of X is observed to occur.)

For those interested, the formula for the density function that generates the normal distribution is:

$$f(X) = \frac{1}{\sigma\sqrt{2\Pi}}(e)^{-(x-\mu)^2/2\sigma^2}$$

In this formula:

Π and e are constants: Π = 3.1416

e = 2.7183

μ is the population mean of the variable X

σ is the population standard deviation of the variable X

X is any score of the variable X.

Thus, as long as the two population parameters are known, this formula can be used to generate a density function that gives the distance between the normal curve and the horizontal axis of the graph for any value of X. If this process is repeated for all possible values of X the result is a complete description of the normal distribution for the population of X that has the specified mean and standard deviation.

The graph of a normal distribution is a symmetrical bell-shaped curve divided exactly into two halves by the mean and with the mean, the median and mode equal in value (see figure 8.1). The curve is asymptotic, meaning that it stretches out to touch the X axis of the graph at infinity in either direction (thus emphasizing that this is a purely theoretical distribution). Its exact shape is determined by the value of the population standard deviation. When that parameter is large the curve is flatter and wider and when it is small the curve is taller and narrower, as shown in figures 8.2a and 8.2b.

An asymptote is any line that converges on a curve without touching it.

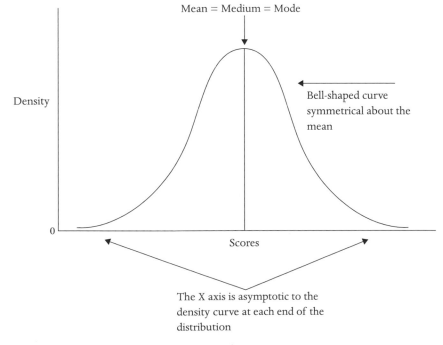

Mean = Medium = Mode

Density

Bell-shaped curve symmetrical about the mean

0

Scores

The X axis is asymptotic to the density curve at each end of the distribution

Figure 8.1   Key characteristics of the normal distribution

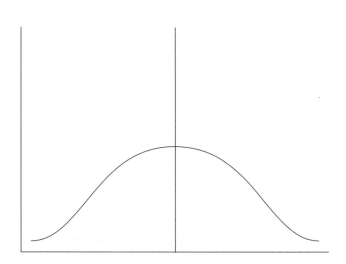

Figure 8.2a   The normal curve when the value of the population standard deviation is large

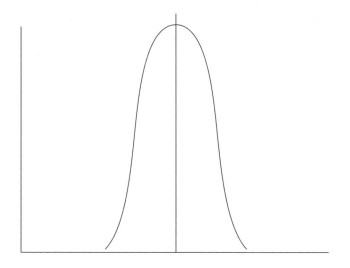

Figure 8.2b   The normal curve when the value of the population standard deviation is small

The standard normal distribution

Earlier, the normal distribution was described as a theoretical distribution. Consequently, a perfect version of the distribution can only be obtained by applying the density function to all possible score values of a specific population whose mean and standard deviation are known. *It cannot be obtained simply by taking a very large sample from some population on a particular variable and drawing a frequency graph of the result*. If such a sampling exercise were to be carried out it *could* produce a distribution that *approaches* normality. However, this would depend on how close the population distribution of X itself is to normality; how easy it has been to obtain accurate measures of the X variable; and the kind of sampling technique used. Nevertheless, there is always some degree of difference between theoretical and empirical distributions.

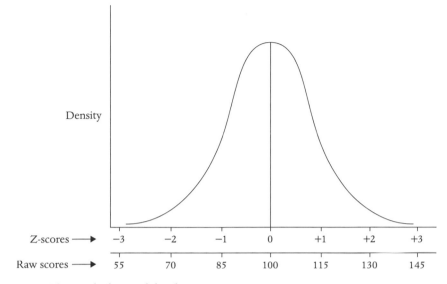

Figure 8.3   The standard normal distribution

BOX 8.1   More about the z-score

The standardization formula $z = \dfrac{x - \mu}{\sigma}$ applied to *any* normally distributed variable X, measures how many standard deviations a particular score is above or below the mean. So if $z = +1.9$ it means that the score is 1.9 standard deviations above the mean; and if $z = -2.3$ it means the score is 2.3 standard deviations below the mean. This will be true of any scores whatever the σ and μ of their population distributions, because, in effect, the raw score values have been re-scaled to become units of standard deviation. We will see how this works in specific instances a little further on.

There is a further difficulty. It is not just that accurate values for the population mean and standard deviation (μ and σ are almost always unavailable, though they can be estimated, as will be shown), but that, for any variable, they can also vary widely from one population to another. It is thus simply not practicable to develop a different distribution for every possible combination of population mean and standard deviation.

The solution has been to use a standardized version of the normal distribution which, because it is the same for all and any values of μ and σ, allows the properties of the normal distribution to be applied to any population whatever. Standardization is achieved simply by assigning zero as the value of the mean and calibrating the X axis of the graph in units of z-score rather than in raw score units of the empirical variable X (see figure 8.3 and box 8.1).

BOX 8.2   How to use the table of areas under the SND curve

A section of table 2 in appendix 4 is shown in figure 8.5. This gives, in decimal form, any fractional area under the curve located between the mean of the SND and any point *above or below* it measured in z-score. The left-hand margin of the table gives z-score values up to the first decimal place, and the top margin gives the values to the second place. By reading across and down the body of the table the proportion of the total area indicated by that value of z-score can be found.

The SND is symmetrical about the mean, so if the area to be found is also symmetrical about the mean you simply double the table value as in example 1 below. If it is not symmetrical you need to use two different values from the table, as in the other examples.

Using the SND to compare different populations

In all normal distributions, the ends of the curve lie at infinity, so the area under the curve includes all possible values of the variable X in the population. One important consequence of this is that any given proportion of the area under the curve will contain exactly the same proportion of all possible values of the variable. For example, any 50% of the area under the curve includes 50% of the scores represented by the whole distribution, and so on.

What makes the SND particularly useful is the fact that the area under the curve is indexed by z-score values above and below the mean, so that it becomes possible to calculate the precise area between any two points on the X axis and collect the results in a table (table 2 in appendix 4). And because it is easy to move between z-scores and raw score values, the table of areas can be used to make inferences about any normally distributed variable whatsoever (box 8.2).

Thus, as figure 8.4 shows, the area lying beneath the curve between the mean and 1 z-score above the mean is 34.13% of the total, the same as lies between the mean and 1 z-score *below* the mean. Similarly, the area lying between the mean and 2 z-scores above the mean is 47.72% of the total, and is the same as the area between the mean and 2 z-scores below the mean. The remainder

To turn the table value into a percentage of the total area simply multiply it by 100.

of the total area lies outside 2 units of z-score above and below the mean at the extreme ends of the distribution; each of these areas comprises 2.28% of the total area.

Some examples of the SND in use

The following examples show how the SND can be used to answer specific questions about any normally distributed variable (a sketch of the distributions may help you follow the reasoning in each case).

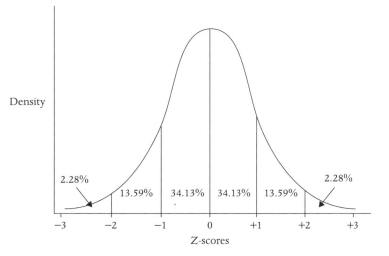

Figure 8.4   The standard normal distribution showing the areas under the curve indicated by integer values of z

Fractional area under the standard normal curve from 0 to z

z	0	1	2	3	4	5	6	7	8	9
0.0	.0000	.0040	.0080	.0120	.0160	.0199	.0239	.0279	.0319	.0359
0.1	.0389	.0438	.0478	.0571	.0557	.0596	.0636	.0675	.0714	.0754
0.2	.0793	.0832	.0871	.0910	.0948	.0987	.1026	.1064	.1103	.1141
0.3	.1179	.1217	.1255	.1293	.1331	.1368	.1406	.1443	.1480	.1517
0.4	.1554	.1591	.1628	.1664	.1736	.1700	.1772	.1808	.1844	.1879
0.5	.1915	.1950	.1985	.2019	.2054	.2088	.2123	.2157	.2190	.2224
0.6	.2258	.2291	.2324	.2357	.2389	.2422	.2454	.2486	.2518	.2549
0.7	.2580	.2612	.2642	.2673	.2704	.2734	.2764	.2794	.2823	.2852
0.8	.2881	.2910	.2939	.2967	.2996	.3023	.3051	.3078	.3106	.3133
0.9	.3159	.3186	.3212	.3238	.3264	.3289	.3315	.3340	.3365	.3389
1.0	.3413	.3438	.3461	.3485	.3508	.3531	.3554	.3577	.3599	.3621
1.1	.3643	.3665	.3686	.3708	.3729	.3749	.3770	.3790	.3810	.3830
1.2	.3849	.3869	.3888	.3907	.3925	.3944	.3962	.3980	.3997	.4015
1.3	.4032	.4049	.4066	.4082	.4099	.4115	.4131	.4147	.4162	.4177
1.4	.4192	.4207	.4222	.4236	.4251	.4265	.4279	.4292	.4306	.4319

Figure 8.5   Extract from statistical table 2: areas under the standard normal distribution

Example 1

Q: *What proportion of the area under the curve lies between z = ± 0.75, (i.e. between 0.75 units of z-score above and below the mean)?*

A: From table 2 in the appendix, the area between the mean and a z-score of z = 0.75 is 0.2734 of the total area under the curve. Therefore the area between the mean and z = 0.75 *in both directions* will be 2 × 0.2734 = 0.5468 (54.68%) of the total area (see figure 8.6).

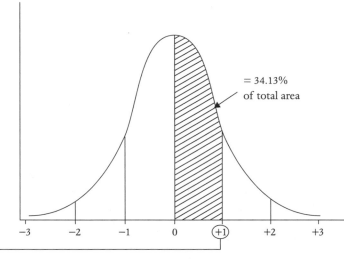

= 34.13%
of total area

Fractional area under the standard normal curve from 0 to z

z	0	1	2	3	4	5	6	7	8	9
0.0	.0000	.0040	.0080	.0120	.0160	.0199	.0239	.0279	.0319	.0359
0.1	.0389	.0438	.0478	.0571	.0557	.0596	.0636	.0675	.0714	.0754
0.2	.0793	.0832	.0871	.0910	.0948	.0987	.1026	.1064	.1103	.1141
0.3	.1179	.1217	.1255	.1293	.1331	.1368	.1406	.1443	.1480	.1517
0.4	.1554	.1591	.1628	.1664	.1736	.1700	.1772	.1808	.1844	.1879
0.5	.1915	.1950	.1985	.2019	.2054	.2088	.2123	.2157	.2190	.2224
0.6	.2258	.2291	.2324	.2357	.2389	.2422	.2454	.2486	.2518	.2549
0.7	.2580	.2612	.2642	.2673	.2704	.2734	.2764	.2794	.2823	.2852
0.8	.2881	.2910	.2939	.2967	.2996	.3023	.3051	.3078	.3106	.3133
0.9	.3159	.3186	.3212	.3238	.3264	.3289	.3315	.3340	.3365	.3389
1.0	.3413	.3438	.3461	.3485	.3508	.3531	.3554	.3577	.3599	.3621
1.1	.3643	.3665	.3686	.3708	.3729	.3749	.3770	.3790	.3810	.3830
1.2	.3849	.3869	.3888	.3907	.3925	.3944	.3962	.3980	.3997	.4015
1.3	.4032	.4049	.4066	.4082	.4099	.4115	.4131	.4147	.4162	.4177
1.4	.4192	.4207	.4222	.4236	.4251	.4265	.4279	.4292	.4306	.4319

Figure 8.6   Part of the table of areas under the normal curve with a sketch of the standard normal distribution

Example 2

Q: *What proportion of the area under the curve lies between z = −0.75 and z = +1.33 (i.e. between 0.75 units of z-score below the mean and 1.33 units above)?*

A: From table 2 in appendix 4, the area between the mean and a z-score of z = 0.75 is 0.2734 of the total area under the curve. The area between the mean and a z-score of z = 1.33 is similarly 0.4082 of the total. Therefore the area between the mean and z = −0.75 and z = +1.33 is 0.2734 + 0.4082 = 0.6816 (68.16%) of the total area.

Example 3

Q: Given a normally distributed population with a mean of 100 and a standard deviation of 15, what proportion of the scores in the population will lie between 80 and 120?

A: First convert the raw scores (80, 120) into their z-score equivalents using, in this case, 1 unit of z-score = 15 units of raw score. (Look again at figure 8.3, if necessary.)

(For this operation, a specific population mean and standard deviation is required. Recall that the 1 unit of z-score = the standard deviation of the population.)

The z-score equivalent of a raw score of 80 lies $20/15 = 1.33$ z-score units below the mean. Similarly, the z-score equivalent of a raw score of 120 also lies $20/15 = 1.33$ z-score units above the mean.

To find the proportion of the area under the curve that lies between $z = \pm 1.33$ consult table 2 in the appendix, which shows that the area is $2 \times 0.4082 = 0.8164$ (81.64%) of the total area. Since the normal distribution represents the entire population in question, we conclude that 81.64% of all the scores lie between raw score values of 80 and 120 in this case.

Using the table of areas to establish probabilities

The relationship between raw score values and z-scores in the standard normal distribution is doubly useful because the table of areas can also be used to determine the probability of obtaining any given range of scores in a sample. As we have seen, we can easily find the proportion of the area under the normal curve associated with any given range of raw scores and this relationship can also be expressed as a probability. The logic of this is the same as that used earlier to introduce the concept of probability, except that instead of dealing with one or more specific outcomes of interest we deal with different proportions of the area under the curve. Thus the entire area under the curve represents all possible outcomes (all possible scores), and any part of that total area may contain the outcome of interest. So, if we are interested in the range of scores that lie within (say) 10% of the total area under the curve, it follows (from the formula for simple probability) that the probability of obtaining scores within that range is $10/100$ or $p = 0.1$. Likewise, the probability of obtaining scores that lie within 5% of the area under the curve is $p = 0.05$, and so on.

Random sample: A sample taken from a population in such a way that all the units in the population have an exactly equal chance of being selected into the sample.

The following further examples show how this reasoning can be combined with z-scores to allow ranges of specific score values to be identified and their probabilities computed.

Example 4

Q: Given a normally distributed population with a mean of 100 and a standard deviation of 15, what is the probability of obtaining a score in the range 100–115?

A: This questions asks for the probability associated with the area immediately adjacent to the mean of the distribution. First, we convert the range of raw scores into its z-score equivalent. In this case, one unit of z-score = 15 raw score units, so a raw score of 115 will be 1 z-score above the mean. From table 2 in appendix 4, the area under the curve located between the mean and one z-score above the mean is 34.13% of the total area. Therefore, in this case the probability associated with raw scores in the range 100 to 115 is $p = 34.13/100 = 0.3413$ (figure 8.7).

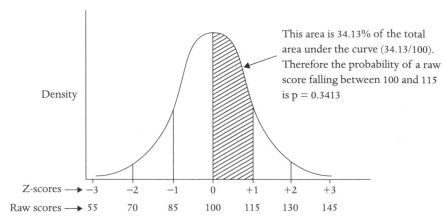

Figure 8.7   Using the area under the standard normal curve to find the probability of scores in a given range

Example 5

Q: *Given a normally distributed population with a mean of 95 and a standard deviation of 10 what is the probability of obtaining a score in the range 115–125?*

A: First, we convert the range of raw scores into its z-score equivalent. In this case, one unit of z-score = 10 raw score units, so a raw score of 115 (20 raw score units above the mean) will be 2 z-scores above the mean and a raw score of 125 will be exactly 3 z-scores above the mean. From table 2 in appendix 4, the area under the curve located between 2 and 3 z-scores above the mean is $0.4987 - 0.4772 = 2.15\%$ of the total area. Note that here we are working with two areas and subtract the smaller one from the larger to find the difference. Thus, the probability associated with scores located between 2 and 3 z-scores above the mean (i.e. raw scores in the range 115–125 taken from a population with the given mean and standard deviation) is found to be $p = 0.0215$, or a little over one chance in 50 (figure 8.8).

   The technique of translating backwards and forwards between z-scores and raw scores allows the table of areas under the curve to be used to answer a variety of questions as long as the distribution is known or believed to be normal and (crucially) the relevant parameters are known. For example, one can also find the probability associated with any specific range of raw scores and also the probability of obtaining values greater than or less than a specific raw score value. Some exercises using these techniques are provided at the end of the chapter.

● PARAMETER ESTIMATION ●

Introduction

The need to know the population mean and standard deviation might seem to limit the usefulness of the standard normal distribution because they are almost never available. However, there is a way around this problem because these, and other, parameters can, under certain

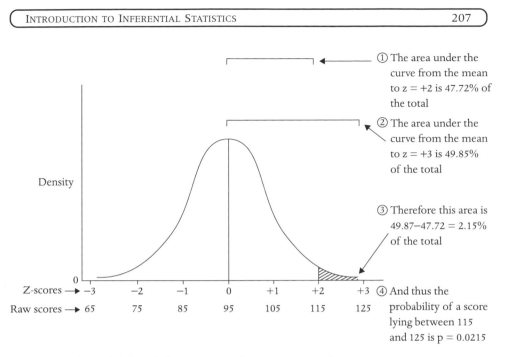

Figure 8.8 The probability of obtaining scores between z = +2 and z = +3

circumstances, be estimated with a degree of confidence. Parameter estimation is the essential technique that allows inferences about population parameters to be constructed from the data in a single sample. From the point of view of the experimenter this is a particularly useful application. Data analysis in psychology frequently involves comparing sets of data that are suspected of having come from different populations, and the principles that underlie parameter estimation are fundamental to this type of inquiry.

Point estimates and their limitations

One might think that, providing a procedure has been rigorously applied to produce a sample that is as representative as possible of the population, any statistic (such as the mean of a sample) should have the same value as its corresponding parameter computed from the whole population. In other words, it is plausible to assume that a point estimate, consisting of a single value will be as close as needed to its corresponding population parameter. In fact, point estimates are a poor guide to parameter values. Not only is it impossible for *any* sampling procedure, no matter how carefully applied, to provide data that lead to accurate estimates but it is also impossible to say how *inaccurate* a point estimate may be – how far it diverges from the true value of the parameter.

Sampling error

This difference is known as sampling error, and it represents the effects of chance within the sampling process (i.e. choosing one individual data item for inclusion rather than another)

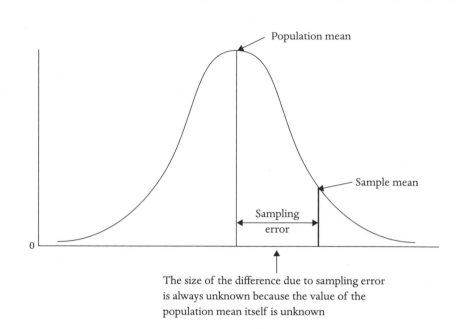

The size of the difference due to sampling error
is always unknown because the value of the
population mean itself is unknown

Figure 8.9   A point estimate of a population mean showing the difference due to sampling error

Sampling error: The
variation, due to chance,
in the value of a statistic
in relation to the
parameter that it
estimates.

on the composition of a sample as a whole. Its effect is to make it
virtually certain that any statistic will deviate from its 'true' parameter value even if the most rigorous and unbiased procedure for
random sampling is applied. In fact, if the population being
sampled is large the probability of any statistic exactly hitting the
value of its corresponding parameter is so small that an infinite
number of samples would be needed to be sure of making the hit
even once (see figure 8.9).

Interval estimation

The better alternative to point estimation is interval estimation. This is slightly more complicated conceptually, but provides a much more reliable way of reasoning from sample statistics to population parameters.

The basic idea is straightforward. Interval estimation makes use of the characteristics of
the normal distribution to generate an estimate of a parameter (such as the population mean)
from the information in a single sample. This estimate takes the form of a range of *possible*
values for the parameter (called the confidence interval) that extend between upper and lower
confidence limits. Attached to this interval is, crucially, a confidence level, expressed either as
a percentage or as a confidence coefficient, that indicates the likelihood that the interval
actually contains the parameter in question. It is essential to include the confidence
level. Interval estimation uses only the information that is available from a sample that
(as we have seen) always contains an unknown proportion of sampling error. The problem

is not so much that the error exists, but that the size of its contribution to a parameter estimate cannot be precisely known. The advantage offered by interval estimation is that it allows the uncertainty to be quantified. We now consider how this important and useful estimate can be generated.

Key concepts in interval estimation

Sampling distributions

The sampling distribution of a statistic is the distribution that would be obtained empirically if a very large number of random samples were drawn from the same population, and a statistic (such as the mean or standard deviation) were computed from each sample. In what follows we concentrate on the sampling distribution of the mean, whose characteristics are defined by a Central Limit Theorem (see figure 8.10).

Standard error

Like all distributions, sampling distributions have both a mean and a standard deviation – standard error is the usual term for the latter quantity. As we shall see, the sampling distribution of the mean can be modelled by the standard normal distribution, so the standard error of the mean translates into standard units of deviation about the mean (called standard variates), in exactly the same way as the standard deviation of the raw scores in a sample translates into z-scores.

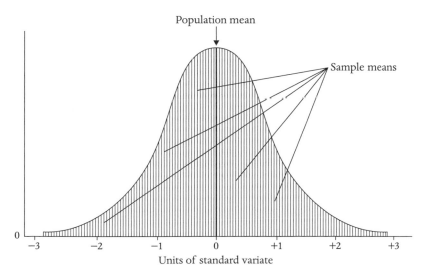

Figure 8.10 The sampling distribution of the mean from a normally distributed population
A sampling distribution of the mean is made up of very many individual sample means, some of which are shown above. One sample mean is equal to the population mean and all others differ from it due to sampling error.

A central limit theorem

The theory behind interval estimation of a population mean is provided by a Central Limit Theorem (there are a number of them). The important conclusions that follow from this theorem are,

1   The mean of the sampling distribution of the mean is equal to the population mean from which the samples were taken ($\mu = \mu_{\bar{x}}$).

2   The standard error of the mean is equal to the population standard deviation divided by the square root of the sample size.

3   If the population distribution is normal and the samples are random samples, then the sampling distribution of the mean will also be normal. *This will always be true no matter what the size of the samples* (see figure 8.10).

4   Even if non-normal, as long as the population distribution is symmetrical (and especially if it is unimodal), then even moderately sized random samples (of, say, N = 30), will still produce a sampling distribution of the mean that is a good approximation to normal. And, if large random samples are taken (of size greater than N = 30), the sampling distribution of the mean will closely approximate to normal *even if the underlying population distribution is highly skewed*.

The formula for standard error of the mean is,

$$\sigma_{\bar{x}} = \frac{\sigma}{\sqrt{N}}$$

μ is the symbol for a population mean
σ is the symbol for a population standard deviation
$\sigma_{\bar{x}}$ is the symbol for the standard error of the mean
N is the symbol for the number of observations in the sample.

To summarize, providing that samples are random and due attention is paid to sample size the central limit theorem makes virtually certain that the sampling distribution of the mean is either normal, or sufficiently close to it, whatever the shape of the population distribution may be. The overall effect is therefore to provide a straightforward way of reasoning about a population mean on the basis of a single set of sample data by applying the characteristics of the normal distribution.

In the following sections the procedure and reasoning involved in the hand computation of an estimate of a population mean are reviewed, since this is the parameter that is most frequently required. The SPSS procedures for generating the same estimate can be found below.

Estimating the population mean when the population deviation is known

Suppose that we wish to estimate the 95% confidence interval of the population mean for a variable on a rare occasion when σ, the population deviation, is known.

Sample size: N = 50
Sample mean: $\bar{X} = 19.67$
Sample standard deviation: s = 9.8
Standard error (population standard deviation): $\sigma = 7.6$

In this case the distribution of the variable in the population is assumed to be normal. Therefore, the sampling distribution of the mean is also normal in this example (from point 3 above), and is centred on the true population mean (from point 1).

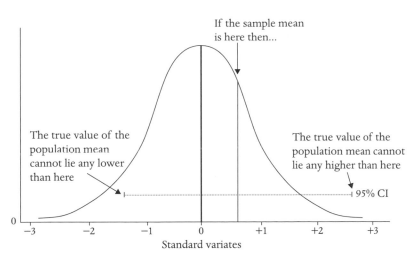

Figure 8.11   Reasoning about a population mean from a single sample mean using a 95% confidence interval (CI)

The procedure is to first obtain a good estimate of the standard error of the mean from the known value of σ from the formula above. This makes it possible to assign values to the units on the X axis of the sampling distribution of the mean (the standard variates), and then to use the table of areas under the normal curve to determine the range of values for μ (remembering that the normal curve represents the sampling distribution of the mean). Thus:

$$\sigma_{\bar{x}} = \frac{\sigma}{\sqrt{N}}$$

$$= \frac{7.6}{\sqrt{50}}$$

$$= \frac{7.6}{7.07}$$

$$= 1.07$$

Next, identify the confidence limits associated with the 95% confidence level, as follows.

The table of areas under the normal curve shows that 95% of the area under the sampling distribution curve is located between $\mu \pm z = 1.96$. To determine how many raw score units lie above and below the population mean we multiply the standard error estimate of 1.07 by the value of the standard variate, 1.96 (the equivalent of z-score), that marks the boundary of the desired area. The 95% confidence limits therefore lie at $1.96 \times 1.07 = 2.10$ raw score units above and below the true population mean (see figure 8.11).

However, the true value of the population mean is unknown so, in the final step, we are forced to reason on the basis of the sample mean itself, which in this example has the value 19.67. The argument goes as follows.

If the sample mean were to be located exactly 1.96 units of standard variate (SV) *below* the population mean then the population mean cannot be higher than 1.96 units of SV *above* that point (it could be something less). The value of the population mean therefore cannot

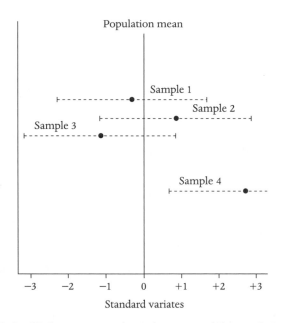

Figure 8.12 The relationship between several sample means and the population mean
The dotted lines represent the extent of the 95% confidence interval for each sample. Samples 1–3 have different means and generate different confidence intervals, but each includes the value of the true population mean. Sample 4, by comparison, generates a confidence interval that does not include its population mean.

be *greater* than the sample mean plus 1.96 units of SV or $19.67 + 2.1 = 21.77$ raw score units. By the same reasoning the *lowest* the population mean can be is 1.96 SV units below the sample mean or $19.67 - 2.1 = 17.57$ raw score units.

Thus, the limits of the 95% confidence interval for the estimate of the population mean obtained from this sample are established as 17.57 to 21.77 raw score units.

The correct interpretation of this result is that, given repeated sampling from the population, 95% of the samples will generate an interval that contains the true value of the population mean, although each one will also generate a *different* interval, as in figure 8.12.

(A less accurate, but frequently used, way of expressing this idea is to say that the 95% confidence interval is that range of values which we can be 95% certain will contain the population mean.)

The confidence level of a parameter estimate is that proportion of repeated samples from the population that generate estimates containing the true value of the parameter in question.

It follows that the interval of 17.57 to 21.77 may or may not be one of the 95% that contains the true population mean. While the likelihood is very high that it is, there is also the possibility that it is one of the 5% that do not, and it is impossible to know for certain one way or the other.

One way of coping with this is to increase the confidence level from 95% to (say) 99%, thereby making it more likely that the estimate contains the true value of the parameter. However, that likelihood is linked to the size of the confidence interval. As the confidence level increases the size of the confidence inter-

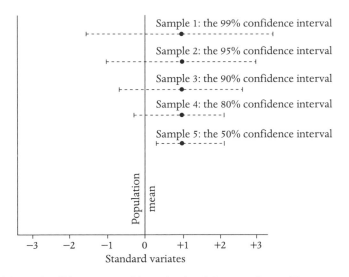

Figure 8.13   The trade-off between confidence level and the size of a confidence interval
Five samples having identical means with different confidence intervals calculated for each. Note that
the most precise CI does not include the population mean.

val estimate widens (see figure 8.13). This is the reason one speaks of 'the 95% confidence
interval', because the interval of the parameter estimate is almost invariably determined by
selecting a confidence level rather than the other way round. In general, users of statistics
will prefer high confidence levels (typically set at 95% or 99%), that deliver near-certainty that
the true value of a parameter lies within the estimate rather than the alternative of dealing
with more precise, but less likely, estimates.

Confidence level and significance level

The confidence level – the degree of certainty attached to an estimate of a population parameter – is closely related to the concept of significance level, symbol α. The level of significance in this case represents the proportion of parameter estimates generated from repeated
sampling that will *not* contain the true value of the parameter. Thus a confidence level of
95% implies a significance level (α) of 5%. The relationship can be expressed as, confidence
level = $1 - \alpha$.

Estimating the population mean when the population deviation is unknown

As it is very unlikely that the value of the population standard deviation is known, an
approach must usually be taken that differs in two respects from that shown earlier. First, in
the absence of definite information, it is necessary to estimate σ, the population standard
deviation. Fortunately, this is straightforward because it can be shown that the standard
deviation of a sample, **s**, provides an *unbiased estimate* of σ, and we can therefore use the
formula given earlier, slightly modified, to estimate the standard error of the mean. Thus,

The unbiased estimate is the property possessed by a statistic (e.g. sample mean) when it can be shown that its *expected value* (the mean of the statistic computed from a very large number of samples) is equal to its corresponding parameter.

Degrees of freedom: the number of data items in a sample that are free to vary while values such as the sum and mean remain unchanged.

$$\sigma_{\bar{X}} = \frac{s}{\sqrt{N}}$$

The second difference is that we use the t-distribution rather than the standard normal distribution to arrive at the interval estimate for the population mean. The reason, as Howell (1997) shows, is that **s** is always likely to over-estimate σ, especially when samples are small (N < 20), and the t-distribution corrects for this. The t-distribution is approximately normal, with a mean of 0, but with the X axis calibrated in t-scores rather than z-scores. The exact shape of the t-distribution varies with N-1, the number of degrees of freedom, so the number of t-scores lying within the distribution also varies with sample size. Apart from these two points, the reasoning is exactly the same as when the standard deviation of the population is known. The following example shows the process.

Suppose a random sample of

Sample size: N = 45
Sample mean: $\bar{X}$ = 83.6
Sample standard deviation: s = 14.2

has been obtained from a population of unknown characteristics and we wish to estimate the population mean for the 99% confidence interval. Given a sample of this size we can assume that the sampling distribution of the mean approaches normal.

First, estimate the standard error of the mean. Note again that this uses the sample deviation **s** instead of the population deviation σ:

$$\sigma_{\bar{X}} = \frac{s}{\sqrt{N}}$$

$$\sigma_{\bar{X}} = \frac{14.2}{\sqrt{45}}$$

$$= 2.12$$

The table of critical values of t (table 9 in appendix 4) gives one- and two-tailed values for t for the p = 0.05 and p = 0.01 significance levels for a range of degrees of freedom.

The 2-tailed t-value is always required because a confidence interval is symmetrical about the population mean, leaving equal proportions remaining in the tails of the sampling distribution. You will also recall that confidence level = (1 − α). As we wish to find the 99% confidence interval we therefore use the significance level of α = 0.01 with N-1 degrees of freedom.

Consulting appendix table 9 for α = 0.01 (two-tailed) with N-1 = 44 degrees of freedom we find the value of t for exactly the required number of degrees of freedom is not available, so it is necessary to take the closest available, namely df = 40, finding t = 2.704. To obtain the 99% confidence interval for the population mean we now multiply this t-value by the estimate for the standard error, thus,

$$t = 2.704$$
$$\sigma_{\bar{X}} = 2.12$$
$$2.704 \times 2.12 = 5.73$$

and add and subtract this result from the sample mean. The sample mean is 83.6 so the upper limit of the 99% confidence interval is $83.6 + 5.73 = 89.33$ raw score units, and the lower limit is 83.6 minus $5.73 = 77.87$ raw score units. We conclude that the true value of the population mean is highly likely to lie within this interval since only 1% of repeated samples from the population can be expected not to contain this parameter.

Beyond the sampling distribution of the mean

The same basic procedure is used to obtain estimates of other population parameters such as the population standard deviation, but these require the use of other distributions such as the χ^2 to determine the estimated values. If you need to estimate these parameters consult an advanced text such as Howell (1997).

Parameter estimation in SPSS

An estimate of the population mean for any desired confidence level together with the standard error estimate on which it was based can be obtained, once data have been entered, by following

ANALYZE > Descriptive Statistics > Explore
In the **Explore** dialogue box
    Click on the name of the variable to highlight
    Click on the top arrow button to move it to the **Dependent** box [**v. 13: Dependent List**]
    Click on the **Statistics** button
In the **Explore: Statistics** dialogue box
    Click to tick **Descriptives**
    Set the desired confidence level (e.g. 95%) in the box **Confidence Interval for Mean**
    Click **Continue**
    Click **OK**.

The program shows upper and lower bound parameter values for the desired confidence level, as in table 8.1.
    Alternatively, to see the t-value on which the estimate is based use

ANALYZE > General Linear Model > Univariate
    In the **Univariate** dialogue box
    Click on the name of the variable to highlight
    Click on the arrow button to move it to the **Dependent Variable** box
    Click on **Options**
    Click to tick **Parameter estimates**
    (Changing the **Significance level shown** at the foot of this dialogue box will change the
        Confidence Interval; $p = 0.05$ gives a confidence level of 95%; $p = 0.01$ a confidence
        level of 99%.)

Table 8.1 SPSS output showing the upper and lower bounds of the 90% confidence interval for the mean

Descriptives			Statistic	Std error
VAR00001	Mean	Lower bound	44.1707	2.79130
	90% Confidence	Upper bound	39.4706	
	Interval for mean		48.8709	
	5% Trimmed mean		44.3767	
	Median		45.0000	
	Variance		319.445	
	Std deviation		17.87303	
	Minimum		3.00	
	Maximum		76.0	
	Range		73.0	
	Interquartile range		21.5000	
	Skewness		−.080	.369
	Kurtosis		−.276	.724

Table 8.2 SPSS output showing upper and lower bound estimates and t-value

Parameter estimates

Dependent variable: VAR00001

Parameter	B	Std error	t	Sia	95% Confidence interval	
					Lower bound	Upper bound
Intercept	44.171	2.791	15.824	.000	38.529	49.812

The sample mean is the value in column B.

Click on **Continue**
Click on **OK.**

The resulting output (table 8.2) gives upper and lower bound parameter values for the desired confidence level, the t-value employed, and the estimate of standard error. The sample mean is the value in the column labelled B.

To obtain the standard error estimate alone,

ANALYZE > Descriptive Statistics > Descriptives
In the **Descriptives** dialogue box
    Click on the name of the variable to highlight
    Click on the arrow button to move it to the **Variable(s)** box
    Click on the **Options** button
In the **Descriptives:Options** dialogue box
    Click to tick **SE Mean**
    Click on **Continue**
    Click on **OK**
The output is as shown in table 8.3.

Table 8.3 SPSS output showing the standard error estimate

Descriptive statistics

	N Statistic	Mean Statistic	Std error	Std deviation Statistic
VAR2	40	42.6000	2.1097	13.34320
Valid N (listwise)	40			

● HYPOTHESIS TESTING ●

A further important application of inferential techniques is the testing of statistical hypotheses, where typically one wishes to assess the likelihood that different sets of data could have been taken from different populations. Hypothesis testing for this purpose takes place within a precise framework of concepts, consisting of:

- The statistical hypotheses, null and alternate
- The sampling distribution of the test statistic
- The critical value and the region of rejection on the sampling distribution of the test statistic
- The significance level (α).

Statistical hypotheses

In every test of data a pair of statistical hypotheses is used to limit the decision to two, mutually exclusive, possibilities expressed as statements, called the null and alternate hypotheses. These are so designed that each excludes the possibility that the other could be true. The role of the test is to provide the basis for a reasoned decision about which of the two should be retained as probably correct, and which should be rejected.

Null hypothesis

The null hypothesis (symbol H_0) is generally a hypothesis of nil difference applied to one or more populations. (The exception in this book is that required for the sign test.)

Thus, the null hypothesis required when a 2 (or more) samples test is planned, asserts that, whatever the observed difference between them, the samples came from the same population. For example, if a t-test is to be used, then the specific form of the null hypothesis says that the samples came from populations with equal means: in effect, from the same population. (The variety of null hypothesis appropriate to each test will be found in chapter 9.)

The null hypothesis plays a crucial role in statistical testing. In general, the sampling distribution of a test statistic (see below) is established on the assumption that the null

---

BOX 8.3   Directional and non-directional alternate hypotheses – which to choose?

In most research an expected outcome is often understood, implied either by the theory being tested, or by simple common sense. Statistical purists tend to prefer the directional alternate hypothesis, arguing that the non-directional version should be reserved for those (perhaps rare), occasions when there is *genuine* uncertainty about the outcome of the investigation.

However, some (e.g. Howell, 1997) think this approach is excessively scrupulous, not least because it is harder to find the evidence needed to accept a non-directional hypothesis compared to a directional one. Consequently, the null hypothesis may be retained under circumstances where the opposite decision could be justified.

One solution to this disagreement, that also maintains the integrity of the decision procedure, is to ensure that the alternate hypothesis is specified before data are collected. Then, whatever expectation may be held of the result, the possibility that the appearance of the data could have influenced the choice of alternate hypothesis has been prevented.

---

hypothesis is correct. All testing of data therefore starts from the position that it will be retained (note the terminology), unless there is strong contrary empirical evidence, and for this reason statistical hypothesis testing essentially means testing the null hypothesis.

Alternate hypothesis

The alternate hypothesis (symbol H_1) takes the directly contradictory position to the null hypothesis: that a difference *is* expected in relation to the population(s) sampled. In a 2-sample comparison, for example, the alternate hypothesis says that the samples *were* drawn from different populations which, in experimental research, is generally attributed to the effect of the different treatments.

The assertion of difference may be either *non-directional* (simply that a difference exists with no prediction about its direction), or *directional*, if it specifies which sample is expected to contain the higher values of the variable of interest (box 8.3).

Test statistics and their sampling distributions

Once data have been collected they are fed into the computation of a test statistic and a value of that statistic, *for those data*, is produced. That result is required in the decision on whether to retain or reject the null hypothesis and for this its location on the sampling distribution of the statistic must be considered (see box 8.4).

Most test statistics generate a family of theoretical sampling distributions – one for each possible degree of freedom (or sample size). Each of these distributions represents all poss-

---

BOX 8.4   A summary of the decision sequence

1   Compute a value for the test statistic from data and compare it with the critical value on the appropriate table.
2   The critical value represents that value on the sampling distribution of the null hypothesis that has an associated probability equal to the significance level.
3   Therefore, if the computed value is more extreme than the table value (and the data match the direction of difference stated in the alternate hypothesis), then the probability of obtaining that value *when the null hypothesis is correct* is no greater than the significance level. The null hypothesis can therefore be rejected.

---

ible values of the statistic for the given number of degrees of freedom *when the null hypothesis is true*. Since these tend to be normal or near normal in form it follows that it is possible to use the characteristics of the normal distribution in order to assign a probability to the obtained value of the test statistic. The decision about the null hypothesis therefore turns on the question,

Does this computed value of the test statistic lie in a region of the sampling distribution that indicates that it has a low probability of occurrence?

Or, more formally,

Is this computed value of the test statistic, for this number of degrees of freedom, so extreme that it would be unlikely to occur when the null hypothesis is true?

If the answer is affirmative, the null hypothesis is in line to be rejected. Before that can happen, however, it is necessary to have a definition of what is meant by 'extreme' in this case. This function is performed by the significance level of the test. This identifies a point of demarcation on the sampling distribution that separates the (low) probabilities that require an affirmative answer from the remainder.

Significance level

The significance level of a test (α) is a (low) level of probability selected by the researcher before the test is computed. Its purpose is to mark the point on the sampling distribution that separates those values of the test statistic that are to be regarded as 'unlikely' (at the chosen level of probability) from the others. On one side lie those values that are *more* likely than the significance level when the null hypothesis is true and on the other lie those that are less likely. The convention in psychology is to use the $\alpha = 0.05$ or $\alpha = 0.01$ levels of significance and to reject the null hypothesis when the computed value of the test statistic has an associated probability equal to, or below, those values so that it lies in the 'region of rejection' on the distribution.

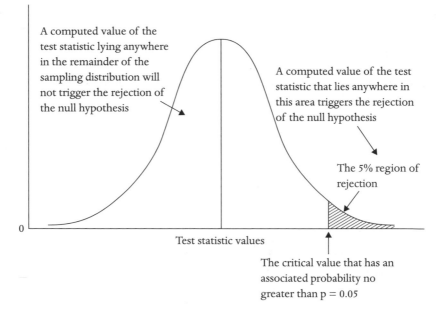

A computed value of the test statistic lying anywhere in the remainder of the sampling distribution will not trigger the rejection of the null hypothesis

A computed value of the test statistic that lies anywhere in this area triggers the rejection of the null hypothesis

The 5% region of rejection

Test statistic values

The critical value that has an associated probability no greater than p = 0.05

Figure 8.14   The sampling distribution of a test statistic showing the one-tailed region of rejection and critical value for $\alpha = 0.05$

The region of rejection

The region of rejection lies at the extreme end(s) of the sampling distribution of the test statistic and contains all those values whose probability of occurrence is equal to, or lower than, the significance level. It gets its name from the fact that any computed value of the test statistic lying in that area will trigger the rejection of the null hypothesis. Thus the 5% region of rejection of a sampling distribution is indicated by a significance level of $\alpha = 0.05$ and is that part that contains the *most extreme* 5% of the values of the sampled statistic.

Critical value of the test statistic

The role of the 'critical value' is to provide a convenient way of deciding where a computed value of a test statistic lies on its sampling distribution. The critical value of a test statistic is the value that lies exactly on that point of the sampling distribution that is identified by the significance level. A straightforward comparison with a computed value is therefore enough to determine whether the latter lies in the region of rejection, or not. Tables of critical values for each statistic, for the usual significance levels and a range of degrees of freedom, can be found in appendix 4.

The relationship between significance level, region of rejection and critical value of the sampling distribution is shown in figures 8.14 and 8.15. Figure 8.14 shows how a sampling distribution is used to support a decision when the alternate hypothesis is directional. If the

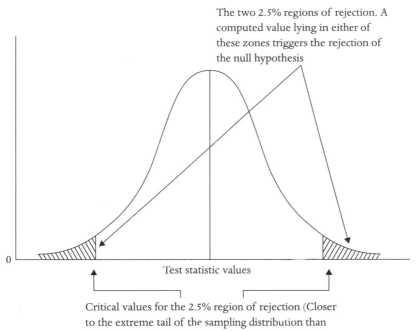

The two 2.5% regions of rejection. A computed value lying in either of these zones triggers the rejection of the null hypothesis

Test statistic values

Critical values for the 2.5% region of rejection (Closer to the extreme tail of the sampling distribution than the critical value for the 5% region of rejection)

Figure 8.15   The sampling distribution of a test statistic showing the two-tailed regions of rejection and critical values for $\alpha = 0.05$
Because the computed value cannot lie in both regions of rejection, the two-tailed test is less liberal than a one-tailed test at any significance level.

computed value of the statistic is more extreme than the critical value (and thus has an associated probability below the significance level), the null hypothesis can be rejected.

Figure 8.15 shows how the same decision is made for a non-directional hypothesis. In this case, the region of rejection is divided between the two extremes of the sampling distribution of the test statistic. For an $\alpha = 0.05$ this means 0.025 of the area of the whole distribution at each end and the critical value that marks the cut-off is therefore correspondingly reduced.

Note that the rejection of a null hypothesis does not mean that it has been shown to be incorrect. Although the greater probability (95% or more for a $\alpha = 0.05$ significance level), is that it *is* incorrect, there always remains the small probability (at equal to or less than the significance level), that it *is* correct *despite having been rejected*. This draws our attention to the ever-present possibility of decision errors.

Depending on whether the alternate hypothesis is directional or not, the region of rejection can lie either at one end or both ends of a distribution. If the former, the test is called a one-tailed test, and if the latter, a two-tailed test.

Table 8.4   Decisions about the null hypothesis

Decision	The true situation	
	H_0 True	H_0 False
Reject H_0	Type 1 error	Correct decision
	$p = \alpha$	$p = 1 - \beta$ = Power
Retain H_0	Correct decision	Type 2 error
	$p = 1 - \alpha$	$p = \beta$

Decision errors in hypothesis testing

The type 1 (or α) error

The type 1 ('false positive') error is made when the null hypothesis is rejected when in fact it should really have been retained. As we saw above, the probability of making this error is set by the significance level. This type of decision error occurs when sampling and/or measurement error causes the computed value of the test statistic to fall in the rejection region of the sampling distribution.

The type 2 (or β) error

A type 2 ('false negative') error is made when the null hypothesis is retained when it should not have been, again because of sampling and/or measurement error that causes the value of the test statistic to lie *outside* the region of rejection. β has some value greater than the probability of making a type 1 error that increases as the significance level becomes smaller.

Table 8.4 shows the two correct and two erroneous decisions that can be made about the null hypothesis.

It is impossible to avoid making both type 1 and type 2 errors, so the usual strategy is to set the probability of a type 1 error to an acceptable level (via the significance level), having previously checked that the sample size gives sufficient power (see below) to ensure that the probability of making a type 2 error is also as low as possible.

Test power ($1 - \beta$)

The power of a test is defined as the probability that it will lead to the correct rejection of the null hypothesis. This represents a measure of the test's ability to perform the task for which it was designed, given appropriate data. Some tests – the parametric tests – are based on statistical models that define the situations for which they were designed in some detail and are more powerful (i.e. approach more closely the theoretical value of $1 - \beta$) than their non-parametric equivalents, as long as the assumptions in the model are satisfied. Power is clearly a desirable characteristic of a test and box 8.5 suggests some ways in which test power can be increased.

BOX 8.5   Strategies for maximizing the power of a test

1   Increase sample size by as much as possible. This increases the probability of a correct rejection of the null hypothesis. Howell (1997) provides a detailed discussion of this, and other aspects of test power.

2   Reduce the variability in the samples by removing (as far as possible) all sources of error variance from the design, sampling and measurement. The greater the number of independent levels of a variable in an experiment the higher the variability of the data and the lower the power of the test. Therefore, consider using a matched subjects design and ensure that research participants generate scores under identical conditions.

3   Use a directional hypothesis instead of a non-directional one.

4   Consider increasing the significance level from (say) $\alpha = 0.05$ to 0.1 providing this does not increase the probability of making a type 1 error to an unacceptable degree.

EXTENSION ACTIVITIES

(Unless otherwise stated, assume that data have been obtained by random sampling.)

Activity 1

1   In a standard normal distribution find the proportion of the total area under the curve that lies between the mean and a z-score of

   (a) 0.66   (b) 2.89   (c) 1.92   (d) 3.0

2   What proportion of the area under the curve will lie between the following z-score values?

   (a) −1.7 and +1.7   (b) −0.5 and +2.6   (c) −1.4 and + 2.6

3   What z-score value indicates the upper boundary of the area above the mean that makes up 16.64% of the total area under the curve?

4   What z-score value lies at the upper boundary of an area above the mean which makes up 45% of the total?

5   Suppose we have a normally distributed population with a mean of 100 and a standard deviation of exactly 15.0. What is the probability of obtaining a score greater than 123?

6   Suppose the raw score in Q. 5 came from a different population with a mean of 110 and a standard deviation of 12.5. What is the effect on the probability of obtaining a score greater than 123?

Continued

7   Given a population with a mean of 90 and a standard deviation of 8, what is the probability of obtaining a score smaller than 75?

8   Given a population with a mean of 112 and a standard deviation of 9 what is the probability of obtaining a score between 115 and 125?

9   Given a population with a mean of 150 and a standard deviation of 12.5, which raw scores have a probability of occurrence below $p = 0.05$? Below $p = 0.01$?

Answers to Activity 1

1   (a) 24.54%   (b) 49.81%   (c) 47.26%   (d) 49.87%

2   (a) 91.08% (2×45.54)   (b) 68.68% ($19.15 + 49.53$)   (c) 91.45% ($41.92 + 49.53$)

3   $z = +0.43$

4   $z = +1.645$

5   A score of 123 is equal to $23/15$ units of z-score above the mean, so $z = 1.53$. The area underneath the curve between the mean and $z = 1.53$ is 43.70% of the total area. As the question concerns a raw score *greater* than 123 the area *above* the z-score point must be found by subtracting 43.70 from 50.0% = 6.3 %. Therefore, the probability of obtaining a score greater than 123 is $p = 0.063$.

6   The reasoning is the same. A score of 123 is equal to $13/12.5$ units of z-score above the mean, so $z = 1.04$. The area underneath the curve between the mean and $z = 1.04$ is 35.08% of the total area and so the area above a z-score of $z = 1.04$ is $50 - 35.08 = 14.92\%$. In this case, the probability of obtaining a score greater than 123 is $p = 0.1492$.

7   This is basically the same question as number 6. The answer in this case is $p = 0.0307$.

8   The z-score equivalents of the raw scores 115 and 125 are, respectively, $3/9$ or $z = 0.33$ and $14/9$ or $z = 1.44$. The area between the mean and $z = 0.33$ is 12.93% and between the mean and $z = 1.44$, 42.51%. The difference between these two areas is the area between the z-scores, $42.51 - 12.93 = 29.58\%$ and the probability of obtaining a score in the range 115 to 125 is $p = 0.2958$.

9   Raw scores of very low probabilities of occurrence are to be found at the extreme ends of the distribution. Those with a probability of $p = 0.05$ or below lie in the very bottom 2.5% and the very top 2.5% of the area under the curve (leaving 47.5% of the total area remaining in each half). The z-score that indicates the boundary of each of these small areas in each half of the distribution is found by locating the area of 47.5% in the body of the table and then reading back to get $z = 1.96$. The raw score equivalents of this z-score above the mean is $150 + (1.96 \times 12.5) = 174.5$ and below the mean $150 - (1.96 \times 12.5) = 125.5$. Scores more extreme than these have a probability of occurrence that is no greater than $p = 0.05$.

The same process is applied to find the raw score values that lie outside 99% of the area under the curve, having a probability of occurrence of $p = 0.01$ or less. The answer here is 182.19 and 117.83.

Table 8.5 Apparent difference between the length of horizontals in a Muller–Lyer figure (mm), N = 40

11.0	5.5	0	3.0	7.0	2.5	9.0	4.0	10.0	12.0
7.0	4.0	2.0	1.0	4.0	6.0	8.5	8.0	5.0	3.5
1.0	9.5	2.0	4.0	6.5	12.5	5.0	7.0	3.5	9.0
2.5	8.0	1.0	4.0	7.0	0	4.5	8.0	4.0	6.5

Table 8.6 Upper and lower bounds of a confidence interval for a range of confidence levels

Confidence level	α	Lower bound of CI	Upper bound of CI
0.99			
0.95			
0.90			
0.80			
0.75			
0.50			

Activity 2

1   A random sample of N = 50 scores on a memory test is found to have a mean of 24.2 items with a standard deviation of 5.67. Obtain an estimate of the 95% confidence interval for the population mean, μ.

2   A second random sample, also of size N = 50 and from the same population gives new values for the mean and standard deviation statistics of 26.13 and 4.87 respectively. How does the estimate of the population mean change?

3   A sample of N = 20 intelligence test scores from a population that is assumed to be normally distributed has a mean of 96.42 and a standard deviation of 12.2. Obtain an estimate of the 99% confidence interval for the population mean, μ. Write out in full the precise meaning of the interval you have obtained.

4   Assume that the scores in the dataset in table 8.5 have been obtained by random sampling and, using SPSS, complete table 8.6

5   Given an estimate for a population mean of 90 − 112 units at the 99% confidence level, based on random samplings of size N = 50, which of the following statements is *not* true?

- 99% of the population lies within the given range.
- There is a 99% probability (p = 0.99) that the estimate is correct.
- There is a 99% probability (p = 0.99) that the estimate contains the true value of the population mean.
- 99% of random samples from this population generate estimates that place the population mean within the specified limits.
- The true value of the population mean will lie in the given range 99% of the time.

Continued

- The probability that the true value of the population mean does NOT lie within the given range is p = 0.01.
- 1% of random samples from this population will return estimates of the population mean that lie outside the specified limits.

Answers

1   The sample locates the lower bound of the 95% confidence interval for the population mean of memory test scores at 22.59 and the upper bound at 25.81 items.
2   The second sample locates the lower bound of the 95% confidence interval for the population mean of memory test scores at 24.74 and the upper bound at 27.52 items.
3   From this sample, the 99% confidence interval for the population mean of scores stretches from 88.64 to 104.2 units. This means that given a very large number of random samples from this population 99% of them will generate a confidence interval that includes the true value of the population mean.
5   The correct answers are (d) and (g).

Chapter Summary

1   Inferential statistics are techniques that allow conclusions to be drawn about populations from samples of data, using probability theory to express the likelihood of particular outcomes.
2   The normal distribution is a theoretical population distribution whose graph is a symmetrical bell shape among whose properties are that the mean = median = mode, and the X axis is asymptotic. The standardized normal distribution has a mean of zero and standard deviation expressed in units of z-score, allowing any normally distributed populations with different parameter values to be easily compared.
3   As long as the appropriate parameters are known, or can be estimated, the SND allows the characteristics of the normal distribution to be used to find the probability that any given range of scores will be obtained by random sampling from the population.
4   Parameter estimation is the process that uses the information in a sample in order to say something about the population from which it was taken. Point estimates of parameters are unreliable due to the presence of sampling error that cannot be quantified. Interval estimates, however, offer a better approach. These express a parameter as a range of possible values (the confidence interval), attached to a statement (the confidence level) that specifies the proportion of samples that, under repeated sampling, will generate an estimate containing the true value of the parameter.
5   The confidence limits of a parameter estimate are set by the choice of confidence level. The larger the confidence level selected the greater the width of the interval, and therefore the greater the certainty that it contains the true value of the parameter. The significance level (1- confidence level) conversely indicates the degree of uncertainty attached to an estimate.
6   Parameter estimation depends crucially on a central limit theorem. This states that given large (N > 30) random samples, the sampling distribution of the mean is always close

to normal whatever the shape of the population distribution. This allows the standard normal distribution, or the t-distribution, to be used to identify the confidence interval at the chosen confidence level.

7   Decision-making about quantitative data proceeds by the testing of statistical hypotheses – the null and alternate – within a clear framework. This framework is composed of four key elements in addition to the hypotheses themselves – the sampling distribution of the test statistic, its region of rejection, the significance level (alpha), and the appropriate critical value of the test statistic.

8   The null hypothesis forms the base assumption of all test statistics, and is a hypothesis on nil difference relating to one or more populations, such as a nil difference between the values of some parameter. The alternate hypothesis represents the logically opposite statement.

9   Testing a null hypothesis involves locating a computed value of a test statistic on its sampling distribution. If it lies within a predetermined region of rejection, where it would be unlikely to have occurred when the null hypothesis is correct, then the null hypothesis may be rejected. The probability level that identifies the region of rejection on the sampling distribution is known as the significance level (α).

10 The critical value of a statistic is that value on the sampling distribution that has an associated probability equal to the significance level. Because each test statistic generates a different sampling distribution for each sample size, tables of critical values allow a computed value to be located in relation to a region of rejection.

11 All decisions on hypotheses are subject to error. The most important kind of error, designated type 1, occurs because the region of rejection contains values that are still possible (though unlikely) when the null hypothesis is true. Therefore, there always remains a small probability (which is the same as the significance level), that the null hypothesis will be incorrectly rejected.

● FURTHER READING ●

Frank, H and Althoen, S. C. (1994). *Statistics: Concepts and applications.* Cambridge: Cambridge University Press.

Howell, D. C. (1997). *Statistical methods for psychology,* 4th edn. Belmont, CA: Duxbury Press.

Howell, D. C. (1995). *Fundamental statistics for the behavioural sciences,* 3rd edn. Belmont, CA: Duxbury Press.

9

TEST STATISTICS

CHAPTER MAP

Test Selection

The statistical model
    Parametric tests
    Non-parametric tests
Robustness of a test

Test Statistics

One-sample tests
    Chi-square test for goodness of fit
Two-sample tests
    Sign test
    Multi-dimensional Chi-square test
    Wilcoxon test
    Mann–Whitney U-test
    Independent and related t-tests
More-than-two-sample tests
    One-factor ANOVA for independent samples
    One-factor ANOVA for matched samples
Tests of non-causal relations between two samples
    Spearman's rank order coefficient
    Pearson's product moment coefficient

THIS CHAPTER

- *Contains information about procedures for analysing quantitative data.*
- *Provides information on the statistical model underlying each test, including an overview of the reasoning involved, instructions for hand computation with a worked example, and the procedure for computing the statistic using SPSS.*

KEY CONCEPTS

Statistical model
parametric tests
non-parametric tests

robustness
test power

● TEST SELECTION ●

A key decision in hypothesis testing involves selecting the appropriate statistical test for a given set of data. How does one choose the right test? Although other criteria are sometimes suggested (as in Searle, 1999) the most satisfactory approach is to consider the whole statistical model on which each test is based when deciding which test to use.

A reminder of the basic rules of mathematics can be found in appendix 2.

The statistical model

Every test statistic is based on a statistical model (see figure 9.1) also sometimes referred to as the 'assumptions' of the test. This defines the required characteristics of the population and samples around which the test was designed and thus specifies the conditions for its valid use.

The parametric tests

Parametric tests, such as the t-test, are based on statistical models that specify in some detail the kind of population(s) from which data must be obtained if the test is to be used appropriately. In general, parametric tests require a population distribution that is close to normal.

The non-parametric tests

Non-parametric tests are those that are based on models that do not necessarily specify the properties of the population distribution, and for this reason they are also known as 'distribution-free' tests. This means they can be used when the nature of the underlying distribution is unknown or, if known, is non-normal in form.

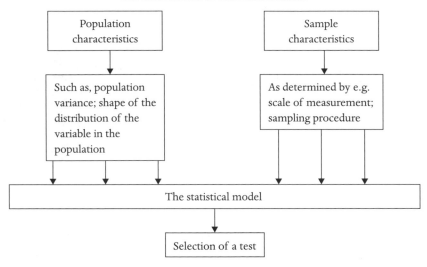

The constituents of a statistical model

The statistical model defines the conditions of use for each test statistic

Figure 9.1   Statistical model

Table 9.1   A guide to test selection

Statistical model	Research design				
	1 sample	2 samples		More than 2 samples	
		Related	Independent	Related	Independent
Parametric		Repeated measures t-test	Independent t-test	Related ANOVA	Independent ANOVA
Non-parametric	Chi-square (goodness of fit)	Wilcoxon test Sign test	Multi-dimensional Chi-square test of association Mann–Whitney test		Multi-dimensional Chi-square test of association

Correlation coefficients	
Nominal or ordinal data	Spearman's rank order correlation coefficient
Interval or ratio data	Pearson's product moment correlation coefficient

Table 9.1 shows the tests mentioned in this book divided according to the parametric/ non-parametric distinction, and the number of samples to be tested. Information about the statistical model on which each test is based is to be found at the beginning of each test.

Robustness of a test

The robustness of a test refers to the extent to which the provisions of the statistical model can be disregarded without invalidating the test result. This chapter describes tests that are all relatively robust, meaning that their assumptions can probably be violated to some degree. It may not always be possible to establish that the requirements of the statistical model have been satisfied with certainty, but it must at least be possible to assume that they have been satisfied with a reasonable degree of likelihood. It is also safe to assume that, in general, non-parametric tests are more robust than parametric tests. However, since 'reasonable degree of likelihood' is impossible to define more precisely it is always best to try to ensure that all the requirements of the model are satisfied fully.

There is also an important relationship between the robustness of a test and the size of the sample that it is given to work with. As one might expect, robustness, like power, increases with sample size.

Test Statistics

- The One-sample Chi-square 'Goodness of Fit' Test
- The Sign Test
- The Chi-square Multidimensional Test
- The Wilcoxon Signed Ranks Test
- The Mann–Whitney U Test
- The t Test for Independent Samples
- The t Test for Related Samples
- The One-factor Analysis of Variance for Independent Samples (ANOVA)
- The One-factor Analysis of Variance for Matched Samples (ANOVA)
- Spearman's Rank Order Correlation Coefficient
- Pearson's Product Moment Correlation Coefficient

● THE ONE-SAMPLE CHI-SQUARE 'GOODNESS OF FIT' TEST ●

Purpose

This procedure tests the null hypothesis that an empirically obtained distribution of frequencies across N categories has been drawn from a population with a specified distribution. The latter frequently, but not invariably, takes the form that there are an equal number of cases in each of the N categories in the population.

The statistical model

The test requires data consisting of frequencies, obtained by counting the number of independent observations in each of several mutually exclusive categories. If there are only two categories of data then the usual rule is that the sample must contain a minimum of twenty scores in total. If there are more than two categories, then sample size must be such that an equal division of scores among the different categories results in at least five observations being placed in each category. When these requirements are observed the chi-square distribution is approximately normal. Howell (1997) provides a comprehensive explanation.

Overview of the test

The chi-square statistic expresses the difference between a set of empirically obtained frequencies distributed across a number of categories (the 'observed') and those that could be expected when the null hypothesis is true (the 'expected'). If the difference between 'observed' and 'expected' score values is small for a given number of degrees of freedom the value for chi-square is also small, and vice versa. The smaller the value of the chi-square statistic, therefore, the greater is the probability that the difference between 'observed' and 'expected' could have been obtained when the null hypothesis is true.

Degrees of freedom here refers to the number of categories across which frequencies are able to vary. There is a different distribution of the chi-square statistic for each degree of freedom.

Table 8 in appendix 4 gives the critical values of chi-square for the alpha levels of 0.05 and 0.01 for a range of degrees of freedom. If the computed value is greater than that in the table then the probability of obtaining the observed frequencies when the null hypothesis is true is no greater than the significance level that has been selected and the null hypothesis may be rejected.

Computation of the chi-square (gf) test

Formula:

$$\chi^2 = \sum \frac{(O-E)^2}{E}$$

It is suggested that researchers in psychology benefit from a version of the 'halo effect', that leads them to be seen as highly competent simply because they carry out research. An investigation into this phenomenon obtained data from 50 individuals who took part in an experiment and were each subsequently asked to rate the researcher's competence using a five-point scale,

- Very competent
- Competent
- No opinion
- Incompetent
- Very incompetent.

The frequencies of the ratings in each of the five categories are shown in table 9.2.

Table 9.2   Ratings of researchers in five categories

Very competent	Competent	No opinion	Incompetent	Very incompetent
6	17	10	10	7

As each observation is independent and the data consist of a single sample of frequencies the chi-square test of goodness of fit is appropriate, testing the null hypothesis that the data were drawn from a population in which the frequencies are equal across the categories. The alpha value chosen is $\alpha = 0.05$.

Step 1 Cast the observed frequency O for each category into a table 1 cell deep and n cells long and calculate the row total by adding the cell frequencies together.

Step 2 For each cell in the table calculate E, the expected frequency. If, as in this case, the null hypothesis is that the frequencies in the population are equally distributed among the categories, then the value for E is found by:

$$E = \frac{\text{Total frequency (i.e. the row total)}}{\text{number of cells}}$$

	Very competent	Competent	No opinion	Incompetent	Very incompetent	
Step 1	O = 6	O = 7	O = 10	O = 10	O = 7	Row total = 50
Step 2	E = 10	E = 10	E = 10	E = 10	E = 10	

Step 3 Calculate (O – E) for each cell, square each result, and divide by the E value for that cell.

$(O - E)^2/E$	$\dfrac{(6-10)^2}{10}$	$\dfrac{(17-10)^2}{10}$	0	0	$\dfrac{(7-10)^2}{10}$
	= 1.6	= 4.9	0	0	= 0.9

Step 4 Sum the values obtained in step 3 to obtain a value for *chi-square*.

$$\chi^2 = 1.6 + 4.9 + 0.9 = 7.4$$

Step 5 Determine the number of degrees of freedom by n – 1 (the number of cells in the table minus 1).

$$df = (n-1) = (5-1) = 4$$

Step 6 Consult table 8 in appendix 4 to find the critical values of chi-square for the required number of degrees of freedom and significance level.

The critical value of chi-square at the $\alpha = 0.05$ significance level for 4 degrees of freedom is 9.488.

Step 7 *Decision about hypotheses.* When the computed value for chi-square is equal to or greater than the critical value obtained from the table it indicates that the probability of obtaining the observed difference between the observed and expected distributions when the null hypothesis is true is no greater than the significance level. Therefore reject the null hypothesis and accept the alternate hypothesis.

Otherwise retain the null hypothesis that the observed frequencies are likely to have been drawn from the population with the specified characteristics, with a probability greater than the alpha value.

In this case, as the table value exceeds the computed value, the null hypothesis is retained.

Step 8 *Results.* The result should be reported in the format required by your document. The guidance of the APA is that the computed value for the chi-square statistic, its exact probability (if available), the significance level (α), and the number of degrees of freedom should be presented (APA, 1994).

With an alpha level of 0.05, $\chi^2 = 7.4$ and df $= 4$ the observed data are concluded to have been drawn from a population in which the five ratings are equally distributed. Therefore, no evidence has been found for the suggestion that researchers in psychology benefit from a 'competence halo'.

Chi-square (goodness of fit) in SPSS

(Data from the example above.)

Data entry

In the **Data View** screen click on the **Variable View** tab at the bottom left of the screen.

In **Variable View**
In the column under **Name** enter a name for the set of categories into which observations have been sorted (the maximum is 8 characters e.g. 'competen(ce)'). Then click on the **Data View** tab.

In **Data View**
Each category must be labelled with a number (e.g. if there are five categories number them from 1 to 5). Each row in **Data View** represents *one* observation in *one* of the categories so the values to be placed in the first column (in this case) consist of the numbers 1–5 that identify the categories of the observations. Each category number must be entered as many times as there are observations in that category. For example, there are 6 observations in category 1 and 17 in category 2 in the worked example. Therefore, the number 1 should be entered 6 times in the first column and the number 2 entered 17 times beneath . . . and so on.

Data analysis

ANALYZE > Nonparametric Tests > Chi-square
In the **Chi-square Test** dialogue box
      Click to highlight the variable name in the left-hand box
      Click on the arrow button to move it into the **Test Variable List** box

Table 9.3 SPSS output from the chi-square goodness of fit test (example data)

COMPETEN

	Observed N	Expected N	Residual
1.00	7	10.0	−3.0
2.00	10	10.0	.0
3.00	10	10.0	.0
4.00	17	10.0	7.0
5.00	6	10.0	−4.0
Total	50		

Test statistics

	COMPETEN
Chi-Square[a]	7.400
df	4
Asymp. Sig.	.116

[a] 0 cells (.0%) have expected frequencies less than 5. The minimum expected cell frequency is 10.0.

Click on the **All categories equal** radio button if the Null Hypothesis asserts that the probabilities are equal that an observation will fall into any of the categories.

(Alternatively, click on the **Values** radio button to insert a different probability for each category. To obtain brief advice put the cursor on **Values** and right click.)
Click on **OK**.

The output from SPSS appears as in table 9.3. The upper table gives observed and expected frequencies while the lower table gives chi-square value, degrees of freedom and the exact probability under H_0. The APA guidance on reporting the results of this test can be found at the end of the instructions for hand computation.

● THE SIGN TEST ●

Purpose

The sign test offers an alternative to the Wilcoxon signed ranks test when only the direction of difference between pairs of scores can be reliably determined. The null hypothesis to be tested is that, for any pair of scores in two related samples, the probability that one score will be greater than the other is exactly $p = 0.5$. Thus it is expected that in half the cases the direction of difference will be in one direction, and in the opposite direction for the other half.

The statistical model

The sign test does not assume that the two samples could have been taken from the same population. It requires only that the measured variable has a continuous distribution and the data consist of a set of paired scores, obtained by measuring participants twice under different conditions using an ordinal scale

Overview

This test requires less information from the data than the Wilcoxon test. Whereas the Wilcoxon test requires that both the direction and magnitude of difference between pairs of scores can be established, the sign test needs only the direction of the difference to be known. If these are marked with either a plus, a minus or a zero the probability of the number of plus or minus signs can be determined.

This makes the sign test useful for analysing subjective data, such as judgements about the relative intensity of different smells. Typically, participants are able to report different intensities of smells (i.e. they can say whether they are strong or faint), but cannot assign a precise magnitude to the difference. The Wilcoxon test would be inappropriate for these data, whereas the sign test may be used.

Computation of the sign test

A researcher was interested in whether people experience smells more intensely when they are blind-folded than when they are able to see. Fifteen participants were asked to rate the strength of a standard odour on a 9-point scale under the two conditions – blindfolded and non-blindfolded.

The researcher was confident that the participants would be able to report accurately the subjective strength of the odour under the two conditions, but was less sure that the magnitude of such differences could be accurately assessed, so the sign test was appropriate. The null hypothesis tested was that the number of positive differences between scores would equal the number of negative differences. As no prediction of the direction of difference was made in the alternate hypothesis a 2-tailed test was appropriate at a significance level of $\alpha = 0.05$.

Step 1   Cast the data into columns ensuring that scores from the same participant are placed on the same line. In a third column place the sign of the difference (+ or −) between each pair of scores. If there is no difference place a zero (see table 9.4).

Step 2   Determine which sign is least frequent, ignoring any zeros and find N, the effective sample size, by subtracting the number of zeros in column 3 from the number of pairs of scores.

Step 3   *Decision on hypotheses.* Consult table 5 in appendix 4. If the value for S, the smaller in number of the two signs, is equal to or less than the table value then the probability that it could have occurred when the null hypothesis is correct is less than the significance level, and the null may be rejected. In this case,

Table 9.4 Ratings of a standard odour under blindfolded and non-blindfolded conditions

Sample 1 (non-blindfolded)	Sample 2 (blindfolded)	Sign of difference
4	6	Negative
1	4	Negative
3	7	Negative
6	5	Positive
1	6	Negative
3	8	Negative
7	7	0
4	8	Negative
2	2	0
3	4	Negative
4	8	Negative
6	6	0
4	7	Negative
4	6	Negative
4	5	Negative

Number of positive signs = 1
Number of negative signs = 11
Effective sample size = 15 − 3 = 12
The frequency of the least frequent sign found for a
two-tailed $\alpha = 0.05$ in table 5 of appendix 4 is 2.

The computed value of S is less than the table value, so the probability of obtaining S when the null hypothesis is true is smaller than alpha level and the alternate hypothesis may be accepted.

Step 4 *Results.* The result should be reported in the format required by your document. The guidance of the APA is that the computed value for S, the significance level (α), the exact probability of the observed S under H_0 (if available), the number of untied ranks (N), and the direction of the effect should be presented (APA, 1994).

With an alpha level of 0.05 and S = 1 (12), the difference between scores in the non-blind-folded' and 'blindfolded' groups is statistically significant.

It may be concluded that the perceived strength of a standard odour becomes significantly greater when participants are blindfolded than when vision is allowed.

The sign test in SPSS

(Data from the example above.)

Table 9.5 SPSS output from the sign test (example data)

Frequencies

		N
BLIND – NOTBLIND	Negative differences[a]	1
	Positive differences[b]	11
	Ties	3
	Total	15

[a] BLIND < NOTBLIND
[b] BLIND > NOTBLIND
[c] NOTBLIND = BLIND

Test statistics[b]

	BLIND – NOTBLIND
Exact sig. (2-tailed)	.006[a]

[a] Binomial distribution used.
[b] Sign test.

Data entry

In the **Data View** screen click on the **Variable View** tab in the bottom left corner of the screen.

In **Variable View**

Enter name for one of the samples (e.g. 'notblind') in the column under **Name**

　Enter a name for the other sample (e.g. 'blind') below it in the same column

　Click on the **Data View** tab

In **Data View**

　Enter the scores in the appropriate column

Data analysis

ANALYZE > Nonparametric Tests > 2 Related Samples

In the **Two-Related Samples Tests** dialogue box

　Click to highlight both sample names in the left-hand box

　Click on the arrow button to move them into the **Test Pair(s) List** box

　Click to tick the box next to **Sign**

　Click on **OK**

The output from SPSS appears as in table 9.5. The **Frequencies** table gives the frequencies of positive, negative and tied ranks and the **Test Statistics** table shows the exact 2-tailed probability of S (the smaller number of the two signs) under H_0. To obtain a one-tailed probability halve the two-tailed value.

The APA guidance on reporting the results of this test can be found at the end of the instructions for hand computation.

● THE CHI-SQUARE MULTIDIMENSIONAL TEST ●

Purpose

This test can be used either to test for difference between two or more groups when the observations are divided among two or more categories or as a test of association between two variables. The null hypothesis being tested in each case is that the samples were drawn from the same population.

The statistical model

The test requires data obtained by counting the number of independent observations that have been placed in each of several mutually exclusive categories. Siegal and Castellan (1988) suggest that the minimum sample size required when there are three or more rows should follow the rule that no more than 20% of the cells should have a expected value (E) of less than 5 and no cell should have an E of less than 1. However, a more conservative rule of thumb is that the test requires an E of at least 5 in each cell. When these requirements are satisfied, the sampling distributions of the chi-square statistic (one for each degree of freedom) approximate the (theoretical) chi-square distribution.

Overview

The points made in the earlier introduction to the one-sample chi-square 'goodness of fit' test also apply here.

The computation described below can be used when data have been collected from any number of samples (groups). However, when the number of groups exceeds two the results can be difficult to interpret, requiring techniques that lie outside the scope of this book. For this reason the discussion below confines itself to the 2-sample case when the data are arranged in a table of 2 columns and n rows. Siegal and Castellan (1988) provide a full account of the necessary techniques for analysing the results of research designs employing more than 2 groups.

Computation of the multidimensional chi-square test

The chi-square formula is:

$$\chi^2 = \sum \frac{(O-E)^2}{E}$$

Table 9.6 Frequencies of play styles in families with different parenting styles

		Play style		Row total
		Co-operative	Competitive	
Parenting style	Permissive	9	15	24
	Balanced	24	9	33
	Authoritarian	8	19	27
	Column total	41	43	84

A group of families with young children were studied in order to assess the possible relationship between parenting style and play. Thirty children from different families were observed at play and divided into two groups according to whether their play was identified as predominantly 'co-operative' or 'competitive'. Subsequently, their parents completed a questionnaire that identified their parenting style as either 'permissive', 'balanced' or 'authoritarian'. The research question asked whether parenting style could be predicted from a child's play style.

The chi-square test (see also box 9.1) is appropriate in this case as the investigation concerns a possible difference between two independent groups where the observations, consisting of frequencies, are divided across three categories. The null hypothesis to be tested is that the two groups of children were drawn from the same population. The alpha level selected is $\alpha = 0.05$.

Step 1 Cast the observed frequency O for each category into a table of 2 columns and n rows and calculate the row and column totals by adding the cell frequencies together. Sum these to obtain the grand total N (see table 9.6).

Step 2 For each cell in the table calculate E, the expected frequency for each cell, by taking the totals of the row and column in which it is located, multiplying them, and dividing the result by N, the grand total.

Step 3 Calculate (O – E) for each cell. Square each result, and divide by the E value for that cell.

Step 4 Sum the values obtained at step 3. This is the value for chi-square.

Results of steps 2, 3	Observed frequencies	Expected frequencies	O – E	$(O - E)^2$	$\dfrac{(O-E)^2}{E}$
	9	11.7	−2.7	7.29	0.62
	15	12.3	2.7	7.29	0.59
	24	16.1	7.9	62.41	3.88
	9	16.9	−7.9	62.41	3.69
	8	13.2	−5.2	27.04	2.05
	19	13.8	5.2	27.04	1.96
				Result of step 4	$\chi^2 = 12.79$

BOX 9.1   Chi-square in the 2 × 2 case

The multidimensional chi-square is often required to analyse data arranged into a 2 × 2 table. The formula below, which requires an N above 20 and expected cell frequencies of 5 or more, also incorporates a correction for continuity that brings the sampling distribution of the chi-square statistic closer to the theoretical chi-square distribution. (The frequency in each cell is identified by a letter, beginning with the top left-hand cell as cell A and continuing row by row. N is the total number of observations and df = 1.)

$$\chi^2 = \frac{N\left(|AD - BC| - \dfrac{N}{2}\right)^2}{(A+B)(C+D)(A+C)(B+D)}$$

Step 5   Determine the number of degrees of freedom by finding (no. of rows − 1) × (no. of columns − 1). Consult table 8 in appendix 4 to find the critical values of chi-square for the required number of degrees of freedom.

$$df = (\text{rows minus 1}) \times (\text{columns minus 1})$$
$$= (3 - 1)(2 - 1)$$
$$= 2$$

Step 6   *Decision about hypotheses.* If the computed value for the chi-square statistic is equal to, or greater than, the critical value in table 8 then the probability that the observed difference between the samples occurred when the null hypothesis is true is less than the significance level. In such cases the null hypothesis may be rejected.

From table 8 in appendix 4, the critical value of chi-square at the $\alpha = 0.05$ significance level for 2 degrees of freedom is 5.991. The null hypothesis may therefore be rejected in this case.

Step 7   *Results.* The result should be reported in the format required by your document. The guidance of the APA is that the computed value for the chi-square statistic, its exact probability (if available), the significance level (α), and the number of degrees of freedom should be presented (APA, 1994).

With an alpha level of $\alpha = 0.05$, $\chi^2 = 12.79$ and $df = 2$ the observed frequencies are significantly different from those expected.

The results suggest that there is an association between play style and child-rearing. Children who play co-operatively may be more likely to be experiencing a balanced style of child-rearing and those who play competitively may be more likely to have parents who follow the authoritarian or permissive styles.

The multidimensional chi-square test in SPSS

(Data from the example above.)

Data entry

In **Data View**, click on the **Variable View** tab at the bottom left of the screen.
In **Variable View**,
In the column under **Name** enter a name for one of the variables (e.g. 'parstyle').
Enter a name for the second variable (e.g. 'playst') under the first.
Click on the **Data View** tab.

[SPSS identifies the observations belonging to each cell in a multidimensional table by a combination of digits. For example, 1.1; 1.2; 1.3; 2.1; 2.2; and 2.3 identify the six cells in the 2 × 3 table (see table 9.7). Cell 2.3 thus identifies the third row cell in the second column.]

   Each row of the spreadsheet in **Data View** contains a single observation, so entering an individual item of data requires the insertion of a pair of digits (one for the column and one for the row) on the same row in order to identify *the cell in which each observation is located.* (Note that it is individual observations that are entered and not the total frequencies for each cell: SPSS calculates the totals itself.)

In **Data View**,
Enter a '1' in the column named for the samples (labelled here '**playst**') on as many lines as there are observations in the first column of the data table (the total observations in all three rows).
Enter as many 2s in the same column beneath as there are observations in the second column of the data table.
In the second column in **Data View** (labelled here '**parstyle**') enter the digits that identify each of the cells in the rows of the table, namely a '1' for a first row cell a 2 for a second, and so on, making sure that the number of digits entered matches exactly the number of observations in each cell.

Data analysis

ANALYZE > Descriptive Statistics > Crosstabs
In the **Crosstabs** dialogue box
    Click to highlight the name of the row variable
    Click on the top arrow button to move it to the **Row(s)** box
    Click to highlight the name of the column variable
    Click on the lower arrow button to move it to the **Column(s)** box
    Click on the **Statistics** button

Table 9.7   Identifying the cells in a data matrix in SPSS

Rows	Columns	
	1	2
1	1.1	2.1
2	1.2	2.2
3	1.3	2.3

In the **Crosstabs:Statistics** dialogue box
>   Click to tick the **Chi-square** box
>   Click on **Continue**
>   Click on the **Cells** button

In the **Crosstabs: Cell Display** dialogue box
>   Click to tick both the **Observed** and **Expected** options under **Counts** and the **Total** option in **Percentages** to set up the **Output View** display
>   Click on **Continue**
>   Click on **OK** in the **Crosstabs** dialogue box.

The output from SPSS appears as table 9.8. The **Crosstabulation** box gives observed and expected values for each cell and the associated percentages. The **Chi-square Tests** box gives the computed Chi-square value, its exact probability under H_0 (**Asymp. Sig**) and the no. of degrees of freedom (df).

The APA guidance on reporting the results of this test can be found at the end of the instructions for hand computation.

● THE WILCOXON SIGNED RANKS TEST ●

Purpose

The Wilcoxon signed ranks test is a non-parametric equivalent of the t-test for related samples, testing the null hypothesis that the two samples in question were drawn from the same population.

The statistical model

The test requires that data consist of paired scores (such as those obtained by measuring participants twice under different conditions) representing measures on at least the ordinal scale.

Overview

The computation is based on finding the magnitude (size) of the difference between each pair of scores, ranking the difference and giving each ranking a sign (+ or −) to indicate the direction of difference.

If random factors alone are responsible for differences between the two sets of scores one would expect that the differences between scores (and thus their rankings) would be equally divided between positive and negative directions. That is, about half of the scores in condition 1 should be greater than those in condition 2, and about half of the scores should differ

Table 9.8 SPSS output from the chi-square multidimensional test (example data: crosstabs)

Case processing summary

	Cases					
	Valid		Missing		Total	
	N	Percent	N	Percent	N	Percent
playst * parstyle	84	100.0%	0	.0%	84	100.0%

playst * parstyle crosstabulation

			Parstyle			Total
			1.00	2.00	3.00	
playst	1.00	Count	9	24	8	41
		Expected count	11.7	16.1	13.2	41.0
		% of total	10.7%	28.6%	9.5%	48.8%
	2.00	Count	15	9	19	43
		Expected count	12.3	16.9	13.8	43.0
		% of total	17.9%	10.7%	22.6%	51.2%
Total		Count	24	33	27	84
		Expected count	24.0	33.0	27.0	84.0
		% of total	28.6%	39.3%	32.1%	100.0%

Chi-square tests

	Value	df	Asymp. sig. (2-sided)
Pearson chi-square	12.759[a]	2	.002
Likelihood ratio	13.158	2	.001
Linear-by-linear association	.472	1	.492
N of valid cases	84		

[a] 0 cells (.0%) have expected count less than 5. The minimum expected count is 11.71.

in the other direction, and by about the same amount. Summed separately, the sums of positive and negative ranks will therefore be approximately equal. If, on the other hand, the two sets of scores are different, due to the effect of the experimental treatment, then the rankings will not be equally divided between the two conditions. Consequently, the signs indicating the direction of difference will also be unequally distributed and when summed will be unequal in size, with the difference between the sums reflecting the overall difference between the two sets of scores. However, because the rankings have been carried out over both sets of scores simultaneously, the two sums are related (the larger the size of one, the smaller the size of the other). The test therefore only uses the smaller of the summed rankings, designated 'T'.

Computation of the Wilcoxon signed ranks test

This method is for use when the number of pairs of scores is no greater than 25. When sample sizes are above 25 the sampling distribution of T is approximately normal and table 7 in appendix 4 cannot be used to find a critical value for T. In such cases, a z-score value should be computed and assessed using table 2: areas under the normal curve (Howell, 1997, or Siegal and Castellan, 1988, among others, have the necessary formula).

A forensic psychologist was investigating women's perceptions of their (male) partners following a conviction involving a custodial sentence. A sample of 13 responses to a questionnaire designed to measure the strength of negative attitudes was obtained at the first opportunity after sentence was passed. A year later, the same women were contacted again, and asked to complete the same questionnaire.

Because the data represent measures on an ordinal scale obtained from a repeated measures design, the Wilcoxon test can be used, testing the null hypothesis that the two sets of scores were drawn from the same population. As no prediction of direction of difference has been made, a two-tailed alpha of $\alpha = 0.05$ is employed.

Step 1 Cast the scores in two columns, ensuring that scores generated by the same person lie on the same line. Subtract the first score in column 2 from its corresponding score in column 1 and enter the difference, including the sign of the direction of difference, in a third column. Continue until all differences have been found.

Rank the differences, ignoring the signs in a fourth column, giving the lowest numerical difference the rank of 1, and the highest rank to the highest difference. (See the note below on the treatment of tied rankings.) Transfer the sign of each of the differences to these rankings (see table 9.9).

Step 2 Sum all the positive rankings, and note the result. Do the same for all the negative rankings.

Table 9.9 Scores on a marital attitudes questionnaire

Sample 1 (immediate test)	Sample 2 (1 year test)	Difference	Signed rank of differences
12	14	2	+4
14	16	2	+4
15	12	−3	−8
10	12	2	+4
13	17	4	+10
10	18	8	+12
15	18	3	+8
9	6	−3	−8
14	16	2	+4
10	10	0	0
11	17	6	+11
10	11	1	+1
14	16	2	+4

Sum of negative rankings: $8 + 8 = \mathbf{16}$
Sum of positive rankings: $4 + 4 + 4 + 10 + 12 + 8 + 4 + 11 + 1 + 4 = \mathbf{62}$

Step 3   Take the smaller of the two sums of ranks as the computed value of **T**. (If all the rankings have the same sign, then T = 0.) Consult table 7 in appendix 4 to determine the critical value for T for the appropriate N (the number of pairs of scores with a non-zero difference).

Step 4   *Decision about hypotheses.* If the computed value of T is equal to or less than the critical value in table 7, then it indicates that the two samples of data came from different populations. The probability of such difference having occurred when the null hypothesis is correct is of no greater than the significance level (α). Therefore, the null hypothesis may be rejected

In this case, T = 16 and N = 12. Table 7 gives the critical value of T = 14 for a two-tailed test at α = 0.05. The smaller sum of the signed rankings is greater than the critical value, so the two sets of scores appear to be drawn from the same population, with a probability of the difference occurring when the null hypothesis is correct greater than α = 0.05. The null hypothesis is therefore retained.

Step 5   *Results*: The result should be reported in the format required by your document. The guidance of the APA is that the computed value for T, the significance level (α), the exact probability of the observed T under H_0 (if available), the number of untied ranks (N) and the direction of the effect should be presented (APA, 1994).

With an alpha level of p = 0.05 and T = 16 (12) the difference between scores on the 'immediate' and '1-year' tests is not statistically significant. We conclude from this that the attitudes of women to their incarcerated men do not appear to become significantly more negative during the first year of imprisonment.

Treatment of tied scores and tied ranks

- Where tied scores result in a difference of zero, these are not ranked and N, the number of pairs of scores, is correspondingly reduced.
- Where there are tied difference scores take the median of the rankings that would have been assigned had the difference scores not been the same. For example, suppose three difference scores that would all have a rank of 1. If just different, they would have been given the ranks 1, 2, 3, so a rank of 2 is assigned to all three and the ranking sequence continues at 4.

The Wilcoxon signed ranks test in SPSS

(Data from the example above.)

Data entry

In the **Data View** screen click on the **Variable View** tab at bottom left of the screen. In **Variable View**

Enter name for one of the samples (e.g. 'Immed') in the column under **Name**

Enter a name for the other sample (e.g. 'Oneyear') below it in the same column

Click on the **Data View** tab.

In **Data View**

Enter the scores in the appropriate column

Data analysis

ANALYZE > Nonparametric Tests > 2 Related Samples

In the **Two-Related Samples Tests** dialogue box

Click to highlight both sample names in the left-hand box

Click on the arrow button to move them into the **Test Pair(s) List** box

Click to tick the box next to **Wilcoxon**

Click on **OK**.

The output from SPSS appears as in table 9.10 below. The APA guidance on reporting the results of this test can be found at the end of the instructions for hand computation.

However, SPSS shows the probability of the observed distributions of scores under H_0 rather than a value for T, so this should be reported, along with the number of untied ranks (total N – ties). To obtain a 1-tailed probability halve the value of the two-tailed probability.

Table 9.10 SPSS output from the Wilcoxon signed ranks test (example data)

Ranks

		N	Mean rank	Sum of ranks
Oneyear – Immed	Negative ranks	2[a]	8.00	16.00
	Positive ranks	10[b]	6.20	62.00
	Ties	1		
	Total	13		

[a] Oneyear < Immed.
[b] Oneyear > Immed.
[c] Oneyear = Immed.

Test statistics[b]

	Oneyear – Immed
Z	−1.821[a]
Asymp. sig. (2-tailed)	.069

[a] Based on negative ranks.
[b] Wilcoxon signed ranks test.

● THE MANN–WHITNEY U TEST ●

Purpose

The Mann–Whitney U is a non-parametric equivalent of the t-test for independent samples, testing the null hypothesis that two independent samples were drawn from the same population.

The statistical model

The test requires two independent samples, which need not be of equal size, containing measures on at least the ordinal scale. When these requirements are met the sampling distribution of U is approximately normal, whatever the sample size.

Overview

The ordinal scale captures the relative ordering of the scores, but ignores the exact size of the intervals between them. This characteristic provides the basis for the test. Each score is given a ranking, with the lowest score overall receiving the lowest rank. When the rankings for each of the sets of data are summed and compared, the set with the larger sum will be found to contain the higher scores.

These rankings generate a measure of the difference between the two sets of scores, called 'U'. The value of U is determined by the number of times that a score from one set of data precedes (has been given a lower ranking than) a score from the other set. However, because there are two independently obtained sets of data, these relationships are different for each set of scores, and so there are actually two possible values for 'U', called U and U_1. (read U_1 as 'U complement'). The test requires the smaller of U and U_1.

By means of this procedure it is possible to determine whether the difference between the medians of the two sets of scores is so great that it would be unlikely to occur when the null hypothesis is true. The critical values of U for the 0.05 and 0.01 alpha levels for samples of size N = 9 to N = 20 are given in table 6 of appendix 4.

Computation of the Mann–Whitney U

The following procedure for hand-computation applies only to samples from N = 9 to n = 20. A text such as Siegal & Castellan (1988) should be consulted if the hand computation of the statistic for smaller or larger samples is required. (See also the instructions for computing this statistic by SPSS that follows.)

A psychologist wishes to check the relative effectiveness of two procedures for delivering information about nutrition. Two matched samples of students were shown an official government film followed by either a short, formal talk by a doctor or by an informal discussion session led by a youth

Table 9.11 Scores on a dietary awareness questionnaire

Sample 1 'talk' condition	Ranks of sample 1	Sample 2 'discussion' condition	Ranks of sample 2
17	8	15	5.5
10	1	21	13.5
24	17.5	23	16
11	2.5	19	11
13	4	27	20
19	11	18	9
21	13.5	19	11
11	2.5	26	19
16	7	22	15
15	5.5	24	17.5
	Σranks = 72.5		Σranks = 137.5

worker. After the talk or discussion, the students each completed a 'dietary awareness' questionnaire and these were scored to generate the data for analysis.

As the data represent ordinal measures taken from independent samples the Mann–Whitney U is an appropriate statistic, testing the null hypothesis that the 'talk' and 'discussion' samples were drawn from the same population and thus will have identical medians. As no prediction is made about the direction of difference a two-tailed test is appropriate at a significance level of $\alpha = 0.05$.

Step 1 Cast the data into two columns, leaving space alongside each to enter the rankings. If they are unequal in size make the larger of the two sets column 1.

Step 2 Rank all the items of data by placing a '1' in the rankings column against the *lowest* score in *both* sets of data, a '2' against the next lowest, and so on, until all the scores have been ranked (see below for the treatment of tied scores). Sum the rankings (see table 9.11).

Step 3 If the samples are of *unequal* size, the sum of ranks of the *smaller* of the two is the value for 'U'. If the samples contain *equal* numbers of scores calculate U by summing the ranks for *either* of the two sets of scores, and applying the formula

$$U = n_1 n_2 = \frac{n_1(n_1 - 1)}{2} - R_1$$

[n_1 and n_2 are the number of scores in each sample.
R_1 is the sum of the ranks of *one* of the sets of scores (it doesn't matter which).]

$$= 10 \times 10 + \frac{100 + 10}{2} - 72.5$$
$$= 100 + 55 - 72.5$$
$$= 82.5$$

Step 4 Find the *smaller* of U and U_1 using the following formula and discard the larger value.

$$U_1 = n_1 n_2 - U$$
$$= 10 \times 10 - 82.5$$
$$= 17.5$$

This gives a value for U_1 which is less than that already obtained for U, confirming that 17.5 is the value needed.

Consult table 6 in appendix 4 to determine the critical value for U for the appropriate sample size. In this case U = 23 for a two-tailed test at the $\alpha = 0.05$ significance level when both N_1 and $N_2 = 10$.

Step 5   *Decision on hypotheses.* If the computed value of the smaller of U or U_1 is equal to, or less than, the critical value in table 6, then the probability of obtaining that value (or one more extreme), when the *null hypothesis is correct* is less than the significance level (α) selected.

As 17.5 is below the critical vale in the table the null hypothesis can be rejected. It is concluded that the difference between the two samples is such that they are likely to have been drawn from different populations.

Step 6   *Results*: The result should be reported in the format required by your document. The guidance given by the APA is that the computed value for U, the significance level (α), the probability of the observed U under H_0 (if available), and the direction of the effect should be reported (APA, 1994).

With an alpha level of 0.5 and U = 17.5, the effect of the post-film procedure on a measure of dietary awareness was found to be statistically significant. It is concluded that after watching the film a discussion produces greater dietary awareness than a talk.

Treatment of tied scores

Tied scores are treated by assigning to them the median of those ranks that would have been given had they not been identical. For example, suppose three scores that would all have a rank of 1. If different, they would have been given the ranks 1, 2, 3, so a rank of 2 is assigned to all three and the ranking sequence continues at 4.

The Mann–Whitney U test in SPSS

(Data from the example above.)

Data entry

In the **Data View** screen click on the **Variable View** tab at bottom left of the screen.
In **Variable View**
    Enter a name for all the data (e.g. 'data') in the first row of column 1 under **Name**
    Enter a name for the two conditions (e.g. 'groups') in the row below in the same
       column
    Click on the **Data View** tab.

In **Data View**

Enter the first set of data in the column headed '**data**'

Enter a '1' in the column headed 'groups' against each score

Enter the second set of data under the first in the '**data**' column

Enter a '2' in the column headed 'groups' against each of the second set of scores.

Data analysis

ANALYZE > Nonparametric Tests > 2 Independent Samples

In the **Two-Independent Samples Tests** dialogue box

Click to highlight the name of the data (e.g 'data') in the left-hand box

Click on the top arrow button to move it into the **Test Variable List** box

Click to highlight the name of the groups (e.g. 'groups') in the left-hand box

Click on the arrow button to move it into the **Grouping Variable** box

Click on the **Define Groups** button

In the **Two-Independent Samples: Define Groups** dialogue box

Enter '1' in the **Group 1** box

Enter '2' in the **Group 2** box

Click on **Continue**

Click on **OK.**

The output from SPSS will appear as shown in table 9.12. The general APA guidance for reporting test results can be found at the end of the instructions for hand computation of this test.

Table 9.12   SPSS output from the Mann–Whitney U test (example data)

Ranks

	GROUPS	N	Mean rank	Sum of ranks
DATA	1.00	10	7.25	72.50
	2.00	10	13.75	137.50
	Total	20		

Test statistics[b]

	DATA
Mann-Whitney U	17.500
Wilcoxon W	72.500
Z	−2.464
Asymp. sig. (2-tailed)	.014
Exact sig. [2*(1-tailed sig.)]	.011[a]

[a] Not corrected for ties.

[b] Grouping variable: GROUPS.

Samples of n = 8 and below

The **Exact Sig.** value is used to determine the decision about hypotheses. The SPSS table gives the two-tailed value which must be halved if a one-tailed value is required.

Samples of N = 9 to n = 20

The 2-tailed **Asymp. Sig.** is used to determine the decision about hypotheses. Again halve the two-tailed value to find the one-tailed value which must be smaller than the chosen alpha level if the null hypothesis is to be discarded.

Samples above n = 20

The z-value in the table is used in conjunction with the table of areas under the normal curve (table 2 in appendix 4). For the given value of z subtract the table value from 0.5000. This gives the one-tailed probability associated with a value of z as extreme as the one you have. For a two-tailed probability double the one-tailed value.

● THE T-TEST FOR INDEPENDENT SAMPLES ●

Purpose

This t-test compares the means of two independent samples of scores in order to test the null hypothesis that they were drawn from the same population.

The statistical model

The t-test requires that the measured variable is normally distributed within the populations from which the samples have notionally been drawn and the populations have the same variance.

The data should represent measures on at least the interval scale, obtained by random sampling from the two populations, and each score is obtained independently of the others.

(The t-test is robust and some degree of latitude in meeting the population assumptions is sometimes allowed. See below under Special Issues for further notes.)

Overview

Standard error is the standard deviation of a sampling distribution – in this case the sampling distribution of the differences between two means.

In dealing with two independent samples the t-test works with the difference between score means rather than the raw scores themselves.

In this case, the t-statistic is a ratio:

t = the difference between means/the standard error of the differences between means

The statistic 't' therefore reflects the relationship between the size of an observed difference between two sample means and the dispersion of all possible differences between two samples around *their* population mean. In effect, for any given value of standard error, if the difference between sample means is big, t will also tend to be large.

The sampling distribution of the t-statistic turns out to be approximately normal. However, its precise shape is determined by the size of the samples from which it is computed – so it is, in effect, a *family* of distributions with each member approaching closer to normality as sample size increases. It follows that, because this distribution has a mean of zero, the larger the t-value at any given number of degrees of freedom the more likely it is that the difference in means is significant.

Computation of the t-test for independent samples

(Use this formula when the samples are the same size and have approximately equal variances.)

The top line of the equation is the difference between the two sample means, and the lower line is the estimate of the standard error of the sampling distribution of the differences between two independent means.

$$t = \frac{(\overline{X}_1 - \overline{X}_2)}{\sqrt{\dfrac{s_1^2}{N_1} + \dfrac{s_2^2}{N_2}}}$$

A value for s^2, the population variance of the difference between means, can be found by applying the variance-sum law to give,

$$s^2 = \frac{\sum (X_1 - \overline{X}_1)^2 + \sum (X_2 - \overline{X}_2)^2}{n_1 + n_2 - 2}$$

X_1, X_2 are any individual scores in the samples
$\overline{X}_1$, $\overline{X}_2$ are the means of the samples
n_1, n_2 are the number of observations in the samples

In an investigation into male–female differences in visuo-spatial skills, the participants' performance was measured by the time taken to complete a standard task. This was an independent subjects design, with data representing measures on an interval scale obtained by random sampling.

The variance-sum law states 'The variance of a difference between two independent variables is equal to the sum of their variances.'

As an assumption of equal variances can be made the independent t-test is appropriate, testing the null hypothesis that the two sets of performance scores were drawn from the same population and using an alpha value of $\alpha = 0.05$ with a one-tailed region of rejection.

Step 1 List the scores in two columns, sum each column separately and find their means.

Step 2 Subtract each item of data from its mean, square it and list each squared difference. Sum each list of squared differences separately (see table 9.13).

Table 9.13   Scores on a visuo-spatial task

X_1 Males	X_2 Females	$(X_1 - \bar{X}_1)$	$(X_1 - \bar{X}_1)^2$	$(X_2 - \bar{X}_2)$	$(X_2 - \bar{X}_2)^2$
193	112	45.15	2038.52	−2.08	4.33
143	160	−4.85	23.52	45.92	2108.65
104	73	−43.85	1922.82	−41.08	1687.57
92	121	−55.85	3119.22	6.92	47.89
188	140	40.15	1612.02	25.92	671.85
141	113	−6.85	46.92	−1.08	1.17
120	98	−27.85	775.62	−16.08	258.57
117	127	−30.85	951.72	12.92	166.93
186	155	38.15	1455.42	40.92	1674.45
124	101	−23.85	568.82	−13.08	171.07
217	86	69.15	4781.72	−28.08	788.49
165	94	17.15	294.12	−20.08	403.21
132	103	−15.85	251.22	−11.08	122.77
$\Sigma X_1 = 1922$	$\Sigma X_2 = 1483$				
$\bar{X}_1 = 147.85$	$\bar{X}_2 = 114.08$		$\Sigma(X_1 - \bar{X}_1)^2$ $= 17841.66$		$\Sigma(X_2 - \bar{X}_2)^2$ $= 8106.95$

Step 3   Find the number of degrees of freedom $(n-1) + (n-1)$. Add together the sums of squared differences and divide the result by the number of degrees of freedom. [This is s^2, the estimate of the population variance.]

$$df = (13-1) + (13-1) = 24$$

$$\sum(X_1 - \bar{X}_1)^2 + \sum(X_2 - \bar{X}_2)^2 = 17841.66 + 8106.95 = 25948.61$$

$$s^2 = \frac{25948.61}{24} = 1081.19$$

Step 4   Divide the result of step 3 by the number of observations in one sample. Repeat with the number of observations in the second sample. (If you have the same number of observations in each sample simply double the first answer). Sum the two results and find the square root of *that* result.

$$\sqrt{\frac{1081.19}{13} + \frac{1081.19}{13}} = \sqrt{166.34} = 12.9$$

Step 5   Subtract the smaller of the means of the samples from the larger and divide the result by the result of step 4 to find t. Consult table 9 in appendix 4 to find the critical value for t for the required number of degrees of freedom.

$$t = \frac{147.85 - 114.08}{12.9} = 2.62$$

From table 9, the one-tailed critical value for t with $df = 24$ and $\alpha = 0.05$ is 1.711.

Step 6 *Decision about hypotheses.* If the computed value for t is equal to, or greater than, the critical value in table 9 then the probability of obtaining the observed difference in means when the null hypothesis is true is no greater than the significance level. In such cases the null hypothesis may be rejected.

In this case, the computed value for t exceeds the critical value shown in table 9 and the null hypothesis is therefore not retained.

Step 7 *Results.* The result should be reported in the format required by your document. The guidance of the APA is that the computed value for t, the significance level (α), the exact probability of the observed t under H_0 (if available), the number of degrees of freedom, and the direction of the effect should be reported (APA, 1994).

With an alpha level of 0.05 and df = 24, t = 2.62 (one-tailed), the probability of obtaining the observed difference in sample means when the null hypothesis is true is below α. It is concluded that females are able to perform the standard visuo-spatial task significantly faster than males.

The t-test for independent samples in SPSS

(Data from the example above.)

Data entry

Click on the **Variable View** tab at bottom left of the screen
In **Variable View**
    In the first column under 'Name' type the name of the dependent variable (e.g. 'time')
    Underneath type the name of the independent variable (e.g. 'sex')
    Click on the **Data View** tab
In **Data View**
    In the column under the heading **'time'** enter all the scores in one of the samples.
    In the column under the heading **'sex'** enter a '1' against each score.
    Enter all the scores in the other sample under those of the first sample.
    In the other column enter a '2' against each score in the second set.

Data analysis

ANALYZE > Compare Means > Independent Samples T-test
In the **Independent Samples T-test** dialogue box
    Click to highlight the name of the dependent variable (e.g. 'time')
    Click on the top arrow button to move it into the **Test Variable(s)** box
    Click to highlight the name of the independent variable (e.g. 'sex')
    Click on the lower arrow button to move it into the **Grouping Variable** box

Table 9.14   SPSS output from the Independent t-test (example data)

Group statistics

	Sex	N	Mean	Std deviation	Std error mean
time	1.00	13	147.8462	38.55915	10.69438
	2.00	13	114.0769	25.99186	7.20885

Independent samples test

		Levene's test for equality of variances		t-test for equality of means						
		F	Sig.	t	df	Sig. (2-tailed)	Mean difference	Std error difference	95% confidence interval of the difference	
									Lower	Upper
time	Equal variances assumed	3.141	.089	2.618	24	.015	33.76923	12.89718	7.15076	60.38770
	Equal variances not assumed			2.618	21.039	.016	33.76923	12.89718	6.95110	60.58736

Click on the **Define Groups** button
Click to select the **Use Specified Values** radio button
Enter a '1' in the **Group 1** box
Enter a '2' in the **Group 2** box
Click on **Continue**.

To check and/or modify significance level
Click on the **Options** button
In the **Independent Samples T-test:Options** dialogue box
    Enter the value required in the **Confidence Interval** box (e.g. 99% for $\alpha = 0.01$)
    Check that the **Exclude cases analysis by analysis** radio button has been selected
    Click on **Continue**
    Click on **OK**.

The output from SPSS, as in table 9.14, is divided into two rows – the upper where equality of variances is assumed by the program, and the lower where it is not. The upper line includes the results of Levene's test for equality of variances, (see below).

If the exact probability associated with the reported value of F is greater than $p = 0.05$ then equality of variances can be assumed and the computed value for t, the df value and the exact 2-tailed probability under H_0 (the **Sig** value) found in the top line should be reported. If a one-tailed probability is required, halve the given value. If the result of Levene's test shows $p < 0.05$ then the values in the lower line may be used but the inequality of variances should also be reported along with the results of Levene's test.

The APA guidance on reporting the results of this test can be found at the end of the instructions for hand computation.

Special issues for the t-test

Unequal sample sizes

When the two sets of data are unequal, the assumption that the samples come from populations with equal variances becomes problematic. If two samples are different in size the variances are likely to differ to some degree, even if H_0 is true and if one sample is much larger than the other, it becomes even more likely that the two variances will be different.

The solution to unequal sample sizes is to take a weighted average (known as the pooled variance estimate) of the two variances of the samples. This should give a better estimate of the population variance than either sample variance can individually. The formula is given below.

$$s_p^2 = \frac{(N_1 - 1)s_1 + (N_2 - 1)s_2}{N_1 + N_2 - 2}$$

When this formula is used the formula required for t is as shown below [df = $(n_1 + n_2) - 2$].

$$t = \frac{(\overline{X}_1 - \overline{X}_2)}{\sqrt{s_p^2 \left(\frac{1}{N_1} + \frac{1}{N_2} \right)}}$$

The heterogeneity of variance problem

One of the important assumptions underlying the t-test is that the variances of the two populations from which the samples are drawn are equal. When this assumption can be made, the formulae can be used without difficulty. However, when the variances are heterogeneous (i.e. different), difficulties arise. The ratio of (a) the difference between sample means and (b) the standard error of the difference between the sample means is not distributed as t with df $- (N_1 + N_2 \quad 2)$ but as a statistic called t' about whose distribution there is little agreement (Howell, 1997). The proposed solution, involving a re-calculation of the number of degrees of freedom, can also be found in Howell's book.

Testing for heterogeneity of variance

In the light of the above, it is necessary to be able to determine whether two samples come from populations with heterogeneous or homogeneous variances. Until relatively recently, the preferred solution was the F-test or the variance-ratio test, but this has been shown to be severely affected by the non-normality of the data and Howell (1997) takes the view that it should not be used. Instead, a procedure proposed by Levene (1960), is suggested that involves replacing each value of X by either its absolute deviation from the group mean or by its squared deviation. The standard two-sample t-test is then run on the deviations and the result evaluated in the usual way. Advanced texts, such as Howell (1997), will give the details.

● THE T-TEST FOR RELATED SAMPLES ●

Purpose

This t-test compares the mean difference between two related samples of scores, in order to test the null hypothesis that they were taken from the same population.

The statistical model

The statistical model for the related samples t-test is the same as that for the independent t-test.

Overview

In the related samples design each research participant acts as his own control, so the interest lies in the possibility of a consistent difference emerging, across the sample of participants, when one set of scores is compared to the other. This can be measured by the mean of the individual differences between pairs of scores (the topmost term in the formula below).

If the scores came from similar populations then no consistent differences can be expected between scores and the mean difference will be close to zero (because any differences will be due to sampling error and will tend to cancel each other out). In this case the null hypothesis is retained. However, if the scores in one sample are consistently higher than those in the other, because they came from different populations then the mean difference will also be high and the probability that they came from the same population will be low. In this case the null hypothesis may be rejected at the chosen level of significance (α).

The remainder of the formula is the estimate of the standard error of the sampling distribution. In the same way as was seen in the t-test for independent samples, therefore, 't' reflects the relationship between the size of an observed difference – in this case the mean difference between pairs of scores – and the dispersion of all possible differences between two samples around *their* population mean. Once again, for any given value of standard error, if the difference between sample means is big, 't' will also tend to be large.

The basic formula is, therefore,

$$t = \left(\frac{\overline{D}}{\frac{s_D}{\sqrt{N}}} \right)$$

$\overline{D}$ is the mean difference between the pairs of scores (the mean difference score)
N is the number of pairs of scores
s_D is the standard deviation of the difference scores, found by,

$$s_D = \sqrt{\frac{\sum (D - \overline{D})^2}{N - 1}}$$

Table 9.15   Mean solution times for 'hard' and 'easy' problems (secs)

Step 1

Sample 1 'hard'	Sample 2 'easy'	$X_1 - X_2$	$D - \bar{D}$	$(D - \bar{D})^2$
131.0	64.2	66.8	14.44	208.51
109.1	80.4	28.7	−23.66	559.8
102.0	100.3	1.7	−50.66	2566.44
158.1	70.3	87.8	35.44	1255.99
138.4	102.7	35.7	−16.66	277.56
125.3	83.7	41.6	−10.76	115.78
180.4	55.7	124.7	72.34	5233.08
170.4	123.6	46.8	−5.56	30.91
163.7	89.1	74.6	22.24	494.62
121.2	106.0	15.2	−37.16	1380.87
		$\Sigma X_1 - X_2 = 523.6$		$\Sigma(D - \bar{D})^2 = 12123.56$
		$\bar{D} = 52.36$		

Computation of the related samples t-test

An investigation into the effects of prior expectations on problem-solving employed ten participants as their own controls. Half the participants were asked to solve a problem they believed was 'easy' followed by one which they believed to be 'difficult'. The other half solved the problems in reverse order. In fact, both problems were of the same moderate level of difficulty. The raw data consisted of the mean time taken by each participant to solve each type of problem.

As the investigation assumed that the underlying populations had equal variances and the data were obtained from a repeated measures design using measures on the interval scale this t-test was appropriate, testing the null hypothesis that the two samples were drawn from populations with equal means. A one-tailed significance level of $\alpha = 0.05$ was employed.

Step 1   Cast the data into two columns ensuring that the scores on each line are related. Subtract one score from the other and note the difference in a third column. Sum the difference scores and find their mean. Subtract each difference score from the mean difference and square it. Sum the squared differences (see table 9.15).

Step 2   Divide the sum of the squared difference scores by N − 1 and take the square root of the result. This is the standard deviation of the difference scores.

$$\sqrt{\frac{12123.56}{N-1}} = \sqrt{\frac{12123.56}{9}} = \sqrt{1347.06} = 36.7$$

Step 3   Divide the standard deviation of the difference scores again by the square root of N to find the estimate of the standard error of the differences.

$$\frac{36.7}{\sqrt{10}} = \frac{36.7}{3.16} = 11.61$$

Step 4   Divide the mean of the differences (found at step 1) by the estimate of standard error found at step 3 to find t.

$$t = \frac{52.36}{11.61} = 4.51$$

Consult table 9 of appendix 4 to find the critical value for t for the required number of degrees of freedom.

From table 9, the one-tailed critical value for t with df = 9 and α = 0.05 is 1.833.

Step 5   *Decision about hypotheses.* If the computed value for t is equal to, or greater than, the critical value in table 9, then the probability of obtaining the observed mean difference score when the null hypothesis is true is no greater than the significance level. In such cases the null hypothesis may be rejected.

In this case, the computed value for t exceeds the critical value shown in table 9 and the null hypothesis is therefore not retained.

Step 6   *Results.* The result should be reported in the format required by your document. The guidance of the APA is that the computed value for t, the significance level (α), the exact probability of the observed t under H_0 (if available), the number of degrees of freedom, and the direction of the effect should be reported (APA, 1994).

With an alpha level of 0.05 and df = 9, t = 4.51 (one-tailed) the probability of obtaining the observed mean difference score when the null hypothesis is true is below α.

It is concluded that prior expectations affect the speed with which problems can be solved, with those believed to be 'hard' taking significantly longer than those believed to be 'easy'.

The t-test for related samples in SPSS

(Data from the example above.)

Data entry

Click on the **Variable View** tab at bottom left of the screen
In **Variable View**
In the first column under 'Name' type the name of the first treatment group (e.g. 'hard' for the example data)
Underneath type the name of the second treatment group (e.g. 'easy')
Click on the **Data View** tab
In **Data View**
In the column under the heading '**hard**' enter all the scores for that treatment group
Enter the scores for the other treatment in the other column under the heading '**easy**'

Data analysis

ANALYZE > Compare Means > Paired-Samples T-Test
In the **Paired-Samples T-Test** dialogue box
    Click to highlight both the names of the treatment groups
    Click on the top arrow button to move them into the **PairedVariable(s)** box
    Click on **OK**.

Table 9.16   SPSS output from the related samples t-test (example data)

Paired samples statistics

		Mean	N	Std deviation	Std error mean
Pair 1	HARD	139.9600	10	26.86903	8.49673
	EASY	87.6000	10	20.96987	6.63126

Paired samples correlations

		N	Correlation	Sig.
Pair 1	HARD & EASY	10	−.165	.650

Paired samples test

		Paired differences					t	df	Sig. (2-tailed)
		Mean	Std deviation	Std error mean	95% confidence interval of the difference				
					Lower	Upper			
Pair 1	HARD – EASY	52.3600	36.70232	11.60629	26.1047	78.6153	4.511	9	.001

To check and/or modify significance level before clicking OK

Click on the **Options** button
In the **Paired-Samples T-Test Options** dialogue box
   Enter the value required in the **Confidence Interval** box (e.g. 99% for $\alpha = 0.01$)
   Check that the **Exclude cases analysis by analysis** radio button has been selected
   Click on **Continue**
   Click on **OK**.

The output from SPSS will appear as in table 9.16. This provides descriptive statistics for the differences between pairs of scores as well as the computed value for t, the df value and the exact two-tailed probability associated with the observed t under H_0. If a one-tailed probability is required, halve the two-tailed value. The APA guidance on reporting the results of this test can be found at the end of the instructions for hand computation.

● THE ONE-FACTOR ANALYSIS OF VARIANCE FOR INDEPENDENT SAMPLES (ANOVA) ●

Purpose

This test provides for the analysis of three or more independent samples of data that differ in one dimension, testing the null hypothesis that the samples were all drawn from the same

Table 9.17   Sources of error variance in independent samples

Type of variance	Cause
Variance within a group or sample	Error
Variance between different groups	Effect of treatment + error
Total variance	Variance between different groups + variance within a group

population and therefore have identical means. The alternate hypothesis is non-directional, and at least one of the sample means is significantly different from the others.

The statistical model

This test requires the assumption that the dependent variable is normally distributed in its population, that all observations are obtained by random sampling, and are independent, both within and between groups. Measures should achieve at least the interval scale with homogeneous variance across all groups (i.e. that the variances of each group are approximately equal).

Overview

Different groups of scores analysed by the ANOVA usually represent different experimental treatments, so their means can be expected to differ for the following reasons:

- Difference due to treatment
- Difference due to error.

It is usual to capture this difference in the form of variance so the 1-factor ANOVA sets about comparing the means of three or more independent groups by generating estimates of the population variance attributable to these sources. (Recall that variance is a measure of the variability of a set of scores indicated by the mean of squared individual deviations: see chapter 7.)

Deviation: the difference between a score and a mean to which it has contributed.

Thus, the variances present in samples of scores can be apportioned as in table 9.17.

The ANOVA generates independent estimates of both between and within groups population variance. The ratio of these estimates is the statistic F.

$$F = \frac{\text{between groups variance}}{\text{within groups variance}}$$

Rather than variance, however, the ANOVA computation uses an equivalent quantity called the sums of squares – the sum of squared deviations about a mean. The relationship between variance and sums of squares is straightforward,

$$s^2 = \frac{SS}{df}$$

When H_0 is true and all samples have been drawn from the same population, the ratio of between-groups to within-groups variance is 1 (because both sides of the ratio will consist only of the same amount of error). If the ratio is greater than 1, however, it suggests the presence of other sources of difference between the groups than that caused by error.

The probability of obtaining the observed F ratio under H_0 can be assessed from the sampling distribution of F. (This is a family of positively skewed distributions that vary with each pair of degrees of freedom, one for each variance estimate.) If the ratio exceeds 1 with an associated probability that is below the significance level (α) then H_0 may be rejected.

Computation of the 1-factor ANOVA for independent samples

A memory researcher compared the recall of information that had been presented to participants in one of three ways. In one condition, blindfolded participants were allowed to handle a series of ten objects, in another condition they looked at photographs of the same objects, and in the third condition they read the names of the objects from a projection screen. After the presentations all participants completed the same distractor task for 10 minutes before being tested for recall with the results shown below.

This experiment consists of three independent groups, and the data represent measures on the interval scale. Since the other requirements of the statistical model can be assumed to hold, the 1-factor ANOVA for independent groups is an appropriate test. The null hypothesis being tested is that the three samples will be drawn from populations having identical means (or equivalently, from the same population). A significance level of $\alpha = 0.05$ was selected.

Step 1   (1)   Square each raw score and calculate the sum and mean of both raw and squared scores in each group.

         (2)   Calculate the grand sum (the sum of all scores) and the grand mean, see table 9.18).

Step 2   Find the total sum of squares by:

         (1)   Sum all the squares of raw scores across all groups.

         (2)   Find the correction for the mean by squaring the grand sum and dividing the result by the total number of raw scores.

         (3)   Subtract the result of (2) from the result of (1).

$$SS_{Total} = \sum X^2{}_{Total} - \frac{\left(\sum X_{Total}\right)^2}{N}$$

$$SS_{Total} = (302 + 151 + 110) - \frac{91^2}{16}$$

$$= 45.44$$

Table 9.18   Data from a memory test under three conditions

Handling objects		Viewing pictures of objects		Reading names of objects	
X_1	X_1^2	X_2	X_2^2	X_3	X_3^2
6	36	6	36	6	36
8	64	5	25	2	4
7	49	7	49	3	9
6	36	5	25	6	36
6	36	4	16	5	25
9	81				
$\Sigma X_1 = 42$	$\Sigma X_1^2 = 302$	$\Sigma X_2 = 27$	$\Sigma X_2^2 = 151$	$\Sigma X_3 = 22$	$\Sigma X_3^2 = 110$
$\overline{X}_1 = 7.0$	$\overline{X}_1^2 = 50.33$	$\overline{X}_2 = 5.4$	$\overline{X}_2^2 = 30.2$	$\overline{X}_3 = 4.4$	$\overline{X}_3^2 = 22$

Total N: 16; grand sum: $42 + 27 + 22 = 91$; grand mean: $91 \div 16 = 5.69$.

Step 3   Find the between-groups sum of squares:

(1) Find the square of the sum of the raw scores in each group and divide each by the number of scores in that group. Sum the results (the mean squared sums of scores) across the groups.

(2) Subtract the correction for the mean (step 2) from the result of (1):

$$SS_{Between} = \frac{\left(\sum X_1\right)^2}{n_1} + \frac{\left(\sum X_2\right)^2}{n_2} + \frac{\left(\sum X_n\right)^2}{n_n} - \frac{\left(\sum X_{Total}\right)^2}{N}$$

$$SS_{Between} = \left(\frac{42^2}{6} + \frac{27^2}{5} + \frac{22^2}{5}\right) - \frac{91^2}{16}$$

$$= 19.04$$

Step 4   Find the within-groups sum of squares. As you would expect, total SS = SS within groups + SS between groups so the within-groups sum of squares can be found by subtraction. Alternatively, and to check that the preceding computations have been carried out correctly,

(1) In each group, divide the squared sum of raw scores by the number of scores in the group and subtract the result from the sum of the squared scores for that group.

(2) Sum the results across all groups:

$$SS_{Within} = \left(\sum X_1^2 - \frac{\left(\sum X_1\right)^2}{n_1}\right) + \left(\sum X_2^2 - \frac{\left(\sum X_2\right)^2}{n_2}\right) + \left(\sum X_n^2 - \frac{\left(\sum X_n\right)^2}{n_n}\right)$$

$$SS_{Within} = \left(302 - \frac{42^2}{6}\right) + \left(151 - \frac{27^2}{5}\right) + \left(110 - \frac{22^2}{5}\right)$$

$$= 26.4$$

Table 9.19   Independent ANOVA summary table

Source	Sum of squares	Degrees of freedom	Variance estimate	F ratio
Between	19.04	2	9.52	4.69
Within	26.4	13	2.03	
Total	45.44	15		

Step 5   Convert the sums of squares into variance estimates by dividing the results of steps 3 and 4 by the appropriate number of degrees of freedom.

For between-groups, df = the number of groups (k) minus 1.

$$s^2_{Between} = \frac{SS_{Between}}{k-1}$$

$$s^2_{Between} = \frac{19.04}{2} = 9.52$$

For within-groups, df = the total number of scores (N) minus the number of groups (k).

$$s^2_{Within} = \frac{SS_{Within}}{N-k}$$

$$s^2_{Within} = \frac{26.4}{13} = 2.03$$

Step 6   Calculate the F-ratio.

$$F = \frac{s^2_{Between}}{s^2_{Within}} = \frac{\dfrac{SS_{Between}}{df}}{\dfrac{SS_{Within}}{df}}$$

$$F = \frac{9.52}{2.03} = 4.69$$

Step 7   Insert the computed values in the summary table (table 9.19) and consult table 10 in appendix 4 for the critical values of F at both $\alpha = 0.05$ and 0.01 for pairs of degrees of freedom.

From table 10, the critical value of F for df 2 and 13 and $\alpha = 0.05$ is 3.8.

Step 8   *Decision on hypotheses.* If the computed F equals or exceeds the table value, H_0 may be rejected and it may be concluded that at least one of the population means differed from the others.

In this case, the computed F exceeds the table value and the null hypothesis may be rejected. The probability of obtaining the observed F ratio under the null hypothesis is no greater than α.

[At this point, an *a posteriori* analysis of the data may be required to establish which of the differences between pairs of samples are the significant ones. Glenberg

(1988) and similar sources can provide advice on appropriate techniques, such as the protected t-test.]

Step 9 *Results.* The result should be reported in the format required by your document. Group means and standard deviations should normally be shown in a separate data table. The guidance of the APA is that, in addition, the computed value for F, the number of degrees of freedom of both components of the F ratio, the significance level (α), the exact probability of the observed F under H_0 (if available) and the direction of any observed effect should be reported (APA, 1994).

With an alpha level of 0.05, F (2.13) = 4.69, it can be concluded that the sensory modality in which information is presented appears to influence subsequent ease of recall. Handling the objects produced the highest mean recall score, reading the names of objects produced the lowest, and viewing a picture of the object produced an intermediate score.

The 1-factor ANOVA for independent samples in SPSS

(Data from the example above.)

Data entry

In **Variable View**
In the first column under 'Name' type the name of the independent variable (e.g. 'Tasktype')
Underneath type the name of the dependent variable (e.g. 'Memscore')
[See the introduction to SPSS in the appendix for instructions on how to label the different levels of the IV in Output View.]

Click on the **Data View** tab
In **Data View**
In the column under the heading '**memscore**' enter all the scores in one of the samples
In the column under the heading '**tasktype**' enter a '1' against each score
Enter all the scores from the second sample under those of the first sample
In the other column enter a '2' against each score in the second sample
Enter all the scores from the third sample under those of the second sample
In the other column enter a '3' against each score in the third sample.

Continue in this way until all data from all samples have been entered.

Data analysis

ANALYZE > Compare Means > One-Way ANOVA
In the **One-Way ANOVA** dialogue box
    Click to highlight the name of the dependent variable (e.g. 'memscore')
    Click on the top arrow button to move it into the **Dependent List** box
    Click to highlight the name of the independent variable (e.g. 'tasktype')

Table 9.20 SPSS output from the 1-factor independent samples ANOVA (example data: one way)

ANOVA

MEMSCORE

	Sum of Squares	df	Mean Square	F	Sig.
Between groups	19.037	2	9.519	4.687	.029
Within groups	26.400	13	2.031		
Total	45.437	15			

Click on the lower arrow button to move it into the **Factor** box
Click on **OK**.

The result appears in **Output View** as shown in table 9.20. The APA guidance on reporting the results of this test can be found at the end of the instructions for hand computation.

Alternatively, the general linear model provides more information in Output View, including a reminder of the different levels of the variable under analysis.

ANALYZE > General Linear Model > Univariate
In the **Univariate** dialogue box
    Click to highlight the name of the dependent variable (e.g. 'memscore')
    Click on the top arrow button to move it into the **Dependent Variable** box
    Click to highlight the name of the independent variable (e.g. 'tasktype')
    Click on the second arrow button to move it into the **Fixed Factor(s)** box
    Click on **OK**.

The result appears in **Output View** as shown in table 9.21
[Note that values for between-groups differences (treatment effects) are labelled 'Corrected Model' and within-groups differences are labelled 'Error' in this table.]

● THE ONE-FACTOR ANALYSIS OF VARIANCE FOR MATCHED SAMPLES (ANOVA) ●

Purpose

This test provides for the analysis of three or more related samples of data that differ in one dimension, testing the null hypothesis that the samples were all drawn from the same population and therefore have identical means. The alternate hypothesis is non-directional, that at least one of the sample means is significantly different from the others.

Table 9.21   SPSS output from the general linear model 1-factor
independent samples ANOVA (example data)

Between-subjects factors

		Value label	N
tasktype	1.00	Handle object	6
	2.00	Look at picture	5
	3.00	Read name	5

Tests of between-subjects effects

Dependent variable: memscore

Source	Type III sum of squares	df	Mean square	F	Sig.
Corrected model	19.038[a]	2	9.519	4.687	.029
Intercept	498.071	1	498.071	245.262	.000
tasktype	19.037	2	9.519	4.687	.029
Error	26.400	13	2.031		
Total	563.000	16			
Corrected total	45.438	15			

[a] R squared = .419 (adjusted R squared = .330).

The statistical model

This ANOVA requires the same set of conditions as the 1-factor ANOVA for independent groups, namely that the dependent variable is normally distributed in its population, that all observations are obtained by random sampling, and are independent, both within and between groups. Measures should achieve at least the interval scale with homogeneous variance across all groups (i.e. that the variance of each group is approximately equal).

In addition, it requires that the same degree of relatedness exists between the scores in all pairs of samples (i.e. any pair of samples are related in the same way as any other pair).

Overview

In a related samples design, different groups of scores analysed by this ANOVA represent a series of different experimental treatments applied to the same group of subjects. In this case, the means differ for the following reasons:

- Difference between subjects
- Difference within subjects.

And difference between subjects can further be broken down into:

- Differences due to treatments
- Differences due to error.

Table 9.22   Sources of error variance in matched samples

Type of variance	Cause
Variance within a group or sample	Error
Variance between different groups	Effect of treatment + error
Variance between related scores	Due to the fact that sets of scores are generated by the same, or matched, individuals
Total variance	Variance between different groups + Variance within a group

It is usual to capture this difference in the form of variance, so the 1-factor ANOVA sets about comparing the means of three or more groups by generating estimates of the population variance attributable to these sources. (Recall that variance is a measure of the variability of a set of scores indicated by the mean of squared individual deviations: see chapter 7). The advantage offered by the matched samples ANOVA is that it allows the variability due to interpersonal differences to be estimated and removed from the calculation, thereby resulting in a smaller (or less crude) estimate of error.

> Deviation: the difference between a score and a mean to which it has contributed.

Thus the variances present in samples of related scores can be apportioned as shown in table 9.22.

As with the independent groups ANOVA, the matched groups ANOVA generates independent estimates of population variance and again the ratio of the estimates of the variance between groups and within groups provides the statistic F.

$$F = \frac{\text{between groups variance}}{\text{within groups variance}}$$

In the matched groups ANOVA, however, the estimate of the variance due to individual differences can be computed and subtracted from the total variance when the variance due to error is computed (see step 5 below).

Rather than variance, the matched groups ANOVA computation again uses the sums of squares – the sum of squared deviations about a mean. As noted earlier, the relationship between variance and sums of squares is

$$s^2 = \frac{SS}{df}$$

When H_0 is true and all samples have been drawn from the same population, the ratio of between-groups to within-groups variance is 1 (because both sides of the ratio will consist only of the same amount of error). If the ratio is greater than 1, however, it suggests the presence of other sources of difference between the groups than that caused by error.

The probability of obtaining the observed F ratio under H_0 can be assessed from the sampling distribution of F. (This is a family of positively skewed distributions that vary with each pair of degrees of freedom, one for each variance estimate.) If the ratio exceeds 1 with an associated probability that is below the significance level (α) then H_0 may be rejected.

Table 9.23 Estimates of elapsed time under three conditions

	Silence		Music		Noise			
	X_1	X_1^2	X_2	X_2^2	X_3	X_3^2	ΣX_{Rel}	ΣX_{Rel}^2
1	9.0	81	2.0	4	10.0	100	21	441
2	6.0	36	7.0	49	7.0	49	20	400
3	6.0	36	3.0	9	4.0	16	13	169
4	7.5	56.25	4.5	20.25	6.5	42.25	18.5	342.25
5	5.0	25	4.0	16	7.5	56.25	16.5	272.25
6	5.0	25	5.0	25	5.0	25	15	225
	$\Sigma X_1 =$	$\Sigma X_1^2 =$	$\Sigma X_2 =$	$\Sigma X_2^2 =$	$\Sigma X_3 = 40$	$\Sigma X_3^2 =$	$\Sigma X_{Rel} =$	$\Sigma X_{Rel}^2 =$
	38.5	259.25	25.5	123.25		288.5	104	1849.5
	$\bar{X}_1 = 6.41$		$\bar{X}_2 = 4.25$		$\bar{X}_3 = 6.67$			

Total N: 18; grand sum: 38.5 + 25.5 + 40 = 104; grand mean: 104 ÷ 18 = 5.78.

Computation of the 1-factor ANOVA for matched samples

To control for inter-participant differences, researchers used a 1-factor matched samples ANOVA to assess whether exposure to sounds could affect time perception. The experiment involved estimating the duration of a standard interval in three conditions. In one condition, the interval was completely silent, in the second it was accompanied by strongly rhythmic music, and in the third it was accompanied by un-patterned 'white noise'. Each participant contributed to all three conditions, counterbalanced against order effects. The same standard interval was used throughout.

As the experiment involved a repeated measures design of three groups, and the data involved measures on an interval scale, with the other requirements of the statistical model assumed to hold, the 1-factor ANOVA for matched samples is appropriate. This tests the null hypothesis that the three samples will be drawn from populations having identical means (or equivalently, from the same population). The significance level selected is $\alpha = 0.05$.

Step 1   (1) Square each raw score and calculate the sum and mean of both raw and squared scores in each group.
      (2) Sum each row of scores separately.
      (3) Calculate the grand sum (the sum of all scores) and the grand mean (see table 9.23).

Step 2   Find the total sum of squares by:
      (1) Sum all the squares of raw scores across all groups
      (2) Find the correction for the mean by squaring the grand sum and dividing the result by the total number of raw scores
      (3) Subtract the result of (2) from the result of (1).

$$SS_{Total} = \sum X_{Total}^2 - \frac{\left(\sum X_{Total}\right)^2}{N}$$

$$SS_{Total} = (259.25 + 123.25 + 288.5) - \frac{104^2}{18}$$

$$= 70.11$$

Step 3 Find the between-treatment-groups sum of squares:
(1) Find the square of the sum of the raw scores in each group and divide each by the number of scores in that group. Sum the results (the mean squared sums of scores) across the groups
(2) Subtract the correction for the mean from the result of (1).

$$SS_{Between} = \frac{\left(\sum X_1\right)^2}{n_1} + \frac{\left(\sum X_2\right)^2}{n_2} + \frac{\left(\sum X_n\right)^2}{n_n} - \frac{\left(\sum X_{Total}\right)^2}{N}$$

$$SS_{Between} = \left(\frac{38.5^2}{6} + \frac{25.5^2}{6} + \frac{40^2}{6}\right) - \frac{104^2}{18}$$

$$= 21.2$$

Step 4 Find the sum of squares for related scores (i.e. scores on each line of data).
(1) Square the sum of each set of related scores
(2) Sum the squared totals and divide by the number of groups (k) and subtract the correction for the mean.

$$SS_{Related} = \frac{\sum\left(\sum X_{Related}\right)^2}{k} - \frac{\left(\sum X_{Total}\right)^2}{N}$$

$$SS_{Related} = \frac{1849.5}{3} - \frac{104^2}{18}$$

$$= 15.61$$

Step 5 Find the within-groups sum of squares (the error) by subtracting the SS between treatment groups and SS related scores from the total SS.

$$SS_{Within} = SS_{Total} - SS_{Between} - SS_{Related}$$

$$SS_{Within} = 70.11 - 21.2 - 15.61$$

$$= 33.3$$

Step 6 Convert the sums of squares into variance estimates.
For between-treatment groups, df = the number of group (k) minus 1.

$$s_{Between}^2 = \frac{SS_{Between}}{k-1}$$

$$s_{Between}^2 = \frac{21.2}{2} = 10.6$$

For related scores, df = the number of related scores (n) − 1.

Table 9.24 Matched samples ANOVA summary table

Source	Sum of squares	Degrees of freedom	Variance estimate	F ratio
Between	21.2	2	10.6	3.18
Related	15.61	5	3.12	
Within	33.3	10	3.33	
Total	70.1	17		

$$s^2_{Related} = \frac{SS_{Related}}{n-1}$$

$$s^2_{Related} = \frac{15.61}{5} = 3.12$$

For within-groups, df = the total number of scores (N) minus the number of groups (k) minus the number of related scores (n) + 1.

$$s^2_{Within} = N - k - n + 1$$

$$s^2_{Within} = \frac{33.3}{10} = 3.33$$

Step 7   Calculate the F-ratio

$$F = \frac{s^2_{Between}}{s^2_{Within}} = \frac{\dfrac{SS_{Between}}{df}}{\dfrac{SS_{Within}}{df}}$$

$$F = \frac{10.6}{3.33} = 3.18$$

Step 8   Draw up the summary table as in table 9.24.

Consult table 10 in appendix 4. This gives the critical values of F at both $\alpha = 0.05$ and 0.01 for pairs of degrees of freedom.

From table 10 the critical value of F for df 2 and 10 and $\alpha = 0.05$ is 4.1.

Step 9   *Decision about hypotheses.* If the computed F equals or exceeds the critical value of F in table 10, H_0 may be rejected. In such case it may be concluded that the probability that at least one of the population means differed from the others when the null hypothesis is true is no greater than the significance level α.

Since the computed F does not exceed the table value the probability of obtaining that F under the null hypothesis is greater than α. The null hypothesis, that the data were drawn from populations with the same (or very similar) means is thus retained.

[At this point, further *a posteriori* analyses of the data may be required to establish which differences are significant. Advanced texts, such as Glenberg (1988) can provide advice on appropriate techniques.]

Results. The result should be reported in the format required by your document. Group means and standard deviations should normally be shown in a separate data table. The guidance of the APA is that, in addition, the computed value for F, the number of degrees of freedom, the significance level (α), the exact probability of the observed F under H_0 (if available) and the direction of any effect should all be reported. (APA, 1994).

   With an alpha level of 0.05 F (2,10) = 3.21, it can be concluded that the presence or absence of sound does not significantly affect estimates of duration.

The 1-factor ANOVA for matched samples in SPSS

(Data from the example above.)

Data entry

In **Variable View**,
In the first column under 'Name' type the name of the first level of the IV (e.g. 'silence' in the example)
Enter the names of the other levels in the same column (e.g. 'music' and 'noise')
Click on **Data view**
Enter the scores under the appropriate name of the level.

Data analysis

Select **ANALYZE > General Linear Model > Repeated Measures**
In the **Repeated Measures Define Factors** dialogue box
Enter a name for the within-subjects factor (e.g. 'exposure') after highlighting '**factor 1**' in the top box.
Enter the number of levels (conditions) in the box below.
   Click on the **Add** button
   Click on the **Define** button
In the **Repeated Measures** dialogue box
   Click to highlight a variable name (e.g 'silence')
   Click on the top arrow button to move it into the **Within-Subjects Variables (list)** box.
   Repeat the process for other variable names. (If there is a meaningful order to the variables, such as the expected magnitudes of data values, then it should be followed.)

   Click on the **Options** button to obtain descriptives with the output
   Click on **OK**.

The output table is the **Tests of Within-Subjects Effects table**, shown with the descriptives in table 9.25. This gives the measure of the effect of the experimental treatment on the various conditions.

Table 9.25   SPSS output from the 1-factor ANOVA for matched samples (example data)

Descriptive statistics

	Mean	Std deviation	N
Silence	6.4167	1.56258	6
Music	4.2500	1.72482	6
Noise	6.6667	2.08966	6

Tests of within-subjects effects

Source		Type III sum of squares	df	Mean square	F	Sig.
Cond	Sphericity Assumed	21.194	2	10.597	3.182	.085
	Greenhouse-Geisser	21.194	1.444	14.677	3.182	.110
	Huynh-Feldt	21.194	1.874	11.309	3.182	.090
	Lower-bound	21.194	1.000	21.194	3.182	.135
Error (cond)	Sphericity Assumed	33.306	1.0	3.331		
	Greenhouse-Geisser	33.306	7.220	4.613		
	Huynh-Feldt	33.306	9.371	3.554		
	Lower-bound	33.306	5.000	6.661		

The information required is that in the first line of this table (the one listed as 'sphericity assumed) giving type III sums of squares; df; F value; and exact significance. The APA guidance on reporting the results of this test can be found at the end of the instructions for hand computation.

The table **Tests of Within Subjects Contrasts** gives the results of linear and quadratic trend tests on the different levels of the factor. These are only relevant when the levels have been moved into the **Within-Subjects Variables (list)** box in a meaningful order (see above). As trend tests are outside the scope of this book you will need to consult a text such as Howell (1997) for guidance.

● SPEARMAN'S RANK ORDER CORRELATION COEFFICIENT ●

Purpose

Spearman's rank order correlation coefficient, r_s, describes the co-variance of any two sets of scores, X and Y, and can be used to test the null hypothesis that the population coefficient, ρ_s, is zero (i.e. that the populations from which the two sets of scores were drawn co-vary randomly) and thus that r_s is also zero.

Statistical model

The Spearman coefficient makes only two assumptions:

* The data consist of measures on at least an ordinal scale
* The X and Y samples are dependent, while scores within them are independent.

It is therefore appropriate to use this procedure when the assumptions of the Pearson coefficient cannot be satisfied.

Overview

Because ordinal data preserve only general relationships of magnitude between different scores, Pearson's coefficient cannot be used directly on datasets containing ordinal measures. However, if raw ordinal data are first converted to rankings then the simpler computational formula can be used to produce the same result as would be obtained from the Pearson formula.

When the null hypothesis is true the value of r_s will be close to zero, so the greater the value of r_s the greater the confidence that can be placed in the alternate hypothesis. Critical values for r_s for sample sizes up to n = 30 can be found in table 3 in appendix 4. For sample sizes greater than this consult an advanced text such as Glenberg (1988).

Computation of Spearman's rank order coefficient

The formula is:

$$r_s = 1 - \frac{6 \sum d^2}{n_p^3 - n_p}$$

Where:

n_p is the number of pairs of scores
Σd^2 is the sum of the squared differences in ranks
6 is a constant

A designer of psychometric tests wished to evaluate the validity of a newly constructed test of emotional stability. In order to do this she decided to compare the scores obtained by a sample of 12 subjects on the new test, with the scores obtained by the same individuals on an established test.

The data consist of paired scores from the same individuals representing measures on the ordinal scale so the Spearman coefficient is appropriate, testing the null hypothesis that the correlation between the two sets of scores is zero. The one-tailed alpha level chosen is $\alpha = 0.05$.

Step 1 Rank each set of scores individually, giving the rank of 1 to the lowest score in each set.

Step 2 Find the difference between each pair of ranks and square each difference. Sum the squared differences (see table 9.26).

Step 3 Insert the result of step 2 in the formula to find r_s.

Table 9.26 Scores on 'old' and 'new' tests

Data X old test	X ranks	Data Y new test	Y ranks	Difference in ranks	Difference
17	1	20	11.5	10.5	110.25
48	12	13	4	−8	64
44	10	17	9	−1	1
19	2	11	2	0	0
30	5	20	11.5	6.5	42.25
36	6	16	7.5	1.5	2.25
41	8	19	10	2	4
40	7	12	3	−4	16
42	9	10	1	−8	64
22	3	14	5	2	4
24	4	16	7.5	3.5	12.25
47	11	15	6	−5	25
					$\Sigma d^2 = 345$

$$r_s = 1 - \frac{6 \sum d^2}{(n^3 - n)}$$

$$= 1 - \frac{6(345)}{12^3 - 12}$$

$$= 1 - \frac{2070}{1716}$$

$$= 1 - 1.21$$

$$r_s = -0.21$$

Step 4 *Decision on hypotheses.* Table 3 in appendix 4 gives critical values of r_s for the $p = 0.05$ and $p = 0.01$ significance levels and different sample sizes up to $n = 30$.

   If the computed value for r_s is so different from zero that it equals or exceeds the table value then its probability under the null hypothesis is no greater than the significance level and the null hypothesis may be rejected.

   For a non-directional test, r_s may exceed the table value in either the positive or the negative direction, while for a directional test, the computed r_s must equal or exceed the table value in the predicted direction for the null hypothesis to be rejected.

   In this case, table 3 gives the one-tailed critical value for $\alpha = 0.05$ *and* $n_p = 12$ *of* $r_s = 0.503$.

   As the absolute value of r_s is closer to zero than this value, its probability under the null hypothesis is greater than the significance level, and the null hypothesis is retained.

Step 5 *Results.* The result should be reported in the format required by your document. The guidance of the APA is that the computed value for r_s, the significance level (α), the size of samples, and the exact probability of the observed r_s under H_0 (if available) should be presented (APA, 1994).

For $\alpha = 0.05$ (one-tailed) and $r_s = -0.21$ (12) the correlation between scores on the established and new tests was found to be negative and non-significant. It is therefore concluded that it is likely that the new test of emotional stability is measuring a different variable than the older test, and cannot be used as an alternative to it.

Spearman's correlation coefficient in SPSS

(Data from the example above.)

Data entry

In **Data View**
Click on **Variable View**
Type the name of one variable (e.g. 'old') n the first cell of column 1.
Type the name of the other variable ('new') underneath the first
Click on **Data View**
Enter the scores under the appropriate variable name, ensuring that related scores are on the
    same line.

Data analysis

ANALYZE > Correlate > Bivariate
    Click to highlight the names of the variables in the left-hand box
    Click on the arrow button to move the names into the **Variables** box
    Click to tick the **Spearman Coefficient**
    Click on the appropriate radio buttons to select either the 1- or 2-tailed **Test of Significance** required
    Tick the box in the bottom left-hand corner to select **Flag significant correlations**
    Click on **OK**.

The output from SPSS will appear as shown in table 9.27. This gives the computed value for r_s, the exact probability of that value under H_0 and N the number of pairs of scores. Note that the top and bottom halves of the table contain identical information. The APA guidance for reporting results can be found at the end of the instructions for hand computation of the coefficient.

Missing scores

If any scores are missing from the dataset, before clicking on **OK**
    Click on the **Options** button
In the **Bivariate Correlations:Options** dialogue box
    Click the radio button to select **Exclude cases pairwise**
    Click to tick any descriptive statistics required
    Click on **Continue**
    Click on **OK**.

Table 9.27 SPSS output from the Spearman rank order correlation (example data)

Correlations

			old	new
Spearman's rho	old	Correlation coefficient	1.000	−.211
		Sig. (1-tailed)		.256
		N	12	12
	new	Correlation coefficient	−.211	1.000
		Sig. (1-tailed)	.256	
		N	12	12

● PEARSON'S PRODUCT MOMENT CORRELATION COEFFICIENT ●

Purpose

The Pearson product moment correlation coefficient, r, describes the co-variance of any two sets of scores, X and Y, and can be used as a test statistic testing the null hypothesis that the population coefficient, ρ, is zero (i.e. that the populations from which the two sets of scores were drawn co-vary randomly) and thus that r is also zero.

Statistical model

For appropriate use of this coefficient it should be possible to assume, with a reasonable degree of certainty, that the following requirements have been met.

- The populations of X and Y are normally distributed
- The variance of the Y scores is the same for each value of X (homoscedasticity)
- There is a linear relationship between the X and Y variables
- The X and Y samples are dependent while scores within them are independent
- Data consist of measures on at least the interval scale and represent samples from the whole range of both variables
- There are no extreme scores in either sample
- Neither set of scores was formed by combining data from different groups.

Overview

The co-variance (or correlation) of any two variables, X and Y, refers to the extent to which the values of X vary for different values of Y (see chapter 7 for an introduction). A measure of this relationship is defined in the formula below where, for each pair of scores, the deviations of each score about their respective means are multiplied together and the sum of those products is divided by the number of degrees of freedom. (Note that the formula for s^2, the variance of a single sample, is obtained if the Y term is changed to X.)

$$COV_{XY} = \frac{\sum(X - \bar{X})(Y - \bar{Y})}{N - 1}$$

However, it is also known that the value of COV_{XY} is a function of the standard deviations of X and Y. When the standard deviations are high a given value for COV_{XY} may reflect a low degree of correlation, but when the standard deviations are low the same value could indicate a high degree of correlation. This means that it is necessary to take the standard deviations into account when trying to evaluate the extent to which two variables co-vary. This is what the product-moment coefficient does: r is the ratio between the co-variance of the two sets of scores and the product of their standard deviations, with limits that are always ±1.

$$r = \frac{COV_{XY}}{s_X s_Y}$$

When $\rho = 0$ (i.e. when H_0 is correct) r is distributed approximately normally. The critical values of r for the 0.05 and 0.01 alpha levels for a range of degrees of freedom are given in table 4 of appendix 4.

Computation of Pearson's product moment coefficient

The formula for Pearson's r is:

$$r = \frac{n_p \sum XY - \sum X \sum Y}{\sqrt{\left[n_p \sum X^2 - \left(\sum X\right)^2 \right]\left[n_p \sum Y^2 - \left(\sum Y\right)^2 \right]}}$$

Where n_p is the number of pairs of scores.

A study of problem solving asked whether the ability to solve pencil and paper problems in a laboratory test was related in any way to the ability to solve problems in everyday life. Two sets of problems were put together. One set were logic problems – statements that required a decision about whether they were 'true' or 'false'. The other were 'real-life' problem scenarios requiring a decision about the 'best' course of action.

Half of the ten participants attempted the logic problems first followed by the real-life problems and the other half attempted them in the reverse order. The data consisted of measures of the time in minutes to answer each set of problems.

As the data represent interval scale measures of a continuous variable, the Pearson product-moment correlation, it is appropriate, testing the null hypothesis that the correlation between the two sets of scores is zero. The two-tailed significance level chosen is $\alpha = 0.05$.

Step 1 Cast the data into two columns, X and Y, ensuring that related scores are placed on the same line. Then,
- Square each raw score and
- Find the product of each pair of raw scores
- Sum each column of raw scores, each column of squared scores and the column of raw score products separately (see table 9.28).

Table 9.28   Scores on problem solving

Data X logic problems	X^2	Data Y real-life problems	Y^2	XY
16	256	19	361	304
16	256	17	289	272
12	144	18	324	216
19	361	4	16	76
7	49	7	49	49
14	196	23	529	322
24	576	12	144	288
3	9	8	64	24
21	441	17	289	357
13	169	12	144	156
$\Sigma X = 145$	$\Sigma X^2 = 2457$	$\Sigma Y = 137$	$\Sigma Y^2 = 2209$	$\Sigma XY = 2064$

Step 2   Find: $n_p\Sigma X^2 - (\Sigma X)^2$ and $n_p\Sigma Y^2 - (\Sigma Y)^2$

Square the sum of the X scores and subtract the result from the sum of the squared scores multiplied by n_p. Repeat for the Y scores.

$$n_p\sum X^2 - \left(\sum X\right)^2 = 10(2457) - 145^2$$
$$= 24570 - 21025$$
$$= 3545$$

$$n_p\sum Y^2 - \left(\sum Y\right)^2 = 10(2209) - 137^2$$
$$= 22090 - 18769$$
$$= 3321$$

Step 3   Multiply together the results of step 2 and find the square root of the result.

$$\sqrt{(3545)(3321)} = 3431.17$$

Step 4   Find $n_p\Sigma XY - \Sigma X\Sigma Y$

Multiply the sum of X and the sum of Y scores and subtract the result from the sum of the products of X and Y multiplied by the number of pairs of scores.

$$n_p\sum XY - \sum X\sum Y = 10(2064) - (145)(137)$$
$$= 20640 - 19865$$
$$= 775$$

Step 5   Divide the result of step 3 into the result of step 4 to find Pearson's **r**.

$$\mathbf{r} = \frac{775}{3431.17} = 0.226$$

Step 6 *Decision on hypotheses.* Table 4 in appendix 4 gives critical values of r for the p = 0.05 and p = 0.01 significance levels and a range of degrees of freedom (df = n_p − 2). If the computed value for **r** is so different from zero that it equals or exceeds the table value then its probability under the null hypothesis is no greater than the significance level and the null hypothesis may be rejected.

Table 4 gives the two-tailed critical value for α = 0.05 and df = 8 as r = 0.632.

*As the computed value for **r** is lower than this value, its probability under the null hypothesis is greater than the significance level. The null hypothesis is therefore retained.*

(For a non-directional test, r may exceed the table value in either the positive or the negative direction, while for a directional test, the computed r must equal or exceed the table value in the predicted direction for the null hypothesis to be rejected.)

Step 7 *Results.* The result should be reported in the format required by your document. The guidance of the APA is that the computed value for r, the significance level (α), the number of degrees of freedom (n_p − 2) and the exact probability of the observed r under H_0 (if available) should be presented (APA, 1994).

For α = 0.05 (two-tailed) and r = 0.226 (8) the correlation between scores on the logic and 'real-life' tests was found to be non-significant. It is therefore concluded that the knowledge and abilities required to answer the logic test items and the 'real-life' items are not related.

Pearson's correlation coefficient in SPSS

(Data from the example above.)

Data entry

In **Data View**,
Click on **Variable View**
Type the name of one variable (e.g. 'logic') in the first cell of column 1.
Type the name of the other variable ('real') underneath the first
Click on **Data View**
Enter the scores under the appropriate variable name, ensuring that related scores are on the same line.

Data analysis

ANALYZE > Correlate > Bivariate
Click to highlight the names of the variables in the left-hand box
Click on the arrow button to move the names into the **Variables** box
Click to tick the **Pearson Coefficient**
Click on the radio buttons below to select the **Test of Significance** required (either 1- or 2-tailed).

Table 9.29 SPSS output from the Pearson product moment correlation (example data)

Correlations

		logic	real
logic	Pearson Correlation	1	.226
	Sig. (2-tailed)		.530
	N	10	10
real	Pearson Correlation	.226	1
	Sig. (2-tailed)	.530	
	N	10	10

Tick the box in the bottom left-hand corner to select **Flag significant correlations**.
     Click on **OK**.

Missing scores

If any scores are missing from the dataset, before clicking on **OK**,
     Click on the **Options** button
In the **Bivariate Correlations: Options** dialogue box
     Click the radio button to select **Exclude cases pairwise**
     Click to tick any descriptive statistics required
     Click on **Continue**
     Click on **OK**.

The output from SPSS will appear as shown in table 9.29. This gives the computed value for r (identified as Pearson correlation), its exact probability under H_0 and N the number of pairs of scores. Note that the top and bottom halves of the table contain identical information. The APA guidance for reporting results can be found at the end of the instructions for hand computation of the coefficient.

APPENDICES

1

ETHICAL PRINCIPLES IN PSYCHOLOGICAL RESEARCH

The following is a summary of the current guidance on research ethics published by the British Psychological Society (BPS, 1992). The full version is available on the British Psychological Society website at www.bps.org.uk.

Introduction

- People who give up their time to assist psychological research by acting as research participants, whether with or without payment, should be confident that they will receive the highest standards of treatment. The purpose of these ethical principles, by making clear the distinction between acceptable and unacceptable research practice, is to allow participants to have that confidence.

The principles

- The ethical implications of research must always be considered from the standpoint of prospective participants with a view to identifying and removing any identifiable threats to well-being, health, values or dignity.
- All participants should normally be fully informed of the purpose of the research so that they may give real consent, and the researcher should answer any further questions that a participant might have especially if these may have a bearing on willingness to take part. Special safeguards are required for participants, such as children, who may not fully understand the information provided.
- Deception, in the form of withholding information or deliberately misleading participants, should be avoided. If either appears necessary for scientific reasons there is a procedure for safeguarding the interests of participants.
- Post-investigation debriefing should be a normal part of procedure. This permits participants to be given any information omitted before the research began, and provides a

period during which they can review and discuss their experience of participation with the investigator.

- Participants should be informed of their right to withdraw from the research at any time, including after debriefing, and to require their data to be destroyed.
- All information about a participant is held in confidence and is subject to the requirements of the Data Protection Act 1998.
- The researcher's prime responsibility is to protect participants from mental or physical harm, including the effects of stress, during an investigation. The test is whether there is likely to be exposure to risks greater than would normally be encountered in everyday life.
- Observational research requires informed consent unless observation is conducted where participants could normally expect to be observed by strangers.
- If a participant solicits the advice of a researcher as a consequence of having been involved in research, and the matter appears serious, a recommendation to seek appropriately qualified professional advice should be given.

● FURTHER READING ●

Gale, A. (1995). Ethical issues in psychological research. In A. M. Colman (ed.), *Psychological research methods and statistics*. London: Longman.

Oliver, P. (2003). *The student's guide to research ethics*. Maidenhead: Open University Press.

2

SPSS VERSIONS 11, 12 AND 13

SPSS is a widely used statistics software package for the social sciences that removes the need for laborious hand calculation. It is a complex piece of software and this book therefore aims to offer only essential guidance, and an aid to memory, rather than a complete introduction. For more information a dedicated text, such as those listed below, should be consulted.

The SPSS procedures described in this book have been checked against the three most recently released versions of the program, namely versions 11, 12 and 13. (It may also be possible to use the book with version 10, although this has not been checked.) Most of the procedures and dialogue boxes are the same in all three versions, but where differences exist the points at which versions 12 and/or 13 diverge from version 11 are indicated in the text by the presence of square brackets [ ]. Except where otherwise indicated, the figures and tables were generated by SPSS version 11 and these may also differ when produced by later versions of the software.

BOX 1

In the following pages,

- The names of the main menus in SPSS are in bold upper-case thus, **ANALYZE**
- Dialogue box items or menu items are shown in bold title case thus, **Compare Means**
- The successive selection of menu or dialogue box items is indicated by the right facing arrowhead: **ANALYZE > Descriptive Statistics > Frequencies**

Data entry into SPSS

Select SPSS from the **Programs** menu
   The first screen presents you with a number of options.

Click on a radio button to select either **Type in data** or **Load Data** [In v. 12 & 13 the latter command is **Open an existing Data Source**].
Click on **OK.**

If you chose **Type in data** the next screen you will see is the spreadsheet interface of the Data Editor. Note the tab at the bottom left of the screen indicates that you are now in **Data View.**

Click on the tab next to **Data View** to switch to **Variable View** (note that the column labels change). In this view you are able to set up headings for the columns in **Data View** and tell the program what kind of data to expect.

- The **Name** column identifies the subsets of data. When you type something in this column the system provides default entries for the other columns. Type 'Group 1' in the first cell of the first column, press **>Return<** and observe the effect – the defaults should appear.
- The **Type** column is where you can tell the system whether or not to expect Numeric data – this should almost always show **Numeric.**
- The **Width** column is where you set the number of characters you want to have room for – re-set it if it doesn't already show 8.
- The **Decimals** column is where you set the number of decimal places you want the system to accommodate. Re-set it if it isn't set at 2. (You can experiment with different settings later, if you wish.)
- The **Values** column is where you enter data labels to identify different levels of variables (especially useful when carrying out an ANOVA).
- The **Missing** column is where you indicate how many missing data items are in your dataset.
- The **Columns** column is where you indicate the number of columns of data to be used.
- The **Align** column allows you to align data items (right, left or centre) for that variable.
- The **Measures** column allows selection of a scale of measurement.

Adding data labels

In **Variable View** (once variable names have been entered in column 1).
Click on the empty **Values** cell on a line containing a variable name
Click on the grey shaded area that appears
In the **Variable Labels** dialogue box
Enter the number identifying the first level of the variable in the **Value** box
Enter a name for that level in the **Value Label** box
Click on the **Add** button

Repeat for as many labels as needed, changing the identifying number and label name each time. When all levels have been labelled,
Click on **OK**
The labels will appear in **Output View.**

Analysis using SPSS

Most of the data treatments needed are accessed through the **ANALYZE** pull-down menu and will be found under the headings,

- **Compare Means** (t-tests and ANOVAs)
- **Correlate** (Correlation coefficients)
- **Nonparametric tests** (Nonparametric tests)
- **Descriptive Statistics** (Descriptive statistics of all kinds)
- **Descriptive Statistics > Explore** provides the boxplot and stem and leaf display.

The **GRAPHS** pull-down menu provides a range of line and bar graphs, histograms, scatterplots.

Once data have been processed by the program, the result is displayed in **Output View**. Both graphs and tables from **Output View** can be cut and pasted directly into a word processor document if desired.

To obtain online help with the interpretation of SPSS output tables

In **Output View** click to activate any table.

Right click on the mouse and select **Results Coach** to obtain a series of annotated example screens for the current statistic.

● FURTHER READING ●

Brace, N., Kemp, R. and Snelgar, R. (2003). *SPSS for psychologists*, 2nd edn. Basingstoke: Palgrave Macmillan.

Miller, R. L., Acton, C., Fullerton, D. A. and Maltby, J. (2002). *SPSS for social scientists*. Basingstoke: Palgrave Macmillan.

Pallant, J. (2005). *SPSS survival manual*, 2nd edn. Buckingham: Open Universaity Press.

3

THE BASIC RULES OF MATHEMATICS

Expressions with and without brackets

The contents of any pair of brackets will be reducible to a single value. If a formula includes an expression in brackets carry out the calculations inside the brackets first of all.

When brackets are placed back to back, as they are below, multiply the contents of the brackets together. Thus:

$$(7+4)(5-3) = (11)(2) = 22$$

If there are no expressions in brackets carry out all multiplication and division operations first, then add and subtract.

$$e.g. \quad 15 \div 3 + 8 = 13 \quad not \quad 1.36$$

If there are only additions and subtractions work through them systematically from left to right.

Positive and negative values

Values can be either positive or negative. The relationship between positive and negative values for a small selection of integers (whole numbers) is shown below.

$$\Leftarrow etcetera \quad -4 \quad -3 \quad -2 \quad -1 \quad 0 \quad +1 \quad +2 \quad +3 \quad +4 \quad etcetera \Rightarrow$$

The rules for manipulating positive and negative values are:

- Adding positive values gives a positive answer
- Adding negative values gives a negative answer
- Adding positive to negative values is the same as subtracting positive from positive values. Thus, $(-7) + (9) = 9 - 7 = 2$
- Multiplying two positive values gives a positive answer
- Multiplying two negative values also gives a positive answer

- Multiplying a positive by a negative value gives a negative answer
- Dividing a positive value by a negative one (or vice versa) always gives a negative answer
- Dividing a negative value by a negative one gives a positive answer.

Squares and cubes

The square of a value is that value multiplied by itself: $2^2 = 2 \times 2 = 4$.

The cube of a value is the value multiplied by itself twice: $2^3 = 2 \times 2 \times 2 = 8$.

The square root of a value is the value that you need to multiply by itself to arrive at the value you already have. Thus, $\sqrt{64} = 8$ and $8 \times 8 = 64$.

Similarly the cube root of a value is the value that must be multiplied by itself twice to arrive at the initial value – the cube root of 125 is 5 because $5 \times 5 \times 5 = 125$.

Rounding

Rounding makes unwieldy decimal numbers more manageable and comprehensible. In psychology, where measurement processes are subject to error anyway, rounding to two decimal places is a sensible practice.

To round a long decimal value to two places, start with the number furthest to the right of the decimal point. If it is a 5 or more remove it and increase the number to its left by 1. If it is 4 or less remove it without changing the next number. Continue until only two numbers remain to the right of the decimal point.

4

STATISTICAL TABLES

Table 1 Random numbers

2889	6587	0813	5063	0423	2547	5791	1352	6224	1994	9167	4857
1030	2943	6542	7866	2855	8047	4610	9008	5598	7810	7049	9205
1207	9574	6260	5351	5732	2227	1272	7227	7744	6732	2313	6795
0776	3001	8554	9692	7266	8665	6460	5659	7536	7546	4433	6371
5450	0644	7510	9146	9686	1983	5247	5365	0051	9351	3080	0519
2956	2327	1903	0533	1808	5151	7857	2617	3487	9623	9589	9993
3979	1128	9415	5204	4313	3700	7968	9626	6070	3983	6656	6203
5586	5777	5533	6202	0585	4025	2473	5293	7050	4821	4774	6317
2727	5126	3596	2900	4584	9090	6577	6399	2569	0209	0403	3578
1979	9507	2102	8448	5197	2855	5309	4886	2830	0235	7130	3206
4793	7421	8633	4990	2169	7489	8340	6980	9796	4759	9756	3324
8736	1718	1690	4675	2728	5213	7320	9605	6893	4169	9607	9750
8179	5942	3713	8183	9242	8504	3110	8907	7621	4024	7436	4240
3304	4624	3563	0231	6134	5943	3696	9150	2778	3706	0616	2598
1778	8036	8526	4177	6337	7163	9494	3303	4544	6688	9781	2603
8939	4667	2117	9810	3933	1561	6300	2592	8941	5891	6365	9959
9784	9014	7961	5556	1688	8760	3215	9967	4313	4300	9726	1691
2132	4160	2266	7217	3185	3369	0768	4920	4329	7171	0051	7262
0389	2632	3527	9918	2578	1203	0970	5093	1935	5619	2815	0041
9227	7340	3837	1105	7516	9881	9937	2992	2032	3967	5638	3092
3045	5194	6904	0084	1436	3795	6639	0109	2168	4095	7939	2752
8911	0081	0628	4812	0805	7526	0335	6305	7713	1381	2067	5873
1328	5801	0506	4224	0760	6029	9993	7293	7804	3625	7601	5403
8160	8451	5712	6846	5589	6009	7187	8970	8110	9591	8379	6820
6605	6298	0785	0779	2669	6167	8572	3741	8579	7648	2361	5887
0805	6297	1629	1852	1616	2356	6295	8097	6332	2534	0336	4884
6037	6531	1363	2108	1601	9258	2148	7974	7372	0864	8091	3807
2866	6159	9738	3534	1989	8405	3447	4788	0931	5488	9796	8601
6946	1395	6596	3211	7833	8251	9998	4439	1275	1060	3680	6639
9497	4236	3116	5981	9913	3705	0812	6039	2361	7384	8918	2602
0437	9596	1869	0630	4574	0003	0569	9947	2652	4806	3000	1803
3028	5559	6610	7144	0511	8413	6901	8891	2879	5071	4214	9655
9859	9601	3688	7790	4559	1466	1287	2259	4527	0851	8564	2385
4164	7208	5944	6798	3665	5640	2567	8782	8427	1730	3748	6949
0258	9802	5058	1195	3906	3563	4448	9749	4365	4553	4107	1483
4674	1176	6663	6008	9054	3365	8441	9454	0657	4828	0183	8409
1121	9173	9728	4474	0622	3095	6972	0712	1558	8493	1831	8345
5452	6229	9153	5854	6605	4719	6392	7564	2790	4352	1826	3296
8350	5845	2757	1496	3964	8573	8796	7623	8071	8641	0345	6263
4088	3569	3410	9432	2252	0474	6963	2183	4127	0608	0992	2622
5928	2738	5822	1479	2432	1238	4233	5690	9257	5468	9720	5433
2674	0330	7422	1913	4830	2801	9249	5861	5227	0302	9265	6899
0553	1526	7004	6922	6407	0473	2574	8278	3522	2188	8352	5778
6298	6170	4822	6850	6455	7542	7032	0960	5870	6143	9782	8276
3133	8513	4138	1016	4761	4377	8327	1970	4134	7877	6025	3861
3409	4904	4166	0976	2050	7340	9524	7795	9573	2047	4280	6103
0101	1188	3803	1016	8224	3958	2012	3982	7702	1888	3311	4915
1621	1438	2854	0818	0704	9217	6336	7533	1411	1178	9730	5362
3832	2930	6959	6850	3331	4715	6488	7527	0451	4161	9686	6293
6671	0459	2165	4739	9089	8677	4686	8688	8650	0913	2491	5480
6778	6638	6450	0736	5650	4594	2548	2848	3051	6073	7303	8768
4737	1084	4833	5083	5359	7764	5990	5892	6250	1893	9945	8906

Source: Taken from table XXXIII of R. A. Fisher and F. Yates (1953), *Statistical tables for biological, agricultural and medical research*, published by Longman Group UK Ltd, 1974, 6th edn.

Table 2   Areas under the normal distribution curve from the 0 to z

This table gives the area beneath the curve between the mean and any point on the X axis denoted by a z-score.

To read the table, first determine the values of z required up to the first decimal place in the leftmost column, then read across to find the area in the column indicated by the second decimal position. For example, the area under the curve between the mean and a z-score of 1.37 is 0.4147.

The table can also be read in reverse to find the z-score marking off any given area above or below the mean, by reading from the body of the table out to the margins.

z	00	01	02	03	04	05	06	07	08	09
0.0	.0000	.0040	.0080	.0120	.0160	.0199	.0239	.0279	.0319	.0359
0.1	.0398	.0438	.0478	.0517	.0557	.0596	.0636	.0675	.0714	.0754
0.2	.0793	.0832	.0871	.0910	.0948	.0987	.1026	.1064	.1103	.1141
0.3	.1179	.1217	.1255	.1293	.1331	.1368	.1406	.1443	.1480	.1517
0.4	.1554	.1591	.1628	.1664	.1700	.1737	.1772	.1808	.1844	.1879
0.5	.1915	.1950	.1985	.2019	.2054	.2088	.2123	.2157	.2190	.2224
0.6	.2258	.2291	.2324	.2357	.2389	.2422	.2454	.2486	.2518	.2549
0.7	.2587	.2612	.2642	.2673	.2704	.2734	.2764	.2794	.2823	.2852
0.8	.2882	.2910	.2939	.2967	.2996	.3023	.3051	.3079	.3106	.3133
0.9	.3159	.3186	.3212	.3238	.3264	.3289	.3315	.3340	.3365	.3389
1.0	.3414	.3438	.3461	.3485	.3508	.3531	.3554	.3577	.3599	.3621
1.1	.3643	.3665	.3686	.3708	.3729	.3749	.3770	.3790	.3810	.3830
1.2	.3849	.3859	.3888	.3907	.3925	.3944	.3962	.3980	.3997	.4015
1.3	.4032	.4049	.4066	.4082	.4099	.4115	.4131	.4147	.4162	.4177
1.4	.4192	.4207	.4222	.4236	.4251	.4265	.4279	.4292	.4306	.4319
1.5	.4332	.4345	.4358	.4370	.4382	.4394	.4406	.4418	.4430	.4441
1.6	.4452	.4463	.4474	.4485	.4495	.4505	.4515	.4525	.4535	.4545
1.7	.4554	.4564	.4573	.4582	.4591	.4599	.4608	.4616	.4625	.4633
1.8	.4641	.4649	.4656	.4664	.4671	.4678	.4686	.4693	.4700	.4706
1.9	.4713	.4719	.4726	.4732	.4738	.4744	.4750	.4756	.4762	.4769
2.0	.4772	.4778	.4783	.4788	.4793	.4798	.4803	.4808	.4812	.4817
2.1	.4821	.4826	.4830	.4834	.4838	.4842	.4846	.4850	.4854	.4857
2.2	.4861	.4865	.4868	.4871	.4875	.4878	.4881	.4884	.4887	.4890
2.3	.4893	.4896	.4898	.4901	.4904	.4906	.4909	.4911	.4913	.4916
2.4	.4918	.4920	.4922	.4925	.4927	.4929	.4931	.4932	.4934	.4936
2.5	.4938	.4940	.4941	.4943	.4945	.4946	.4948	.4949	.4951	.4952
2.6	.4953	.4955	.4956	.4957	.4959	.4960	.4961	.4962	.4963	.4964
2.7	.4965	.4966	.4967	.4968	.4969	.4970	.4971	.4972	.4973	.4974
2.8	.4975	.4975	.4976	.4976	.4977	.4978	.4979	.4980	.4980	.4981
2.9	.4981	.4982	.4983	.4983	.4984	.4984	.4985	.4985	.4986	.4986
3.0	.4987	.4987	.4987	.4988	.4988	.4988	.4989	.4989	.4989	.4990
3.1	.4990	.4990	.4991	.4991	.4991	.4992	.4992	.4992	.4992	.4993
3.2	.4993	.4993	.4993	.4994	.4994	.4994	.4994	.4994	.4995	.4995
3.3	.4995	.4995	.4995	.4996	.4996	.4996	.4996	.4996	.4996	.4997
3.4	.4997	.4997	.4997	.4997	.4997	.4997	.4997	.4997	.4997	.4998
3.5	.4998	.4998	.4998	.4998	.4998	.4998	.4998	.4998	.4998	.4998
3.6	.4998	.4999	.4999	.4999	.4999	.4999	.4999	.4999	.4999	.4999
3.7	.4999	.4999	.4999	.4999	.4999	.4999	.4999	.4999	.4999	.4999
3.8	.4999	.4999	.4999	.4999	.4999	.4999	.4999	.5000	.5000	.5000

Table 3 Critical values for Spearman's rank order correlation coefficient at the p = 0.01 and p = 0.05 significance levels

No. of pairs of scores	One-tailed test		Two-tailed test	
	p = 0.01	p = 0.05	p = 0.01	p = 0.05
5	1.000	.900		1.000
6	.943	.829	1.000	.886
7	.893	.714	.929	.786
8	.833	.643	.881	.738
9	.783	.600	.833	.700
10	.745	.564	.794	.648
11	.709	.536	.755	.618
12	.671	.503	.727	.587
13	.648	.484	.703	.560
14	.622	.464	.675	.538
15	.604	.443	.654	.521
16	.582	.429	.635	.503
17	.566	.414	.615	.485
18	.550	.401	.600	.472
19	.535	.391	.584	.460
20	.520	.380	.570	.447
25	.466	.337	.511	.398
30	.425	.306	.467	.362

Source: Taken from table 1 of J. H. Zar (1972), Significance testing of the Spearman rank correlation coefficient. *Journal of the American Statistical Association*, *67*, 578–80. Reproduced by permission. Copyright 1972 by the American Statistical Association. All rights reserved.

Table 4 Critical values for Pearson's correlation coefficient at
$p = 0.01$ and $p = 0.05$ significance levels

Degrees of freedom	One-tailed test		Two-tailed test	
	$p = 0.01$	$p = 0.05$	$p = 0.01$	$p = 0.05$
5	.833	.669	.875	.755
6	.789	.622	.834	.707
7	.750	.582	.798	.666
8	.716	.549	.765	.632
9	.685	.521	735	.602
10	.658	.497	.708	.576
11	.640	.476	.684	.553
12	.612	.458	.661	.532
13	.592	.441	.641	.514
14	.574	.426	.623	.497
15	.558	.412	.606	.482
16	.543	.400	.590	.468
17	.529	.389	.575	.456
18	.516	.378	.561	.444
19	.503	.369	.549	.433
20	.492	.360	.537	.423
25	.445	.323	.487	.381
30	.409	.296	.449	.349

Source: Taken from table VII of R. A. Fisher and F. Yates (1953),
Statistical tables for biological, agricultural and medical research,
published by Longman Group UK Ltd, 1974, 6th edn.

Table 5 One- and two-tailed critical values of S for the sign test at the $p = 0.01$ and $p = 0.05$ significance levels

N	One-tailed test		Two-tailed test	
	$p = 0.01$	$p = 0.05$	$p = 0.01$	$p = 0.05$
5	–	0	–	–
6	–	0	–	0
7	0	0	–	0
8	0	1	0	0
9	0	1	0	1
10	0	1	0	1
11	1	2	0	1
12	1	2	1	2
13	1	3	1	2
14	2	3	1	2
15	2	3	2	3
16	2	4	2	3
17	3	4	2	4
18	3	5	3	4
19	4	5	3	4
20	4	5	3	5
25	6	7	5	7
30	8	10	7	9

Source: Taken from table 12.1 of D. B. Owen (1972), *Handbook of statistical tables*, © 1962 by Addison-Wesley Publishing Company Inc. Reprinted by permission.

Table 6 One- and two-tailed critical values of U for the Mann–Whitney test at the p = 0.01 and p = 0.05 significance levels

To use this table: Find the appropriate value for n2, the number of scores in the larger of the two samples (if there is one), followed by n1, the number of scores in the other sample. Then read off the critical value for the chosen significance level and decision type. Where there is no entry in the table, it means that no critical value can be computed, and you will need either to use a different significance level or decision type or collect more data.

n2	n1	1-tailed test		2-tailed test	
		p = 0.01	p = 0.05	p = 0.01	p = 0.05
5	2	–	0	–	–
	3	–	1	–	0
	4	0	2	–	1
	5	1	4	0	2
6	2	–	0	–	–
	3	–	2	–	1
	4	1	3	0	2
	5	2	5	1	3
	6	3	7	2	5
7	2	–	0	–	–
	3	0	2	–	1
	4	1	4	0	3
	5	3	6	1	5
	6	4	8	3	6
	7	6	11	4	8
8	2	–	1	–	0
	3	0	3	–	2
	4	2	5	1	4
	5	4	8	2	6
	6	6	10	4	8
	7	7	13	6	10
	8	9	15	7	13
9	1	–	–	–	–
	2	–	1	–	0
	3	1	4	0	2
	4	3	6	1	4
	5	5	9	33	7
	6	7	12	5	10
	7	9	15	7	12
	8	11	18	9	15
	9	14	21	11	17
10	1	–	–	–	–
	2	–	1	–	0
	3	1	4	0	3

Table 6 *Continued*

n2	n1	1-tailed test		2-tailed test	
		p = 0.01	p = 0.05	p = 0.01	p = 0.05
	4	3	7	2	5
	5	6	11	4	8
	6	8	14	6	11
	7	11	17	9	14
	8	13	20	11	17
	9	16	24	13	20
	10	19	27	16	23
11	1	–	–	–	–
	2	–	1	–	0
	3	1	5	0	3
	4	4	8	2	6
	5	7	12	5	9
	6	9	16	7	13
	7	12	19	10	16
	8	15	23	13	19
	9	18	27	16	23
	10	22	31	18	26
	11	25	34	21	30
12	1	–	–	–	–
	2	–	2	–	1
	3	2	5	1	4
	4	5	9	3	7
	5	8	13	6	11
	6	11	17	9	14
	7	14	21	12	18
	8	17	26	15	22
	9	21	30	18	26
	10	24	34	21	29
	11	28	38	24	33
	12	31	42	27	37
13	1	–	–	–	–
	2	0	2	–	1
	3	2	6	1	4
	4	5	10	3	8
	5	9	15	7	12
	6	12	19	10	16
	7	16	24	13	20
	8	20	28	17	24
	9	23	33	20	28
	10	27	37	24	33
	11	31	42	27	37
	12	35	47	31	41
	13	39	51	34	45

Table 6 *Continued*

n2	n1	1-tailed test		2-tailed test	
		p = 0.01	p = 0.05	p = 0.01	p = 0.05
14	1	–	–	–	–
	2	0	3	–	1
	3	2	7	1	5
	4	6	11	4	9
	5	10	16	7	13
	6	13	21	11	17
	7	17	26	15	22
	8	22	31	18	26
	9	26	36	22	31
	10	30	41	26	36
	11	34	46	30	40
	12	38	51	34	45
	13	43	56	38	50
	14	47	61	42	55
15	1	–	–	–	–
	2	0	3	–	1
	3	3	7	2	5
	4	7	12	5	10
	5	11	18	8	14
	6	15	23	12	19
	7	19	28	16	24
	8	24	33	20	29
	9	28	39	24	34
	10	33	44	29	39
	11	37	50	33	44
	12	42	55	37	49
	13	47	61	42	54
	14	51	66	46	59
	15	56	72	51	64
16	1	–	–	–	–
	2	0	3	–	1
	3	3	8	2	6
	4	7	14	5	11
	5	12	19	9	15
	6	16	25	13	21
	7	21	30	18	26
	8	26	36	22	31
	9	31	42	27	37
	10	36	48	31	42
	11	41	54	36	47
	12	46	60	41	53
	13	51	65	45	59
	14	56	71	50	64

Table 6 *Continued*

n2	n1	1-tailed test		2-tailed test	
		p = 0.01	p = 0.05	p = 0.01	p = 0.05
	15	61	77	55	70
	16	66	83	60	75
17	1	–	–	–	–
	2	0	3	–	2
	3	4	9	2	6
	4	8	15	6	11
	5	13	20	10	17
	6	18	26	15	22
	7	23	33	19	28
	8	28	39	24	34
	9	33	45	29	39
	10	38	51	34	45
	11	44	57	39	51
	12	49	64	44	57
	13	55	70	49	63
	14	60	77	54	69
	15	66	83	60	75
	16	71	89	65	81
	17	77	96	70	87
18	1	–	–	–	–
	2	0	4	–	2
	3	4	9	2	7
	4	9	16	6	12
	5	14	22	11	18
	6	19	28	16	24
	7	24	35	21	30
	8	30	41	26	36
	9	36	48	31	42
	10	41	55	37	48
	11	47	61	42	55
	12	53	68	47	61
	13	59	75	53	67
	14	65	82	58	74
	15	70	88	64	80
	16	76	95	70	86
	17	82	102	75	93
	18	88	109	81	99
19	1	–	0	–	–
	2	1	4	0	2
	3	4	10	3	7
	4	9	17	7	13
	5	15	23	12	19

Table 6 *Continued*

n2	n1	1-tailed test		2-tailed test	
		p = 0.01	p = 0.05	p = 0.01	p = 0.05
	6	20	30	17	25
	7	26	37	22	32
	8	32	44	28	38
	9	38	51	33	45
	10	44	58	39	52
	11	50	65	45	58
	12	56	72	51	65
	13	63	80	57	72
	14	69	87	63	78
	15	75	94	69	85
	16	82	101	74	92
	17	88	109	81	99
	18	94	116	87	106
	19	101	123	93	113
20	1	–	0	–	–
	2	1	4	0	2
	3	5	11	3	8
	4	10	18	8	14
	5	16	25	13	20
	6	22	32	18	27
	7	28	39	24	34
	8	34	47	30	41
	9	40	54	36	48
	10	47	62	42	55
	11	53	69	48	62
	12	60	77	54	69
	13	67	84	60	76
	14	73	92	67	83
	15	80	100	73	90
	16	87	107	79	98
	17	93	115	86	105
	18	100	123	92	112
	19	107	130	99	119
	20	114	138	105	127

Source: Taken from table 11.4 of D. B. Owen, *Handbook of statistical tables*, © 1962 by Addison-Wesley Publishing Company Inc. Reprinted by permission.

Table 7 One- and two-tailed critical values of T for the Wilcoxon test at the p = 0.01 and p = 0.05 significance levels

N	One-tailed test		Two-tailed test	
	p = 0.01	p = 0.05	p = 0.01	p = 0.05
5	–	1	–	–
6	–	2	–	1
7	0	4	–	2
8	2	6	0	4
9	3	8	2	6
10	5	11	3	8
11	7	14	5	11
12	10	17	7	14
13	13	21	10	17
14	16	26	13	21
15	20	30	16	25
16	24	36	19	30
17	28	41	23	35
18	33	47	28	40
19	38	54	32	46
20	43	60	37	52
25	//	101	68	90

Source: Taken from table 23 of E. S. Pearson and H. O. Hartley (1966), *Biometrika tables for statisticians*, vol. 1, 3rd edn, 1966, Cambridge University Press. Reproduced by permission of the Biometrika Trustees.

Table 8 Critical values of χ^2 at the p = 0.01 and p = 0.05 significance levels

df	Critical values of χ^2	
	p = 0.01	p = 0.05
1	6.635	3.841
2	9.210	5.991
3	11.345	7.815
4	13.277	9.448
5	15.086	11.070
6	16.812	12.592
7	18.475	14.067
8	20.090	15.507
9	21.666	16.919
10	23.209	18.307
11	24.725	19.675
12	26.217	21.026
13	27.688	22.362
14	29.141	23.685
15	30.578	24.996
16	32.000	26.296
17	33.409	27.587
18	34.805	28.869
19	36.191	30.144
20	37.566	31.410
21	38.932	32.671
22	40.289	33.924
23	41.638	35.172
24	42.980	36.415
25	44.314	37.652
26	45.642	38.885
27	46.963	40.133
28	48.278	41.337
29	49.588	42.557
30	50.892	43.773

Source: Taken from table IV of R. A. Fisher and F. Yates (1953),
Statistical tables for biological, agricultural and medical research,
published by Longman Group UK Ltd., 1974, 6th edn.

Table 9 One- and two-tailed critical values of t for the t-test at the
p = 0.01 and p = 0.05 significance levels

df	One-tailed test		Two-tailed test	
	p = 0.01	p = 0.05	p = 0.01	p = 0.05
1	31.821	6.314	63.657	12.706
2	6.965	2.920	9.925	4.303
3	4.541	2.353	5.841	3.182
4	3.747	2.132	4.604	2.776
5	3.365	2.015	4.032	2.571
6	3.143	1.943	3.707	2.447
7	2.998	1.895	3.499	2.365
8	2.896	1.860	3.355	2.306
9	2.821	1.833	3.250	2.262
10	2.764	1.812	3.169	2.228
11	2.718	1.796	3.106	2.201
12	2.681	1.782	3.055	2.179
13	2.650	1.771	3.012	2.160
14	2.624	1.761	2.977	2.145
15	2.602	1.753	2.947	2.131
16	2.583	1.746	2.921	2.120
17	2.567	1.740	2.898	2.110
18	2.552	1.734	2.878	2.101
19	2.539	1.729	2.861	2.093
20	2.528	1.725	2.845	2.086
21	2.518	1.721	2.831	2.080
22	2.508	1.717	2.819	2.074
23	2.500	1.714	2.807	2.069
24	2.492	1.711	2.797	2.064
25	2.454	1.708	2.787	2.060
26	2.497	1.706	2.779	2.056
27	2.473	1.703	2.771	2.052
28	2.467	1.701	2.763	2.048
29	2.462	1.699	2.756	2.045
30	2.457	1.697	2.750	2.042
40	2.423	1.684	2.704	2.021
60	2.390	1.671	2.660	2.000
120	2.358	1.658	2.617	1.980
∞	2.326	1.645	2.576	1.960

Source: Taken from table III of R. A. Fisher and F. Yates (1953),
Statistical tables for biological, agricultural and medical research,
published by Longman Group UK Ltd, 1974, 6th edn.

Table 10 One-tailed critical values of F for the variance ratio test at the p = 0.05 and 0.01 significance levels

$\alpha = 0.05$

Degrees of freedom in denominator	Degrees of freedom in numerator																	
	1	2	3	4	5	6	7	8	9	10	12	15	20	24	30	40	60	120
1	161.4	199.5	215.7	224.6	230.2	234.0	236.8	238.9	240.5	241.9	243.9	245.9	248.0	249.1	250.1	251.1	252.2	253.3
2	18.51	19.00	19.16	19.25	19.30	19.33	19.35	19.37	19.38	19.40	19.41	19.43	19.45	19.45	19.46	19.47	19.48	19.49
3	10.13	9.55	9.28	9.12	9.01	8.94	8.89	8.85	8.81	8.79	8.74	8.70	8.66	8.64	8.62	8.59	8.57	8.55
4	7.71	6.94	6.59	6.39	6.26	6.16	6.09	6.04	6.00	5.96	5.91	5.86	5.80	5.77	5.75	5.72	5.69	5.66
5	6.61	5.79	5.41	5.19	5.05	4.95	4.88	4.82	4.77	4.74	4.68	4.62	4.56	4.53	4.50	4.46	4.43	4.40
6	5.99	5.14	4.76	4.53	4.39	4.28	4.21	4.15	4.10	4.06	4.00	3.94	3.87	3.84	3.81	3.77	3.74	3.70
7	5.59	4.74	4.35	4.12	3.97	3.87	3.79	3.73	3.68	3.64	3.57	3.51	3.44	3.41	3.38	3.34	3.30	3.27
8	5.32	4.46	4.07	3.84	3.69	3.58	3.5	3.44	3.39	3.35	3.28	3.22	3.15	3.12	3.08	3.04	3.01	2.97
9	5.12	4.26	3.86	3.63	3.48	3.37	3.29	3.23	3.18	3.14	3.07	3.01	2.94	2.90	2.86	2.83	2.79	2.75
10	4.96	4.10	3.71	3.48	3.33	3.22	3.14	3.07	3.02	2.98	2.91	2.85	2.77	2.74	2.70	2.66	2.62	2.58
11	4.84	3.98	3.59	3.36	3.20	3.09	3.01	2.95	2.90	2.85	2.79	2.72	2.65	2.61	2.57	2.53	2.49	2.45
12	4.75	3.89	3.49	3.26	3.11	3.00	2.91	2.85	2.80	2.75	2.69	2.62	2.54	2.51	2.47	2.43	2.38	2.34
13	4.67	3.81	3.41	3.18	3.03	2.92	2.83	2.77	2.71	2.67	2.60	2.53	2.46	2.42	2.38	2.34	2.30	2.25
14	4.60	3.74	3.34	3.11	2.96	2.85	2.76	2.70	2.65	2.60	2.53	2.46	2.39	2.35	2.31	2.27	2.22	2.18
15	4.54	3.68	3.29	3.06	2.90	2.79	2.71	2.64	2.59	2.54	2.48	2.40	2.33	2.29	2.25	2.20	2.16	2.11
16	4.49	3.63	3.24	3.01	2.85	2.74	2.66	2.59	2.54	2.49	2.42	2.35	2.28	2.24	2.19	2.15	2.11	2.06
17	4.45	3.59	3.20	2.96	2.81	2.70	2.61	2.55	2.49	2.45	2.38	2.31	2.23	2.19	2.15	2.10	2.06	2.01
18	4.41	3.55	3.16	2.93	2.77	2.66	2.58	2.51	2.46	2.41	2.34	2.27	2.19	2.15	2.11	2.06	2.02	1.97
19	4.38	3.52	3.13	2.90	2.74	2.63	2.54	2.48	2.42	2.38	2.31	2.23	2.16	2.11	2.07	2.03	1.98	1.93
20	4.35	3.49	3.10	2.87	2.71	2.60	2.51	2.45	2.39	2.35	2.28	2.20	2.12	2.08	2.04	1.99	1.95	1.90
21	4.32	3.47	3.07	2.84	2.68	2.57	2.49	2.42	2.37	2.32	2.25	2.18	2.10	2.05	2.01	1.96	1.92	1.87
22	4.30	3.44	3.05	2.82	2.66	2.55	2.46	2.40	2.34	2.30	2.23	2.15	2.07	2.03	1.98	1.94	1.89	1.84
23	4.28	3.42	3.03	2.80	2.64	2.53	2.44	2.37	2.32	2.27	2.20	2.13	2.05	2.01	1.96	1.91	1.86	1.81
24	4.26	3.40	3.01	2.78	2.62	2.51	2.42	2.36	2.30	2.25	2.18	2.11	2.03	1.98	1.94	1.89	1.84	1.79
25	4.24	3.39	2.99	2.76	2.60	2.49	2.40	2.34	2.28	2.24	2.16	2.09	2.01	1.96	1.92	1.87	1.82	1.77
26	4.23	3.37	2.98	2.74	2.59	2.47	2.39	2.32	2.27	2.22	2.15	2.07	1.99	1.95	1.90	1.85	1.80	1.75
27	4.21	3.35	2.96	2.73	2.57	2.46	2.37	2.31	2.25	2.20	2.13	2.06	1.97	1.93	1.88	1.84	1.79	1.73
28	4.20	3.34	2.95	2.71	2.56	2.45	2.36	2.29	2.24	2.19	2.12	2.04	1.96	1.91	1.87	1.82	1.77	1.71
29	4.18	3.33	2.93	2.70	2.55	2.43	2.35	2.28	2.22	2.18	2.10	2.03	1.94	1.90	1.85	1.81	1.75	1.70
30	4.17	3.32	2.92	2.69	2.53	2.42	2.33	2.27	2.21	2.16	2.09	2.01	1.93	1.89	1.84	1.79	1.74	1.68
40	4.08	3.23	2.84	2.61	2.45	2.34	2.25	2.18	2.12	2.08	2.00	1.92	1.84	1.79	1.74	1.69	1.64	1.58
60	4.00	3.15	2.76	2.53	2.37	2.25	2.17	2.10	2.04	1.99	1.92	1.84	1.75	1.70	1.65	1.59	1.53	1.47
120	3.92	3.07	2.68	2.45	2.29	2.17	2.09	2.02	1.96	1.91	1.83	1.75	1.66	1.61	1.55	1.50	1.43	1.35

$$\alpha = 0.01$$

Degrees of freedom in numerator

	1	2	3	4	5	6	7	8	9	10	12	15	20	24	30	40	60	120
1	4052.0	4999.5	5403.0	5625.0	5764.0	5859.0	5928.0	5982.0	6022.0	6056.0	6106.0	6157.0	6209.0	6235.0	6261.0	6287.0	6313.0	6339.0
2	98.50	99.00	99.17	99.25	99.30	99.33	99.36	99.37	99.39	99.40	99.42	99.43	99.45	99.46	99.47	99.47	99.48	99.49
3	34.12	30.82	29.46	28.71	28.24	27.91	27.67	27.49	27.35	27.23	27.05	26.87	26.69	26.60	26.50	26.41	26.32	26.22
4	21.20	18.00	16.69	15.98	15.52	15.21	14.98	14.8	14.66	14.55	14.37	14.20	14.02	13.93	13.84	13.75	13.65	13.56
5	16.26	13.27	12.06	11.39	10.97	10.67	10.46	10.29	10.16	10.05	9.89	9.72	9.55	9.47	9.38	9.29	9.20	9.11
6	13.75	10.92	9.78	9.15	8.75	8.47	8.26	8.10	7.98	7.87	7.72	7.56	7.40	7.31	7.23	7.14	7.06	6.97
7	12.25	9.55	8.45	7.85	7.46	7.19	6.99	6.84	6.72	6.62	6.47	6.31	6.16	6.07	5.99	5.91	5.82	5.74
8	11.26	8.65	7.59	7.01	6.63	6.37	6.18	6.03	5.91	5.81	5.67	5.52	5.36	5.28	5.20	5.12	5.03	4.95
9	10.56	8.02	6.99	6.42	6.06	5.80	5.61	5.47	5.35	5.26	5.11	4.96	4.81	4.73	4.65	4.57	4.48	4.40
10	10.04	7.56	6.55	5.99	5.64	5.39	5.20	5.06	4.94	4.85	4.71	4.56	4.41	4.33	4.25	4.17	4.08	4.00
11	9.65	7.21	6.22	5.67	5.32	5.07	4.89	4.74	4.63	4.54	4.40	4.25	4.10	4.02	3.94	3.86	3.78	3.69
12	9.33	6.93	5.95	5.41	5.05	4.82	4.64	4.50	4.39	4.30	4.16	4.01	3.86	3.78	3.70	3.62	3.54	3.45
13	9.07	6.70	5.74	5.21	4.86	4.62	4.44	4.30	4.19	4.10	3.96	3.82	3.66	3.59	3.51	3.43	3.34	3.25
14	8.86	6.51	5.56	5.04	4.69	4.46	4.28	4.14	4.03	3.94	3.80	3.66	3.51	3.43	3.35	3.27	3.18	3.09
15	8.68	6.36	5.42	4.89	4.56	4.32	4.14	4.00	3.89	3.80	3.67	3.52	3.37	3.29	3.21	3.13	3.05	2.96
16	8.53	6.23	5.29	4.77	4.44	4.20	4.03	3.89	3.78	3.69	3.55	3.41	3.26	3.18	3.10	3.02	2.93	2.84
17	8.40	6.11	5.18	4.67	4.34	4.10	3.93	3.79	3.68	3.59	3.46	3.31	3.16	3.08	3.00	2.92	2.83	2.75
18	8.29	6.01	5.09	4.58	4.25	4.01	3.84	3.71	3.60	3.51	3.37	3.23	3.08	3.00	2.92	2.84	2.75	2.66
19	8.18	5.93	5.01	4.50	4.17	3.94	3.77	3.63	3.52	3.43	3.30	3.15	3.00	2.92	2.84	2.76	2.67	2.58
20	8.10	5.85	4.94	4.43	4.10	3.87	3.70	3.56	3.46	3.37	3.23	3.09	2.94	2.86	2.78	2.69	2.61	2.52
21	8.02	5.78	4.87	4.37	4.04	3.81	3.64	3.51	3.40	3.31	3.17	3.03	2.88	2.80	2.72	2.64	2.55	2.46
22	7.95	5.72	4.82	4.31	3.99	3.76	3.59	3.45	3.35	3.26	3.12	2.98	2.83	2.75	2.67	2.58	2.50	2.40
23	7.88	5.66	4.76	4.26	3.94	3.71	3.54	3.41	3.30	3.21	3.07	2.93	2.78	2.70	2.62	2.54	2.45	2.35
24	7.82	5.61	4.72	4.22	3.90	3.67	3.50	3.36	3.26	3.17	3.03	2.89	2.74	2.66	2.58	2.49	2.40	2.31
25	7.77	5.57	4.68	4.18	3.85	3.63	3.46	3.32	3.22	3.13	2.99	2.85	2.70	2.62	2.54	2.45	2.36	2.27
26	7.72	5.53	4.64	4.14	3.82	3.59	3.42	3.29	3.18	3.09	2.96	2.81	2.66	2.58	2.50	2.42	2.33	2.23
27	7.68	5.49	4.60	4.11	3.78	3.56	3.39	3.26	3.15	3.06	2.93	2.78	2.63	2.55	2.47	2.38	2.29	2.20
28	7.64	5.45	4.57	4.07	3.75	3.53	3.36	3.23	3.12	3.03	2.90	2.75	2.60	2.52	2.44	2.35	2.26	2.17
29	7.60	5.42	4.54	4.04	3.73	3.50	3.33	3.20	3.09	3.00	2.87	2.73	2.57	2.49	2.41	2.33	2.23	2.14
30	7.56	5.39	4.51	4.02	3.70	3.47	3.30	3.17	3.07	2.98	2.84	2.70	2.55	2.47	2.39	2.30	2.21	2.11
40	7.31	5.18	4.31	3.83	3.51	3.29	3.12	2.99	2.89	2.80	2.66	2.52	2.37	2.29	2.20	2.11	2.02	1.92
60	7.08	4.98	4.13	3.65	3.34	3.12	2.95	2.82	2.72	2.63	2.50	2.35	2.20	2.12	2.03	1.94	1.84	1.73
120	6.85	4.79	3.95	3.48	3.17	2.96	2.79	2.66	2.56	2.47	2.34	2.19	2.03	1.95	1.86	1.76	1.66	1.53

Degrees of freedom in denominator

REFERENCES

Ainsworth, M. D. S. and Bell S. M. (1969). Exploratory behaviour of 1 year olds in a strange situation. In B. M. Foss (ed.), *Determinants of infant behaviour*, vol. 4. London: Methuen.

American Psychological Association (1994). *Publication manual of the American Psychological Association*, 4th edn. Washington, DC: American Psychological Association.

Anderson, B. F. (1971). *The psychology experiment*, 2nd edn. Belmont, CA: Brooks/Cole.

Antaki, C. (2002). *Discourse analysis means doing analysis: A critique of six analytic shortcomings.* [Web-page available at http://www.shu.ac.uk/daol/articles/open/2002/002/antaki/2002002-paper.html, accessed on 17/01/05.]

Argyris, C. (1968). Some unintended consequences of rigorous research. *Psychological Bulletin, 70*, 185–7.

Asch, S. (1955). Opinions and social pressure. *Scientific American, 193*, 31–5.

Bales, R. F. (1950a). A set of categories for the analysis of small group interaction. *American Sociological Review, 15*, 257–68.

Bales, R. F. (1950b). *Interaction process analysis*. Reading, MA: Addison-Wesley.

Banister, P. (1994). Observation. In P. Banister, E. Burman, I. Parker, M. Taylor and C. Tindall (eds), *Qualitative methods in psychology: A research guide*. Buckingham: Open University Press.

Barton, E. J. and Ascione, F. R. (1984). Direct observation. In T. H. Ollendick and M. Hersen (eds), *Child behavioural assessment*. New York: Pergamon.

Baumrind, D. (1964). Some thoughts on the ethics of research: After reading Milgram's 'behavioural study of obedience'. *American Psychologist, 19*, 421–3.

Beck, C. T. (1993). Teetering on the edge: A substantive theory of postpartum depression. *Nursing Research, 42* (1), 42–8.

Berger, P. and Luckman, T. (1967). *The social construction of reality*. Harmondsworth: Penguin.

Bell, C. and Roberts, H. (eds) (1984). *Social researching: Politics, problems, practice*. London: Routledge.

Beloff, J. (1973). *Psychological science: A review of modern psychology*. London: Crosby, Lockwood, Staples.

Bernstein, D. A., Clarke-Stewart, A., Roy, E. J. and Wickens, C. D. (1997). *Psychology*, 4th edn. Boston, MA: Houghton Mifflin.

Brace, N., Kemp, R. and Snelgar, R. (2003). *SPSS for psychologists*, 2nd edn. London: Palgrave Macmillan.

Brigham, J. C. (1986). *Social psychology*. Boston, MA: Little, Brown.

British Psychological Society (1992). *Ethical principles for conducting research with human participants*. Leicester: British Psychological Society.

Broadbent, D. E. (1958). *Perception and communication*. Oxford: Pergamon.

Brown, R., Cazden, C. B. and Bellugi, U. (1969). The child's grammar from 1 to 3. In J. P. Hill (ed.), *Minnesota symposium on child psychology*, vol. 2. Minneapolis, MN: University of Minnesota Press.

Burman, E. (1994a). Interviewing. In P. Banister, E. Burman, I. Parker, M. Taylor and C. Tindall, *Qualitative methods in psychology: A research guide*. Buckingham: Open University Press.

Burman, E. (1994b). Feminist research. In P. Banister, E. Burman, I. Parker, M. Taylor and C. Tindall, *Qualitative methods in psychology: A research guide*. Buckingham: Open University Press.

Coolican, H. (2004). *Research methods and statistics in psychology*, 4th edn. London: Hodder Arnold.

Coyle, A. (2000). Discourse analysis. In G. Breakwell, S. Hammond and C. Fife-Schaw (eds), *Research methods in psychology*, 2nd edn. London: Sage.

Creative Research Systems (2003). *Sample size calculator.* [Webpage available at http://www.surveysystem.com/sscalc.htm, accessed on 15/2/05.]

Cronbach, L. J. (1951). Coefficient alpha and the internal structure of tests. *Psychometrika, 16*, 297–334.

Crutchfield, R. A. (1955). Conformity and character. *American Psychologist, 10*, 191–8.

Dane, F. C. (1995). Survey methods, naturalistic observations and case-studies. In A. M. Colman (ed.), *Psychological research methods and statistics*. London: Longman.

Darley, J. M. and Latane, B. (1968). Bystander intervention in emergencies: Diffusion of responsibility. *Journal of Personality and Social Psychology, 8*, 377–83.

Dement, W. and Kleitman, N. (1957). The relation of eye-movements during sleep to dream activity: An objective method for the study of dreaming. *Journal of Experimental Psychology, 53*, 339–46.

Dollard, J., Doob, L. W., Miller, N. E., Mowrer, O. H. and Sears, R. R. (1939). *Frustration and aggression.* New Haven, CT: Yale University Press.

Doob, A. N. and Gross, A. E. (1968). Status of frustrator as an inhibitor of horn-honking responses. *Journal of Social Psychology, 76*, 213–18. Also in M. P. Golden (ed.) (1972). *The research experience*. Itasca, IL: Peacock.

Dukes, W. F. (1965). N = 1. *Psychological Bulletin, 64*, 74–9.

Ebbinghaus, H. (1885/1913). *Memory*. New York: Teacher's College Press.

Eysenck, M. W. (2000). *Psychology: A student's handbook*. Hove: Psychology Press.

Fife-Schaw, C. (2000a). Surveys. In G. Breakwell, S. Hammond and C. Fife-Schaw (eds), *Research methods in psychology*, 2nd edn. London: Sage.

Fife-Schaw, C. (2000b). Levels of measurement. In G. Breakwell, S. Hammond and C. Fife-Schaw (eds), *Research methods in psychology*, 2nd edn. London: Sage.

Foster, D. L., Bell-Dolan, S. J. and Burge, D. A. (1988). Behavioral observation. In A. S. Bellack and M. Hersen (eds), *Behavioural assessment: A practical handbook*. Oxford: Pergamon.

Foster, J. J. and Parker, I. (1995). *Carrying out investigations in psychology*. Leicester: B. P. S. Books.

Fuller, S. (2003). *Kuhn vs. Popper*. London: Icon Books.

Gale, A. (1995). Ethical issues in psychological research. In A. M. Colman (ed.), *Psychological research methods and statistics*. London: Longman.

Galton, F. (1869). *Hereditary genius*. London: Macmillan.

Gellert, E. (1955). Systematic observation: A method in child study. *Harvard Educational Review, 25*, 179–95.

Gilhooly, K. and Green, K. (1996). Protocol analysis: Theoretical background. In J. T. E. Richardson (ed.), *Handbook of qualitative research methods for psychology and the social sciences*. Leicester: B. P. S. Books.

Gill, R. (1996). Discourse analysis: Practical implementation. In J. T. E. Richardson (ed.), *Handbook of qualitative research methods for psychology and the social sciences*. Leicester: B. P. S. Books.

Gillett, G. (1995). The philosophical foundations of qualitative psychology. *The Psychologist*, March, 111–14.

Glaser, B. G. and Strauss, A. L. (1967). *The discovery of grounded theory: Strategies for qualitative research*. Chicago, IL: Aldine.

Glenberg, A. M. (1988). *Learning from data: An introduction to statistical reasoning*. London: Harcourt Brace Jovanovich.

Goffman, E. (1961). *Asylums*. Harmondsworth: Penguin.

Gold, R. L. (1969). Roles in sociological field observation. In G. McCall and J. Simmons (eds), *Issues in participant observation: A text and reader*. London: Addison-Wesley.

Gray, J. A. and Wedderburn, A. A. (1960). Grouping strategies with simultaneous stimuli. *Quarterly Journal of Experimental Psychology, 12*, 180–4.

Hammersley, M. and Atkinson, P. (1995). *Ethnography: Principles in practice*, 2nd edn. London: Routledge.

Hammond, S. (2000). Using psychometric tests. In G. Breakwell, S. Hammond and C. Fife-Schaw (eds), *Research methods in psychology*, 2nd edn. London: Sage.

Harre, R. (1986). *Varieties of realism: A rationale for the natural sciences*. Oxford: Blackwell.

Harre, R. and Seccord, P. F. (1972). *The explanation of social behaviour*. Oxford: Blackwell.

Hayes, N. (1997). *Doing qualitative research in psychology*. Hove: Lawrence Erlbaum.

Heath, C. and Luff, P. (1993). Explicating face-to-face interaction. In N. Gilbert (ed.), *Researching social life*. London: Sage.

Held, R. and Hein, A. (1963). Movement-produced stimulation in the development of visually-guided behaviour. *Journal of Comparative and Physiological Psychology, 56*, 872–6.

Henwood, K. L. and Nicolson, P. (1995). Qualitative research. *The Psychologist*, March, 109–29.

Henwood, K. L. and Pidgeon, N. F. (1992). Qualitative research and psychological theorising. *British Journal of Psychology, 83*, 97–111.

Henwood, K. L. and Pidgeon, N. F. (1995). Grounded theory and psychological research. *The Psychologist*, March, 115–18.

Herrman, D. J., Crawford, M. and Holdsworthy, M. (1992). Gender-linked differences in everyday memory performance. *British Journal of Psychology, 83*, 221–31.

Honorton, C. and Harper, S. (1974). Psi-mediated imagery and ideation in an experimental procedure for regulating perceptual input. *Journal of the American Society for Psychical Research, 68*, 156–68.

Howell, D. C. (1997). *Statistical methods for psychology*, 4th edn. Belmont, CA: Duxbury Press.

Humpheys, L. (1970). *Tea-room trade: Impersonal sex in public places*. Chicago: Aldine.

Jahn, R. (1982). The persistent paradox of ESP: An engineering perspective. *Proceedings of the IEEE, 70*, 136–70.

Jenni, D. A. and Jenni, M. A. (1976). Carrying behaviour in humans: Analysis of sex differences. *Science, 194*, 859–60.

Koocher, G. P. (1977). Bathroom behaviour and human dignity. *Journal of Personality and Social Psychology, 35*, 120–1.

Kruskal, W. H. (1968). Statistics: The field. *The International Encyclopaedia of the Social Sciences*, vol. 15. New York: Macmillan/The Free Press.

Kuhn, T. S. (1970). *The structure of scientific revolutions*, rev. edn. Chicago: University of Chicago Press.

Latane, B. and Darley, J. M. (1968). Group inhibitions of bystander intervention in emergencies. *Journal of Personality and Social Psychology, 10*, 215–21.

Latane, B. and Darley, J. M. (1969). Bystander apathy. *American Scientist, 5*, 224–68.

Latane, B. and Darley, J. M. (1970). *The unresponsive bystander: Why doesn't he help?* New York: Appleton-Century-Crofts.

Latane, B. and Rodin, J. (1969). A lady in distress: Inhibiting effects of friends and strangers on bystander intervention. *Journal of Experimental Social Psychology, 5*, 189–202.

Leahy, T. H. (1992). *A history of psychology*, 3rd edn. Englewood Cliffs, NJ: Prentice Hall.

Levene, H. (1960). Robust tests for the equality of variance. In I. Olkin (ed.), *Contributions to probability and statistics*. Palo Alto, CA: Stanford University Press.

Lewin, K., Lippett, R. and White, R. K. (1939). Patterns of aggressive behaviour in experimentally created social climates. *Journal of Social Psychology, 10*, 271–9.

Liebert, R. M. and Liebert, L. L. (1995). *Science and behavior: An introduction to methods of psychological research*. New York: Prentice Hall.

Lloyd, P., Mayes, A., Manstead, A. S. R., Meudell, P. R. and Wagner, H. L. (1984). *Introduction to psychology: An integrated approach*. London: Fontana.

MacRae, A. W. (1995). Descriptive and inferential statistics. In A. M. Colman (ed.), *Psychological research methods and statistics*. London: Longman.

May, T. (2001). *Social research: Issues, methods and process*, 3rd edn. Maidenhead: Open University Press.

Middlemist, R. D., Knowles, E. S. and Matter, C. F. (1976). Personal space invasion in the lavatory: Suggestive evidence for arousal? *Journal of Personality and Social Psychology, 33,* 541–6.

Middlemist, R. D., Knowles, E. S. and Matter, C. F. (1977). What to do and what to report: A reply to Koocher. *Journal of Personality and Social Psychology, 35,* 122–4.

Milgram, S. (1963). A behavioral study of obedience. *Journal of Abnormal and Social Psychology, 67,* 391–8.

Miller, G. A. (1969). Psychology as a means of promoting human welfare. *American Psychologist, 24,* 1063–75.

Mook, D. G. (1983). In defense of external validity. *American Psychologist, 38,* 379–87.

Nicolson, P. (1991) *Qualitative psychology*. Report prepared for the Scientific Affairs Board of the British Psychological Society.

Oakley, A. (1981). Interviewing women: A contradiction in terms? In H. Roberts (ed.), *Doing feminist research*. London: Routledge & Kegan Paul.

O'Hear, A. (1989). *An introduction to the philosophy of science*. Oxford: Clarendon Press.

Oliver, P. (2003). *The student's guide to research ethics*. Maidenhead: Open University Press.

Orne, M. T. (1962). On the social psychology of the psychological experiment: With particular reference to demand characteristics and their implications. *American Psychologist, 17,* 776–83.

Osgood, C. E., Suci, G. J. and Tannenbaum, P. H. (1957). *The measurement of meaning*. Urbana, IL: University of Illinois Press.

Parker, I. (1994). Discourse analysis. In P. Banister, E. Burman, I. Parker, M. Taylor and C. Tindall (eds), *Qualitative methods in psychology: A research guide*. Buckingham: Open University Press.

Pidgeon, N. (1996). Grounded theory: Theoretical background. In J. T. E. Richardson (ed.), *Handbook of qualitative research methods for psychology and the social sciences*. Leicester: B. P. S. Books.

Polkinghorne, D. E. (1992). Postmodern epistemology of practice. In S. Kvale (ed.), *Psychology and postmodernism*. London: Sage.

Popper, K. R. (1972). *Conjectures and refutations: The growth of scientific knowledge*, 4th edn. London: Routledge & Kegan Paul.

Popper, K. R. (1974). *Unended quest: An intellectual autobiography*. London: Fontana.

Potter, J. (1996). Discourse analysis and constructionist approaches: Theoretical background. In J. T. E. Richardson (ed.), *Handbook of qualitative research methods for psychology and the social sciences*. Leicester: B. P. S. Books.

Potter, J. and Wetherall, M. (1987). *Discourse and social psychology: Beyond attitudes and behaviour*. London: Sage.

Quirk, A. and Lelliott, P. (2002). Acute wards: problems and solutions. *Psychiatric Bulletin, 26,* 344–5.

Rao, K. R. and Palmer, J. (1987). The anomaly called Psi: Recent research and criteria. *Brain and Behaviour Sciences, 10,* 539–643.

Reason, J. T. (1990). *Human error*. Cambridge: Cambridge University Press.

Rees, W. D. (1971). The hallucinations of widowhood. *British Medical Journal, 4,* 37–41.

Richards, L. (2003). *Introducing N6: A workshop handbook*. [Webpages available at www.qsr.com.au/resources/teachingmaterials/N6workbook.pdf, accessed on 25/5/05.]

Richardson, J. T. E. (ed.) (1997). *Handbook of qualitative research methods for psychology and the social sciences*. Leicester: B. P. S. Books.

Riley, D. A. (1962). Memory for form. In L. Postman (ed.), *Psychology in the making*. New York: Knopf.

Robson, C. (2002). *Real world research*, 2nd edn. Oxford: Blackwell.

Rosenhan, D. L. (1973). On being sane in insane places. *Science, 179,* 250–8.

Rosenthal, R. (1963). On the social psychology of the psychological experiment: The experimenter's hypothesis as unintended determinant of experimental results. *American Psychologist, 51*, 268–23.

Rosenthal, R. (1967). Covert communication in the psychological experiment. *Psychological Bulletin, 67*, 356–67.

Rosenthal, R. (1969). Unintended effects of the clinician in clinical interaction. A taxonomy and a review of clinician expectancy effects. *Australian Journal of Psychology, 21*, 1–20.

Rosenthal, R. (1976). *Experimenter effects in behavioural research*, enlarged edn. New York: Irvington Publishers.

Rosenthal, R. (2002). Experimenter and clinician effects in scientific inquiry and clinical practice. *Prevention and Treatment, 5*, 38. [Web page available at http://www.journals.apa.org/prevention/volume5/pre0050038c.html, accessed 29/11/04.]

Rosenthal, R. and Jacobson, L. (1968). *Pygmalion in the classroom*. New York: Holt, Rinehart & Winston.

Rotter, J. B. (1954). *Social learning and clinical psychology*. New York: Prentice Hall.

Rotter, J. B. (1966). Generalized expectancies for internal versus external control of reinforcement. *Psychological Monographs, 80* (whole no. 609).

Sacket, G. P., Ruppnthal, G. C. and Gluck, J. (1978). Introduction. In G. C. Sacket (ed.), *Observing behaviour, vol 2: Data collection and analysis methods*. Baltimore, MD: University Park Press.

Schachter, S. and Singer, J. E. (1962). Cognitive, social and physiological determinants of an emotional state. *Psychological Review, 69*, 379–99.

Schmidt, H. (1969). Precognition of a quantum process. *Journal of Parapsychology, 33*, 99–108.

Scriven, M. (1968). The philosophy of science. *The international encyclopaedia of the social sciences*, vol. 14. New York: Macmillan/The Free Press.

Searle, A. (1999). *Introducing research and data in psychology: A guide to methods and analysis*. London: Routledge.

Segall, M. H., Campbell, D. T. and Herskovits, M. J. (1963). Cultural differences in the perception of geometrical illusions. *Science, 139*, 769–71.

Seligman, M. E. P and Maier, S. F. (1967). Failure to escape traumatic shock. *Journal of Experimental Psychology, 74*, 1–9.

Shaughnessy, J. J. and Zechmeister, E. B. (1994). *Research methods in psychology*, 3rd edn. New York: McGraw Hill.

Shepherd, R. N. and Metzler, J. (1971). Mental rotation of three-dimensional objects. *Science, 171*, 701–3.

Sherif, M. (1935). A study of some social factors in perception. *Archives of Psychology, 27*, 1–60.

Siegal, S. and Castellan, N. J. (1988). *Non-parametric statistics for the behavioural sciences*, 2nd edn. New York: McGraw Hill.

Slonim, M. J. (1960). *Sampling in a nutshell*. New York: Simon & Schuster.

Smith, H. W. (1975). *Strategies of social research: The methodological imagination*. London: Prentice Hall.

Sperling, G. (1960). The information in brief visual presentations. *Psychological Monographs, 74* (498), 1–29.

Stevens, S. S. (1946). On the theory of scales of measurement. *Science, 103*, 677–80.

Stevens, S. S. (1951). Mathematics, measurement and psychophysics. In S. S. Stevens (ed.), *The handbook of experimental psychology*. New York: John Wiley.

Stiles, W. B. (1993). Quality control in qualitative research. *Clinical Psychology Review, 13*, 593–618.

Stratton, P. (1996). Systemic interviewing and attributional analysis applied to international broadcasting. In J. Howarth (ed.), *Psychological research: Innovative methods and strategies*. London: Routledge.

Strauss, A. L. and Corbin, J. (1990). *Basics of qualitative research: Grounded theory procedures and techniques*. Newbury Park: Sage.

Stroop, J. R. (1932). Studies of interference in serial verbal reactions. *Journal of Experimental Psychology, 18*, 643–62.

Swets, J. and Druckman, D. (1988). *Enhancing human performance*. Washington, DC: National Academy of Sciences Press.

Thibaut, J. W. and Kelley, H. H. (1959). *The social psychology of groups*. New York: Wiley.

Toren, C. (1996). Ethnography: Theoretical background. In J. T. E. Richardson (ed.), *Handbook of qualitative research methods for psychology and the social sciences*. Leicester: B. P. S. Books.

Treisman, A. M. (1960). Contextual cues in selective listening. *Quarterly Journal of Experimental Psychology*, *12*, 242–8.

Tukey, J. W. (1977). *Exploratory data analysis*. Reading, MA: Addison-Wesley.

Turner, B. A. (1981). Some practical aspects of qualitative data analysis: One way of organising the cognitive processes associated with the generation of grounded theory. *Quantity and Quality*, *15*, 225–47.

Underwood, B. J. and Shaughnessy, J. J. (1975). *Experimentation in psychology*. New York: Wiley.

Vaughn, S., Schumm, J. S. and Sinagub, J. M. (1996). *Focus group interviews in education and psychology*. London: Sage.

Viney, W. (1993). *A history of psychology: Ideas and context*. London: Allyn & Bacon.

Watson, J. B. and Rayner, R. (1920). Conditioned emotional reactions. *Journal of Experimental Psychology*, *3*, 1–14.

Weick, K. E. (1968). Systematic observational methods. In G. Lindzey and E. Aronson (eds), *The handbook of social psychology*, vol. 2. Reading, MA: Addison-Wesley.

Westen, D. (1999). *Psychology*. New York: Wiley.

Wilkinson, J. (2000). Direct observation. In G. M. Breakwell, S. Hammond and. C. Fife-Schaw (eds), *Research methods in psychology*, 2nd edn. London: Sage.

Wittgenstein, L. (1953). *Philosophical investigations*. (Tr. G. E. M. Anscombe.) Oxford: Blackwell.

Wooffit, R. (1990). On the analysis of interaction: An introduction to conversational analysis. In P. Luff, D. Frohlich and G. N. Gilbert (eds), *Computers and conversation*. New York: Academic Press.

Wooffitt, R. (1993). Analysing accounts. In N. Gilbert (ed.), *Researching social life*. London: Sage.

Wudka, J. (1998). *The scientific method*. [Web-page available at http://www.phyun5.ucr.edu/~wudka/physics7/Notes_www/node5.html, accessed on 20/7/05.]

Youtz, R. P. (1968). Can fingers 'see' colour? *Psychology Today*.

Zimbardo, P. G., Haney, C., Banks, W. C. and Jaffe, D. (1982). The psychology of imprisonment. In J. C. Brigham and L. S. Wrightsman (eds), *Contemporary issues in social psychology*, 4th edn. Monterey, CA: Brooks/Cole.

INDEX